BRM
V16
In Camera

'I do not know the first thing about this thing called the BRM. It might run on rails or maybe it's a racing car, perhaps it is a motor-byke. I think I know what it is – a British Racing Motor. 'It might have too or four cilynders, it might be heavy or light, big or small, it might only go at a speed of two hundred mph.'

The response by a Scottish primary schoolboy in 1952 when asked to write a one-page essay about the BRM.

BRM
V16
In Camera

A photographic portrait of Britain's glorious Formula 1 failure

ANTHONY PRITCHARD

First published in September 2012

A catalogue record for this book is available from the British Library

ISBN 978 0 85733 235 6

Library of Congress control no. 2012936197

Haynes North America, Inc., 861 Lawrence Drive, Newbury Park, California 91320, USA

Published by Haynes Publishing, Sparkford, Yeovil, Somerset BA22 7JJ, UK
Tel: 01963 442030 Fax: 01963 440001
Int. tel: +44 1963 442030
Int. fax: +44 1963 440001
E-mail: sales@haynes.co.uk
Website: www.haynes.co.uk

Printed and bound in the USA by Odcombe Press LP, 1299 Bridgestone Parkway, La Vergne, TN 37086

Jacket photographs
Front Goodwood, September 1952: Ken Wharton finished third behind teammates José Froilán González and Reg Parnell in the *Daily Graphic* Trophy, but retired on the starting grid for the Woodcote Cup because of a fuel-feed problem. *(Guy Griffiths Collection)*
Rear, from top left Painted pale metallic green, the BRM V16 was first seen by the public when Raymond Mays demonstrated it at the European Grand Prix at Silverstone on 13 May 1950 *(Guy Griffiths Collection)*; a mug and two charlatans – chief mechanic Ken Richardson (left) with Peter Berthon (centre), who had overall responsibility for the V16, and Raymond Mays (right), the instigator and head of the project *(Guy Griffiths Collection)*; José Froilán González, a chubby chap who looked a most unlikely racing driver, on the grid at Goodwood in September 1952 *(Guy Griffiths Collection)*; Raymond Mays, cigarette in mouth, about to drive a Mk II BRM in a demonstration at the International Trophy meeting at Silverstone in May 1967, with Anthony Rivers-Fletcher, Public Relations Officer of the Owen Organisation, standing alongside.
(Guy Griffiths Collection)

Endpapers
Front Juan Manuel Fangio during the Formule Libre race supporting the British Grand Prix at Silverstone in July 1953. Mechanically, the BRM was no match for the Ferrari Thin Wall Special driven by Giuseppe Farina, and Fangio had to work very hard for his second place. *(Klemantaski Collection)*
Rear By the time of the Goodwood meeting of September 1952 the V16s were capable of winning short races, as Argentinian José Froilán González proved in the *Daily Graphic* Trophy and the Woodcote Cup. *(Guy Griffiths Collection)*

Title page
José Froilán González in full flow during the Formule Libre race at the 1952 British Grand Prix meeting at Silverstone. *(Grand Prix Library)*

Contents

Acknowledgements

I am very grateful to many people for their help with this book. Both Kathy Ager (at LAT) and Julian Hunt argued that no previous BRM book has adequately illustrated the BRM V16 story. So while Kathy in her researches at LAT produced many of the brilliant images, Julian inspired many of the captions. Not just Kathy, but all the team at LAT are consistently helpful, welcoming, and supportive when I am working on a book.

The interest and help of both Michael Hammond (The Guy Griffiths Collection), a friend for many years, and Peter Sachs (The Klemantaski Collection), who found fascinating photographs in their archives, was also extremely welcome. I am as well very grateful to Tony Greco, another good friend and a very experienced IT man, who understands (or pretends to understand) my computer ignorance and responds quickly to my panic-stricken telephone calls when something goes wrong. I hope that all of us together have done justice to what is a peculiarly British subject.

Especial thanks are reserved for the Institution of Mechanical Engineers, who gave consent for the reproduction of the paper 'Supercharging the 1½-litre V16 BRM Racing Engine', which includes responses from, among others, Harry Mundy and David Bastow. So far as I am aware, this paper has not been widely seen and I understand that it is rare indeed for the Institution to give consent for the reproduction of its papers in this way.

Anthony Pritchard
Wooburn Green
Buckinghamshire
June 2012

Notes

These are to clarify some important points that constantly arise when writing motor racing history.

One point is that only since the introduction of the electronic calculator has it been possible to accurately calculate engine capacities. In most cases a modern calculation by electronic calculator produces a slightly different figure from that published originally.

If any readers want to check engine capacities, the formula is: ½ the bore x ½ the bore x pi (3.14159) x the stroke x the number of cylinders.

Another point relates to the number of laps covered when a car retires. For instance, consider the statement 'Parnell's Ferrari retired on lap 7'. This means what it says: that is that the car retired on lap 7 before it reached the end of the lap. Now consider the statement 'Parnell's Ferrari retired after 7 laps'. This may or may not mean what it says. It is true if the car retired out on the circuit after the end of lap 7, and it is true if the car retires in the pits, provided that the pits are after the start/finish line. But it is not true if the car retires in the pits and the pits are before the start/finish line.

This may seem to state the obvious, but there are constant minor errors made by writers who do not check these points.

A final point relates to the conversion of millimetres to inches. There are 25.4mm to the inch, and when writers make conversions to the Imperial system they will round them off. Then another writer comes along and converts this Imperial figure back to metric and produces an incorrect figure. In essence, Continental measurements will normally have been made in numbers rounded off to the nearest ten. As an example, take 2600mm, which produces an Imperial figure of 8ft 6.36in. We round this off to, say, 8ft 6.4in. Someone then converts 8ft 6.4in back to mm and produces a figure of 2,600.96 rounded to 2,601mm, which is patently wrong.

What I am saying is that great care is needed when making these conversions.

Readers who want to know more about ERA are directed to the definitive but out-of-print *ERA* by David Weguelin or the paperback *ERA Gold Portfolio 1934-1994* (see Bibliography). Likewise, as this is primarily a photographic history of the V16 BRM, for the full and definitive story the reader is referred to Volume 1 of Doug Nye's definitive history, details of which are also given in the Bibliography.

The cartoon is rather subtle, and appreciation of it depends on familiarity with the Stanley Schofield cassette tapes first released in the 1960s. One of these is a record of the sound of the BRM in action and another records the sound of the 1936 W125 Mercedes-Benz.

*"Fangio, B.R.M. * * * * ! ! !"*

Introduction

In the history of motor racing there have been many failures and among the greatest of them was the BRM V16. Unlike most failures that come, go and are quickly forgotten, however, the BRMs are still brought out for public appearances after 60-plus years and still astound all those who see and – more importantly – hear them. The ignominy of their early days has been transformed into awe and astonishment at the complexity of the concept and the potential that was never fulfilled – and probably never could have been.

Admiration for their speed and power, together with something approaching fear at their tremendous, infernal exhaust noise, which makes the ground tremble, is matched by incomprehension at the folly of the men who conceived, built and tried to develop these monsters.

This folly, together with the resulting failures and broken promises, accompanied the history of these cars in the years from 1949 through to 1955, but it has now been replaced by recognition of the immense problems that faced the promoters of the BRM project (even if there can be little respect for the way in which they were tackled) and delight in the spectacle that they now present from time to time at historic displays and meetings.

Built for the 1,500cc supercharged/4,500cc unsupercharged Grand Prix Formula of 1947–53, the BRM V16 ran late throughout its development. It was announced as a project in 1945 and the intention was for it to compete during the 1948 season. It was, however, still hopelessly unready to race when it was shown to the press in December 1949. The first car appeared at the International Trophy in August 1950. It was still not raceworthy, it only reached the circuit at the last minute and, of course, its failure at the start of its heat made the V16 the subject of derision and contempt.

The way the BRM project seemed to be hamstrung by its complexities was emphasised by the success of the early 2-litre HWM Formula 2 cars, which used simple and underpowered Alta four-cylinder engines. Throughout 1950–51 these cars were raced every weekend of the season as the team trekked all over mainland Europe, challenging the might of Ferrari and achieving many good finishes and even the occasional win. By 1952 the HWMs were losing their competitiveness because team boss John Heath did not tackle the need for much greater power output, and by 1953 the team was a busted flush. HWM did, however, achieve great prestige

and a brilliant reputation when the V16 was an unraceworthy disgrace.

Similar potential lay in the four-cylinder Alta Grand Prix cars, which were built by Geoffrey Taylor on a shoestring and sold to private owners. George Abecassis, who was John Heath's business partner, took delivery of an Alta Grand Prix car in 1948, although he lost interest – because of its teething problems – despite being the one man among the three private owners who could have made it really go. Instead of persevering with the car, Heath pushed it into a corner of the HWM workshops at Walton-on-Thames and eventually the chassis was used as the basis for a Jaguar-powered sports car built for Phil Scragg to use in hill-climbs. The other two Alta Grand Prix cars were owned and raced by Geoffrey Crossley and Irish driver Joe Kelly. Both were enthusiastic amateurs of barely average ability, but they raced their cars regularly and finished races – which was more than could be said for the V16 BRM.

The BRM V16 was financed through a trust which Raymond Mays set up and which employed him and Peter Berthon together with the rest of the staff in their various capacities. By 1953 it had become obvious that BRM was heading for oblivion. The finance came from contributions from British industry (a fill list of those concerns that gave financial support can be found on page 297) and this dependence on outside supporters for finance and technical input meant that BRM was always short of money. This was no way to run a Grand Prix team, as many others, including Gordini and Connaught, discovered to their cost. As Mays, however, was determined to build (or, at least, attempt to build) a world-beating Grand Prix car, there was no other that it could be financed. With the benefit of hindsight it was a completely madcap project. There was a BRM Supporters' Club (which later became the Owen Racing Motors Association) but this had no more interest in the funding of the project than does a football supporters' club in the finances of the team that it supports.

By the end of the 1951 season BRM had succeeded in running in only two Formula 1 races, only one of which, the 1951 British Grand Prix, was a World Championship race. It was, fairly obviously, still not 'fit for purpose'. The sheer complexity of the car – and above all its V16 engine – was such that it did not possess anything approaching full development or reasonable reliability, neither with

the original team nor later when the Owen Racing Organisation became the owner of the enterprise.

Alfa Romeo, which had dominated Grand Prix racing since 1946, withdrew from racing at the end of 1951 because its *Tipo* 159 had reached the peak of development and the directors of this state-owned company believed that it had re-established the high image in which Alfa Romeo had been held in pre-war days, so they judged that the company's resources would be better expended on the development of production cars. One consequence was that the

▲ This fascinatingly accurate model of the V16 BRM was made in 1948, and this posed photograph was taken in the panelled study at Mays' family home, Eastgate House in Bourne, Lincolnshire. The seated man is James Sandercombe (later Company Secretary of BRM) and those around him (clockwise) are Alfred Owen (Trust Member), Denis Flather (Trust Member, Director of family Sheffield steel company and 500cc racer), Bernard Scott (Lucas electrics and Trust Member), Bob Henderson Tate (Ministry of Supply), Walter Hill (publicist), Peter Berthon and Raymond Mays. *(Getty Images)*

◄ This less-than-flattering portrait of Raymond Mays was taken on 13 May 1950 when he demonstrated the BRM on its first public (as opposed to press) appearance at the European Grand Prix at Silverstone. *(Getty Images)*

▼ Raymond Mays, bare-headed, drives the V16 along the original Silverstone runway that was adjacent to the paddock at early races. The one thing that was not in short supply at Silverstone in those days was space. *(Getty Images)*

organisers of World Championship Grands Prix could foresee racing in 1952–53 becoming another period dominated by one team, this time Ferrari in place of Alfa Romeo. So it was that the World Championship in 1952–53 was run to the rules of 2,000cc Formula 2. The results were still dominated by Ferrari, but with at least 15 different makers contesting the category there was plenty of variety and a high level of interest.

Mays and Berthon realised that there was no serious future for the V16 cars, so the Trust was persuaded to put the cars and all associated equipment up for sale. The only serious bid came from Alfred Owen of the Owen Racing Organisation, which took control in late 1952. The BRM was

now in the ownership of a single commercial owner and even further removed from being a 'National Racing Car'.

Much has been written about the damage that BRM's failures did to the British motor industry and indeed British prestige generally. The truth is that the BRM debacle was counterbalanced by success in other areas of motorsport. In an era of hope and determination, BRM was one of the very few bad apples in the barrow.

BRM raced in the period when William Lyons' C-type and D-type Jaguars won three times at Le Mans (in 1951, 1953 and 1955) and when David Brown's Aston Martins were also taking on the giants of sports car racing, winning the Index of

Performance at Le Mans in 1950 and taking outright victories in many other international events.

In single-seater racing, apart from John Heath's HWM outfit, the Connaught team – funded by Kenneth McAlpine and headed by brilliant Chief Engineer Rodney Clarke – contested Formula 2 and Formula 1 in the period 1950–57. It was a Connaught driven by young Tony Brooks that won the 1955 Syracuse Grand Prix, the first Grand Prix victory by a British driver at the wheel of a British car since Sir Henry Segrave's win with a Sunbeam in the 1924 San Sebastian Grand Prix.

Cooper of Surbiton had dominated 500cc Formula 3 racing since 1947 and introduced their successful Formula 2 Cooper-Bristol in 1952, when

Mike Hawthorn drove one of these to joint fourth place in the Drivers' World Championship. Perhaps most significantly of all, Tony Vandervell was uniquely inspired by the concept of the BRM. Disillusioned by the management of BRM, Vandervell was moved to spend five seasons (preceded by research and development) struggling to beat 'the bloody red cars' with his Vanwall cars, his efforts culminating in victory in the 1958 Constructors' World Championship.

After the BRM team's failure in the Formule Libre race at the 1952 British Grand Prix meeting, yet another debacle, S.C.H. ('Sammy') Davis – Sports Editor of *The Autocar* and a very experienced driver and team manager – wrote a letter to Alfred Owen

▲ 'Far from the Madding Crowd'. With Raymond Mays at the wheel, the back end of the V16 is jacked up so that he can warm up the engine before taking the BRM out to demonstrate it before the enormous crowd at Royal Silverstone on 13 May 1950. *(Getty Images)*

▶ The bonnet panel has been removed at the May 1950 Silverstone meeting and the mechanics are making adjustments to the V16 engine before Raymond Mays demonstrates the car. *(Getty Images)*

that summed up all that was wrong with BRM. Edited extracts from this letter are set out below. The editing has been done to reduce the length and does not affect the material content:

'My distinct impression is that the best drivers are not willing to drive the BRM not because of the car but because they do not feel they can trust management and do not like the set-up or the method of preparation. This has been so for years, even in the days of the ERA.

'If you can get Moss to talk, you will find that he is definitely sure that he was double-crossed. The other good British drivers are all chary of going near Peter, and to a certain extent, Ray, remembering what happened before and the trouble with Cook.

'Uninstructed opinion is that the whole thing is run not as a business, but as a game out of which comes a good living in the best of circumstances for those concerned, but not the drivers.'

Such matters never change. Five years later Roy Salvadori contracted with BRM to drive the P25, the four-cylinder Grand Prix car that succeeded the V16. After a succession of unpleasant incidents, Roy learned at Monaco that – despite protests to the contrary – BRM staff had been meddling with the Lockheed disc brakes instead of leaving attention and adjustment to the Lockheed technicians as they had promised. Yet again there had been a breakdown of trust and confidence and Salvadori quit the team.

A final word. This book was conceived to be a pictorial feast accompanied by a commentary that gives the factual backbone of the V16 story together with personal conclusions and comments. For the detailed history the reader is referred to Doug Nye's magisterial *BRM: The Saga of British Racing Motors, Volume 1, Front-Engined Cars 1945–60*, which was first published in 1994 and reissued in 2003.

◀ A little over two years later, in 1952, the V16 BRM still has not won a major race, and by this time it is reduced to running mainly in minor Formule Libre British races. At the wheel here is Ken Wharton, a fussy, superstitious driver who could be brilliant on his day, but almost hopelessly inadequate if something had upset him. Wharton is driving in the Formule Libre race at the British Grand Prix meeting at Silverstone on 21 July 1952. He was called in for González to take over his car, which the Argentinian retired soon afterwards because of gearbox problems. *(Getty Images)*

Chapter 1
English Racing Automobiles
The inspiration behind BRM

The greatest single factor that influenced Raymond Mays and Peter Berthon to embark on the BRM project was the success of the ERA Voiturette and to this should be added their overweening ambitions. Whatever one thinks of Mays, it has to be recognised that he was a very fine competition driver who achieved great success in hill-climbing and Voiturette racing.

Circumstances are now so very different from the 1930s and it is difficult to assess his abilities, especially as he only once drove a Grand Prix car before embarking on the V16 BRM project. This was in the 1939 French Grand Prix at Reims where he was at the wheel of the new *monoplace* Talbot, but retired because of a leaking fuel tank. The car was new, but it was powered by an uncompetitive six-cylinder 4,484cc engine derived from that of a touring car. Thereafter he never had the opportunity to hone his skills at the wheel of a Grand Prix car, except for the occasion in 1949 when he drove Tony Vandervell's Ferrari.

The only British driver who handled the most powerful cars at the time was Dick Seaman, who was a works Mercedes-Benz driver. He was beyond doubt the greatest British racing driver of the era, and Mays, with all his successes in Voiturette racing with ERAs, probably ranks as number two.

◀ Raymond Mays and the White Riley in action at Shelsley Walsh in 1933 on his way to breaking the 'unbeatable' hill record set by Hans Stuck at the wheel of an Austro-Daimler. *(LAT Photographic)*

Raymond Mays

Born 1 August 1899, died 6 January 1980

Thomas Raymond Mays was a practising homosexual at a time when the social situation was so very different from now. In the Britain of his time homosexuality was a criminal offence and remained so until the law was reformed in 1963 following the Wolfendon Report.

There have, of course, always been very many people who have taken a relaxed view of homosexuality, notably Mrs Patrick Campbell, who was famously reported as saying of the shenanigans of Oscar Wilde and Lord Arthur Douglas, 'It doesn't matter what they do, as long they don't frighten the horses.' Unfortunately Mays did 'frighten the horses' by his blatant, predatory approaches to young men at all levels of society.

The most notorious incident occurred in 1954 after his attempted seduction of a young, male hotel employee at Bern during the 1954 Swiss Grand Prix when the team was running the 250F Maserati. Mays tried to importune the lift boy at the hotel at which he was staying. The lad reported the matter to the management and the police were called. The matter was hushed up, partly through the intervention of Count Jacques de Wurstemburge, who was a friend of Mays and is said to have had similar inclinations. Mays had to be escorted out of the hotel with a coat over his head to prevent press photography. There were also incidents in Jersey and in Germany in both pre-war days, and another disgrace in Germany in 1962 when the rather odious, loud-mouthed Louis Stanley gave Mays a noisy and scathing dressing-down in public – a case of the rumbustious lambasting the lascivious.

In addition to heavy criticism of the lack of engineering ability of both Mays and Peter Berthon, and their propensity to milk projects in which they were involved to ensure the life style to which they had become accustomed, many who would otherwise have supported a project to build a British Grand Prix car declined to become involved with these men – Mays because of his sexual proclivities and Berthon because of his technical incompetence.

It is also amazing just how many highly respected figures in the motoring world supported the project despite Mays and Berthon; the most notable, until he became disenchanted with lack of progress, was Tony Vandervell, who had an abhorrence of homosexuality. Alfred Owen, who was a lay preacher, with presumably a strong disapproval of sexual deviation, supported the project tirelessly and his industrial conglomerate, the Owen Organisation, took over BRM lock, stock and barrel in 1953.

Lord Hives, Chairman of Rolls-Royce, which was deeply involved with BRM through the development of the twin-stage centrifugal supercharger, described Mays and Berthon as 'those gilded lilies', a remarkably astute comment by a gentleman of the old school. William Lyons (later Sir William) of Jaguar, a man of impeccable taste and judgement, abhorred sexual deviation and this company consistently refused to provide any support for the BRM. To coin a phrase, if you couldn't trust William Lyons, you couldn't trust anybody, even though he described Prince Bira of Siam as being 'a man of colour'.

▶ In the paddock at Brooklands circuit in 1934 Raymond Mays poses for the camera with his 1,500cc ERA before going out on a record-breaking attempt. *(LAT Photographic)*

Mays lived at the family home in Bourne in Lincolnshire where the family wool business was based. There was quite a lot of land and it was to prove an ideal base for a racing car team. He started his competition career in 1920 with a modified 1½-litre Hillman Speed Model, after which he competed with two supercharged Brescia Bugattis named 'Cordon Bleu' and 'Cordon Rouge'. He received a degree of sponsorship from Mumms, the champagne producer, and Mays can be truthfully credited as one of the very first to raise trade sponsorship to support his motor racing activities. The Bugattis were very successful hill-climb cars, and following these he ran a supercharged AC 2-litre car.

At the Chatcombe Pitch hill-climb in 1922 Mays first met Humphrey Cook, an enthusiastic supporter of motor racing and a very wealthy man, who at that time was competing with a Vauxhall 30/98. Mays had made friends with people at the RAF College at Cranwell, which was nearby, and among them was Peter Berthon, who had been injured in a crash landing in 1927. While Berthon was convalescing, he helped Mays with preparation of the 1922 3-litre Vauxhall that had been one of that year's works team cars.

These immensely powerful cars had been designed by Laurence Pomeroy Senior, chief engineer of Vauxhall (and later managing director of Daimler), to compete in the 1922 Tourist Trophy, which they won. There remains a great enigma about these

cars, as it seems unbelievable that Vauxhall should have spent so much on them for just one race. The company seemed oblivious to the fact that the 3-litre capacity limit for the Tourist Trophy was a 'one-off' and that all other major races for Grand Prix cars had a 2,000cc capacity limit.

It is possible, of course, that development had been delayed and the cars should have appeared in 1921 when there was a 3,000cc limit for Grand Prix cars and, after having spent so much, entering them for the Tourist Trophy was probably better than not racing them at all. It is also likely that the development and construction costs of a team of these cars made Vauxhall short of liquidity and more susceptible to the offer for the company that was accepted in 1923.

The TT Vauxhalls, despite the passing of the years, still possessed considerable performance and great potential for development. This particular 3,000cc Vauxhall had previously been owned by Humphrey Cook, who had fitted it with a supercharger designed by Amherst Villiers (together with other modifications), but he never seriously competed with it. Mays completely rebuilt the car, which became known as the 'Vauxhall-Villiers'. The name was changed as part of a scheme to promote the new range of Villiers-designed superchargers that were to be made in different sizes for engines of different capacity.

▼ Humphrey Cook, looking well-pleased with himself, is seen at the wheel of R1A on the launch of the marque at Bourne in 1934. *(LAT Photographic)*

Mays competed in hill-climbs with the Vauxhall-Villiers from July 1928 until the end of the 1929 season. His successes with this car led to a proposal in 1930 from the India Tyre and Rubber Company that he should undertake a promotional tour with an India-shod Invicta powered by a 4½-litre Meadows engine to publicise the Glasgow-based company's products. Mays retained the Invicta after the tour and together the young engine designer Tom Murray Jamieson and Berthon tuned the engine for hill-climbing. Mays' performances in sprints (and hill-climbs) were impressive and led to a proposal by Cook.

Invicta already built the 2/4-seater 'S'-type with a maximum speed of 95mph (153kph), although commonly referred to as the '100mph' Invicta. Total production amounted to only 87 cars, and these were difficult enough to sell with the UK (and most of the rest of the world) in deep recession at the time. But this did not stop Cook proposing to Captain Noel Macklin, the head of Invicta, that he and the company should together finance a supercharged 5-litre sports car. J. R. Buckley (see Bibliography) gave a specification for the proposed new Invicta, although the extent to which it was speculative is far from clear.

Macklin's company was already in financial trouble and he was only too well aware of the difficulties in

selling expensive cars, and the proposal was dropped at an early stage. For 1933, Mays was planning to enter the Vauxhall-Villiers once more, but the car needed repairing after the engine had failed and, because he was short of money, Cook loaned him the cost of repairs, and the money owed to Amherst Villiers, against a lien on the car.

Before the 1933 season had started, Mays had embarked on another project. During the 1930s the Riley company in Coventry was one of the most successful British builders of sports cars, and their cars featured an overhead valve 1,483cc (57.5 x 95.2mm) six-cylinder engine, designed by Victor Riley, which had twin camshafts mounted high on the cylinder block and operated by short pushrods. This resulted in a high-revving, powerful engine without the complexities of the more usual arrangement of twin overhead camshafts mounted in or on the cylinder head.

Mays and Berthon were fully aware of the competition potential of this engine and they came to an arrangement with Victor Riley to build a sprint car powered by a supercharged version of this engine. There was a new cylinder head that, it was claimed, Berthon had designed, but most critics doubt whether he was sufficiently competent to do this and believe it was the work of Jamieson, who

▲ This is a rarely seen photograph of the first ERA chassis number R1A, seen at the Bourne works in 1934 shortly after completion. It is yet to be painted and is still in the bare metal. It was the first of four cars built in 1934, and during their first season they suffered from numerous design faults and teething troubles. This car remained part of the works team through 1936, and in 1937 it was sold to Norwegian driver Björnstad. *(Tom March Collection)*

Peter Berthon

Born 20 September 1906, died 15 January 1971

Born in Burma, Peter Loraine Ashton Berthon was
a Flying Cadet at Cranwell College in late 1926. He
gained his permanent commission as an RAF Fighter
pilot in November 1926, but in May 1927 he crashed
while landing his Gloster Grebe at his home base,
Duxford, and suffered quite severe injuries. During
part of his convalescence he helped Raymond Mays
prepare the Mercedes-Benz that Mays was competing
with in 1927.

In due course he moved into the Mays family
home and both Mays and his mother Anne became
infatuated with this very handsome, dissolute, amoral
young man. Both had intimate relations with him, but
it seems that only his relationship with Mays was long-
term. It was typical of Berthon's sexual ambivalence
that in June 1932 he married Lorna Mary Wiltshire,
who was glamorous in appearance and outrageous in
behaviour.

When ERA was set up, Berthon became a director
and nominally the designer. It does seem that in
reality, however, his contribution to the design of the
ERA was minimal. He had no proper engineering

training, his sole learning experience having been
attendance at a brief, basic engineering course at
Cranwell. During the war he ran his own company,
Mortimer Engineering Limited based in London
E5, and this produced precision tank gun sights and
similar products

In post-war days Berthon became chief engineer
to BRM and he did little more than lay down the
basic principles of the design and left Harry Mundy,
Eric Richter and other engineers to carry out the
engineering design. Even so, because of his overall
command, he was in a position to make many
blunders and work was often delayed awaiting
his decisions, especially when he was away from
Bourne for extended periods sailing his cutter *Ortac*.
Despite years of folly and incompetence, Mays and
Berthon remained in charge at BRM until they were
eventually sacked in 1962.

Berthon died while holidaying in South Africa
in January 1971 ; he was swimming off the coast
at Durban when he suffered a heart attack and
tragically drowned.

▲ This photograph was taken in
1939 before the announcement
of the E-Type ERA and the break-
up of the Bourne set-up. Peter
Berthon, still with plenty of hair,
is flanked by draughtsman Aubrey
Barratt (left) and newly appointed
team manager Philip Mayne
(right). *(LAT Photographic)*

was definitely responsible for a new crankshaft and the supercharger.

Maximum power on the test bed was 147bhp at 6,500rpm and the engine could be taken as high as 8,000rpm. It was installed in a modified chassis, the transmission incorporated a Wilson pre-selector gearbox, and there was a neat off-white body with Mays' favourite blue upholstery. During 1933 Mays, at the wheel of this car, known as the 'White Riley', scored many successes, among them breaking the outright hill record at Shelsley Walsh set in 1930 by Hans Stuck with an Austro-Daimler. This record stood at 42.8sec, which some thought to be unbeatable, but Mays broke it with the White Riley in 42.4sec.

Because the car incorporated so many Riley components and retained the Riley name, it brought substantial publicity and prestige to the Coventry company. Mays was about to enter into further negotiations with Victor Riley when he received a letter from Humphrey Cook, who had concluded that the White Riley could form the basis of a competitive 1,500cc single-seater racing car that could successfully contest Voiturette racing at an international level.

There followed a meeting between Cook, Mays and Berthon at which they agreed to form a limited company to build and race a team of Voiturettes, and to build a few additional cars for private entrants. It was decided that the company would be called English Racing Automobiles Limited and the cars would be known by the abbreviation ERA. There was no formal agreement between the parties and it was all done on a handshake and good faith. Cook held all the shares in the company apart from a nominal number held by Mays and Berthon. It was agreed that Cook, Mays and Berthon would each receive a salary of £250 per annum.

The company was to be based at Bourne, Lincolnshire, because Mays had commitments to his family and the family business, and Berthon had for some while been an employee of the Mays' family business. Mays obtained the consent of his father to build a small workshop/factory in the orchard of the family home, Eastgate House, and this was sold to Cook for the nominal sum of £50. In addition the new company had the use of some outbuildings.

Mays headed the project, and he was the number one driver. Berthon was chief engineer, and that great engineer Reid Railton, employed by Thomson & Taylor, was responsible for the chassis frame, suspension and axles, incorporating some of Berthon's ideas. The six-cylinder block of the White Riley

▲ Marcel Lehoux is seen here at the wheel of a works 1,500cc ERA in the 99-mile (159km) Coupe de Prince Rainier Voiturette race in 1936. The ERAs faced strong Maserati opposition and on the second lap there was a multi-car accident triggered by Omobono Tenni spinning his Maserati on sea-water that had been blown over the protective wall on to the circuit. The Maseratis suffered mechanical problems and the ERAs of Bira, Lehoux, and Nicos Embiricos took the first three places, with Earl Howe fifth. The best Maserati performers were Christian Kautz (fourth) and Luigi Villoresi (sixth).
(LAT Photographic)

◀Although the E-type was basically a simple design, its racing career was as ill-fated as that of the BRM V16. Frequently the cars non-started and they rarely survived to finish a race. This is GP1 owned by Reg Parnell and rebuilt over the winter of 1947–48 with a straight transmission line (in original form the E-Type had 'stepped down' transmission to reduce the overall height of the car) and twin Murray Jamieson superchargers in place of the original Zoller blower. The car is at the Jersey Road Race in April 1948 when it was driven by Joe Ashmore. He was in 14th place when forced to retire because of fuel-feed and steering problems. *(Guy Griffiths Collection)*

was retained, albeit with substantial modifications, and the engine incorporated the 'Berthon' cylinder and the Jamieson counterbalanced crankshaft. Jamieson uprated his supercharger to deliver 15psi boost compared with the 12psi of the White Riley; Jamieson superchargers were of the Roots type and were mounted vertically at the front of the engine. Other modifications included valves of a different design and improved cooling.

Initially, the power output of the 1,500cc ERA engine was 150bhp at 6,500rpm. In addition, ERA built a 1,087.5cc (57.5 x 69.8mm) version with a power output thought to be around 115bhp – the company seems to have fought shy of stating a power output for this version. Although the 1,500cc class was by far the more important of the Voiturette category, many contenders opted to run in the 1,100cc class.

For the transmission, the Armstrong Siddeley company supplied specially-built Wilson pre-selector gearboxes. Throughout the racing career of the cars in pre-war days they were always superbly turned-out and with great attention to the detail of the design and construction. The Riley company actively supported the project, raising no objection to the design rights to the White Riley's engine being assigned to ERA and agreeing to supply components and machining facilities until the new ERA workshop was up and running.

In the middle of May 1934 the team at Bourne rolled out the first ERA, a 1,500cc car, chassis number R1A, bearing a badge (designed by F. Gordon Crosby, illustrator for the weekly magazine *The Autocar*) depicting a stylised sunrise. It was decided that the lettering 'ERA' on the badge was too small and Berthon and an RAF friend, 'Pongo' Lester, redesigned the badge with the letters 'ERA' within three circles, and this was fitted to all the cars.

ERA had hoped to have two cars, a 1,500cc model plus an 1,100cc, for the Mannin Beg and the Manx Cup races to be held on the Douglas circuit on the Isle of Man on 30 May 1934, but it soon became obvious that there was insufficient time to

get both cars ready, so the team concentrated on the 1,500cc, which was tested at Brooklands and then on the Douglas circuit during practice before the race. It rapidly became clear that there were serious handling problems, and there was no alternative but to withdraw the car from the race.

Back at Bourne, modifications were made to the suspension, new rear springs were fitted and the steering was modified. Mays and Cook shared the driving of R1A on its next appearance, in the British Empire Trophy at Brooklands in June. The car was plagued by engine problems resulting in a succession of pit stops, but it finished the race, albeit too far behind to be officially classified. Before their next race, both R1A and the newly completed 1,100cc R2A were extensively tested.

Running on trade plates and fitted with silencers and plywood mudguards, both cars were tested on public roads over a route that ERA used regularly. It ran from Bourne to Colsterworth at the junction with the Great North Road (the A1) and southwards along this, the main highway between London and Scotland, until just short of Stamford where it left the A1 and wound its way back to Bourne on country roads.

R1A next appeared in the Dieppe Grand Prix, where Mays ran sixth in the first heat for some laps, but a pushrod broke and he was forced to retire. At the August Brooklands meeting, Mays at the wheel of R1A laboured under a severe handicap; he finished second in one race and in another set a new class record for the Mountain road circuit of 76.00mph (122.28kph). Cook, at the wheel of 1,100cc R2A, received rather more generous handicapping; he won the 2nd Esher Mountain Handicap and lapped the Mountain circuit at 76.37mph (122.88kph).

ERA then embarked on setting some standing-start records at Brooklands. Cook with the 1,100cc car set a new record for the Standing Kilometre at 79.75mph (128.32kph) and the Standing Mile at 88.91mph (143.06kph). In the 1,500cc class Mays achieved 85.35mph (137.33kph) for the Standing Kilometre and also set a new record for the Standing Mile at 96.08mph (154.46kph). Then ERA entered two cars for Mays at Shelsley Walsh in September. Mays, who drove to the meeting in the new R3A, was always an impressive performer at this power hill-climb and in 1934 there was a stiff battle between him and Whitney Straight (3-litre Maserati 8CM-3000) for BTD (best time of the day).

The first runs were held in wet weather on a slippery track, and with the 1,500cc R1A Mays lost time because of wheelspin at the start, and was third fastest in his class with a time of 47.4sec. With R3A, powered by a 1,985cc (6.7 x 107mm) engine developing around 175bhp, Mays recorded 45.2sec, a time bettered by Straight, who recorded 44.6sec. By the time the second runs took place the rain had stopped, although the track

Humphrey Cook

Born 16 March 1893, died 3 August 1978

Solemn, quiet and introspective, Humphrey Wyndham Cook, who was rather overweight and tubby, had inherited the family's fortunes and its very prosperous and successful wholesale drapery business, Cook, Son & Co (based in the St Pauls area of London), following the death of his father.

He was only 12 when his father died and while the business and wealth were held in trust for him until he attained the age of 21, his affairs were well-managed and the business continued to be run at a substantial profit. Young Cook went to university in Oxford, but it seems that he learned little in the City of Spires. After Oxford he devoted much of his income to the purchase of sporting cars and his time to travelling.

Cook took part in hill-climbs and sprints on a rather half-hearted basis and it was while he was competing with a Vauxhall 30/98 at Chatcombe Pitch Hill Climb in 1922 that he first met Mays. They remained in somewhat distant contact over the years, but when Mays started competing with the White Riley, Cook became excited and inspired by his performances with this car. Cook came to the conclusion that the engine of the White Riley had sufficient potential to be the basis of a 1,500cc single-seater Voiturette racing car. A letter to Mays setting out his proposal led to the formation of English Racing Automobiles Limited. During the years of his involvement with Mays and Berthon, Cook spent around £90,000 on the ERA project – about £8.5 million in today's values.

It can be argued that it was money well spent, but it certainly depleted Cook's resources. When the company split up in 1939, Cook had not only run out of funds but also finally become totally exasperated by the way in which Mays and Berthon milked the company – they had had their hands in the till from the very beginning. Cook never held a grudge against Mays and they remained on comparatively good terms; he saved his wrath and resentment for Berthon, whom he regarded (in modern parlance) as a 'waste of space'.

There was another factor. While Mays, with some justification, stood in the limelight and revelled in the successes of ERA, the useless Berthon shared the glory simply because he was Mays' friend and lover, and Mays had become emotionally dependent on him. Cook did not seek publicity and public popularity, but he deeply resented Berthon's pursuit of it.

When the company split up, Cook moved the new ERA E-type cars to small premises at Donington Park race track. There was an attempt to raise public money to support ERA organised by Rivers-Fletcher through a support fund called the British Motor Racing Fund. It tried hard, but all it could raise was about £1,000. Cook shut down ERA on 26 May 1939 and the goodwill was later sold to Leslie Johnson, who moved the operation to Dunstable and struggled in vain to make the E-type cars reliable and competitive.

▶ Happy Days! This photograph of Cook and Mays was taken in the early days when ERA was supremely successful and there was no friction between the men in the organisation.
(LAT Photographic)

was still wet. Mays with R1A won the 1,500cc class in 46sec and then at the wheel of the 2-litre R3A he took BTD with a time of 44sec dead.

The next event for the ERA team was the handicap 100-mile (161km) Nuffield Trophy at Donington Park, the only road circuit on the UK mainland, on 6 October. The race was held on a wet track and Mays fought his way through the field and into the lead with R1A; despite an intermittent engine misfire and the loss of two gears he won the race at 61.51mph (98.97kph).

The 1934 season had been sufficiently encouraging for ERA to expand and build the first production cars. South African driver Pat Fairfield ordered a 1,100cc car, which was numbered R4A and completed in April 1935; it was fitted with a 1,500cc engine for 1936 and raced with the works team. Subsequent cars were built to B-Type specification with a number of modifications that included additional chassis bracing under the driver's seat and softer springs. The first of these, R1B, was ordered by Dick Seaman and raced by him throughout 1935; R2B was delivered to Siamese Prince Chula Chakrabongse and raced by his cousin, Prince Birabongse Bhanubandh; it was named 'Romulus'.

During 1935 the ERAs were immensely successful, and cars were now run by a coterie of private owners. Pat Fairfield won the 1,100cc Mannin Beg race on the Isle of Man, the Dieppe Grand Prix (with Bira second), and also the Nuffield Trophy at Donington Park. The ERA works team contested the Eifelrennen Voiturette race at the Nürburgring and Mays won from Hans Ruesch (Maserati), with other ERA drivers Tim Rose-Richards third, Dick Seaman fourth with his private car, and Humphrey Cook fifth.

Dick Seaman took his black-painted car on a European tour and won the Coppa Acerbo Voiturette race at Pescara, the Prix de Berne at Bremgarten (with Bira second), and the Circuit of Masaryk Voiturette race on the Brno circuit in Czechoslovakia. He also set second BTD in the Grossglöckner and Freiburg Mountain Hill Climbs. In Britain, Mays made the first ascents in under 40sec of Shelsley Walsh with both 1,500cc and 2,000cc ERAs.

Although ERA faced stronger opposition from Maserati in 1936 following the introduction of the Bologna company's 6CM six-cylinder car, the successes continued. B. Bira with 'Romulus' won the Picardy and Albi 1,500cc races in France, plus the Coupe de Prince Rainier at Monaco, and the International Trophy race at Brooklands. A sad blow was the death of Algerian-born Marcel Lehoux after a collision at Dieppe with Giuseppe Farina, and the wrecked ERA was scrapped.

Mays had a new works car in 1936 (R4B) and this featured a larger Zoller supercharger mounted at the rear of the engine and projecting into the

cockpit. During the winter of 1936–37 ERA rebuilt R4B as the prototype C-Type ERA with modified chassis frame, Porsche torsion bar independent front suspension and hydraulic brakes. ERA also built R12B to the same specification as R4B. During 1937 the ERA was at the peak of success and the marque scored 17 major wins.

Despite these successes and continuing demand for new cars, ERA was beginning to experience financial difficulties. This was partly because of the high level of expenditure incurred by Mays and Berthon, and Cook was gradually becoming disenchanted by their profligate behaviour. The company sold R12B to Prince Chula for Bira to drive, and they named this car 'Hanuman' (after the mischievous monkey god). Bira crashed this car heavily at Reims and the chassis frame was a write-off. The Siamese Princes' White Mouse Stable built a replacement, which the team called 'Hanuman II'.

Overall, less success was achieved in 1937–38 because the Maserati opposition was proving increasingly difficult to beat. The ERA company had decided to build a production car and it was to be powered by a 4.3-litre six-cylinder engine. Much of this project had been entrusted to Tom Murray Jamieson, but he was killed at Brooklands in May 1938 at the International Trophy meeting when Cyril Paul's V12 Delage crashed

▲ The engine of the ERA E-type, which had a shorter stroke than the earlier cars, was fitted with a Zoller supercharger and had an estimated power output of at least 240bhp. *(Guy Griffiths Collection)*

ERA R4D

Raymond Mays continued to compete with ERA chassis number R4D after the organisation broke up. This had been a team car between 1935 and 1939, and during both its ownership by ERA and afterwards it was extensively modified. Known as R4C it had been rebuilt by the works with a 1,950cc engine, heavily drilled chassis frame to reduce weight, Lockheed two-leading-shoe front brakes and extra radius rods to the front suspension. It was the only ERA to have the steering drag-link on the left.

▼ The photograph shows very clearly the revised front suspension fitted to this car in post-war days. Here Mays is at the wheel of R4D at the Bugatti Owners' Club Prescott hill-climb in 1947. *(Guy Griffiths Collection)*

▶ Here Mays inspects the engine of R4D at Shelsley Walsh hill-climb on 24 September 1949. His chief mechanic Ken Richardson is at the wheel of the car. Parked behind the ERA is Mays' Bentley Mk VI standard-steel saloon. *(Guy Griffiths Collection)*

▼ Here Ron Flockhart is at the wheel of R4D, which he bought from Mays in 1951. The race is the Formule Libre event at Silverstone on 18 July 1953, the day of the British Grand Prix. Both BRMs retired in this race, Farina (Ferrari Thin Wall Special) and Villoresi (works Ferrari Tipo 375) took the first two places. The young Scots driver finished fourth with the ERA. *(Tom March Collection)*

A car with two lives: the reformed ERA Company controlled by Leslie Johnson and based at Dunstable built this G-type for Formula 2. It was not ready until nearly half-way through the 1952 season. Stirling Moss drove it and he is seen at the wheel in the British Grand Prix, in which he retired because of engine problems.

The G-type proved less competitive than expected and also Leslie Johnson's health was deteriorating. The car was sold to the Car Division of the Bristol Aeroplane Company for 1953 and it was developed into the 450 competition sports car, a team of which Bristol raced in 1953–55. (Tom March Collection)

into the crowd. This led to the decision to abandon development of the production ERA, and an additional factor was that it was far too ambitious a project for such a small company.

During 1938 further development work was carried out on R4C (see panel). These cars were immensely successful, but Berthon lost his way after Jamieson's death and with Reid Railton going to work in the United States. Ironically, in post-war days this car was to prove capable of beating the V16 BRMs on more tortuous circuits.

In 1939 the company produced the E-type car, but it was a complete failure. Cook lost patience with being ripped off financially by Mays and Berthon and withdrew to small workshops at Donington Park where he continued to develop and enter the E-type, chassis GP1 with Arthur Dobson at the wheel.

The story of the ERA is part of the BRM story. Several striking features emerge from it. Many ERA successes, but by no means all, were in British races against fairly weak opposition. From racing the ERA, the dynamic duo, Mays and Berthon, gained

immense and invaluable experience in international motor racing. They understood the sort of design qualities that were needed to build a successful Grand Prix car, but they remained blissfully ignorant as to how to achieve it.

Announced in 1939, the E-type ERA differed from previous models by having a tubular chassis, de Dion rear axle, shorter-stroke engine, Zoller supercharger, four-speed synchromesh gearbox, and a much sleeker body. But, as the W 165 Mercedes-Benz appeared only a few weeks after the E-type it was quickly realised that the latest product of the British company was unlikely to prove competitive at an international level. The cars were raced only twice before the outbreak of the Second World War.

The ERAs were very simple cars, while the BRM V16s were for their time exceptionally complex. They were far too complex in design (which in itself possessed many shortcomings) for men of the very limited engineering calibre of Mays and Berthon to develop successfully. Ironically, pre-war ERAs beat the V16s on two separate occasions.

▲ One of the leading ERA exponents in post-war days was Bob Gerard ('Mr Bob as he was familiarly known') and he owned a total of three of these cars. His greatest success with R14B was second place to Emmanuel de Graffenried (Maserati 4CLT/48 San Remo) in the 1949 British Grand Prix. *(Guy Griffiths Collection)*

ERA R14B

One of the persistent and successful opponents of the V16 BRMs was Bob Gerard. Initially this was with one of his three ERAs, usually R14B. Although this was built as a B-type, it was fitted with a Zoller-supercharged C-Type engine in 1938 for Johnny Wakefield. Gerard raced this car extensively until 1952 when he took delivery of a Mk II Cooper-Bristol, and with this he proved equally successful at baiting and beating the BRMs on the slower British circuits.

▶ 'Mr Bob' is seen here on a wet track at Goodwood on Easter Monday, 26 March 1951. His ERA in this race was R14B with C-type Zoller-supercharged engine. Gerard scored many successes with this car, which he raced until 1952. He was out of luck at Goodwood and retired because of mechanical problems. *(Guy Griffiths Collection)*

Chapter 2

Grand Prix racing in the 1930s

Its influence on the BRM V16

In order to trace the background and development of the V16 BRM, it is necessary to look back to the early 1930s when Grand Prix racing was transformed by the Association Internationale de Automobile Clubs Reconnus (AIACR), the governing body of motorsport. For 1934 the AIACR introduced a new Grand Prix formula that was intended to rationalise rather than revolutionise Grand Prix racing.

During the preceding few years the most consistently successful Grand Prix contenders had been cars with engines of between 2 and 3 litres: the Alfa Romeo 8C 2300 Monza and 8C 2600 Monoposto; the Maserati 8C-2500 and 8C-3000; and the 2,267cc Bugatti Types 35B and 51. The AIACR was quite happy with these cars that combined reasonably

◀ Once Mercedes-Benz had learned that the ACCI was planning to introduce a 1,500cc supercharged/4500cc unsupercharged Grand Prix formula for 1940, the company put in hand development of the twin-stage supercharged V8 1,493cc W 165 Voiturette. The decision of the government-influenced Italian Royal Automobile Club to hold all Grands Prix on Italian soil (which included Libya) in 1939 gave Daimler-Benz the opportunity to field two of these W 165 cars in the Tripoli Grand Prix. Driven by Hermann Lang (seen here) and Rudolf Caracciola the German entries trounced the Alfa Romeos and the Maseratis to take the first two places. If Daimler-Benz had been able to field a team of W165s in the immediate post-war days, they, not Alfa Romeo, would have dominated Grand Prix racing. *(Daimler)*

powerful engines with (by the standards of the time) good handling, roadholding and steering.

There were, however, certain cars that seemed monstrously powerful. In 1931 Alfa Romeo had built the 3.5-litre *Tipo* A powered by two 1,750cc twin-cam engines on a common crankcase, Maserati had raced their famous 'Sedici Cilindri' cars – the 4-litre *Tipo* V4 and the 5-litre *Tipo* V5 – with two straight-eight engines on a common crankcase (surprisingly, these cars were tractable and handled reasonably well), and, finally, Bugatti had built the Type 54 4.9-litre single-seater.

So the AIACR introduced the famous 750kg Formula that came into force for 1934. This prescribed a minimum weight of 750kg (1,654lb) without fuel, oil, tyres or the driver, and in addition required that the bodywork should present a minimum cross-sectional area of 85 x 25cm at the driving seat. All aspirations that the Formula would encourage the existing 2- to 3-litre cars were dashed by the cars raced by the German Mercedes-Benz and Auto Union teams, which were subsidised by the National Socialist government.

Engine capacities of the German cars were up to 6

litres (Auto Union C Type) and power outputs were as high as 650bhp (Mercedes-Benz W 125). Only the Italian Alfa Romeo and Maserati teams made any real effort to challenge what soon developed into German supremacy but during the years of the Formula the strength of the Italian challenge faded.

Obviously, speeds rose dramatically during the years of the 750kg Formula and for 1938 the AIACR introduced a new Grand Prix Formula with weights and capacity on a sliding scale, but in simple terms the maximum capacities permitted were 3,000cc supercharged and 4,500cc unsupercharged. Once again the German teams dominated. The French Delahaye and Talbot teams built unblown 4,500cc contenders, but what soon became obvious was that there was an imbalance between the supercharged and unsupercharged categories.

So, once again, the AIACR contemplated changing the rules of Grand Prix racing. It was proposed that the capacity limits should be 1,500cc supercharged (the Voiturette category in which the ERAs ran) and 4,500cc unsupercharged. For 1939 the Italian Royal Automobile Club decided that all Grands Prix on Italian soil (which included the

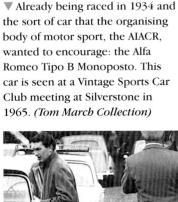

▼ Already being raced in 1934 and the sort of car that the organising body of motor sport, the AIACR, wanted to encourage: the Alfa Romeo Tipo B Monoposto. This car is seen at a Vintage Sports Car Club meeting at Silverstone in 1965. *(Tom March Collection)*

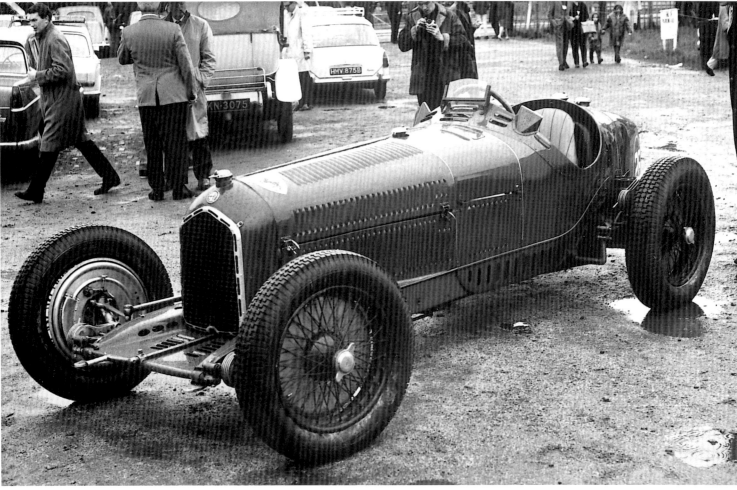

Italian colony of Libya) should be run to 1,500cc supercharged rules. This was partly a move to protect Italian interests, but in addition the body controlling Italian motorsport also recognised the proposals for the new Formula.

Alfa Romeo had introduced their new straight-eight *Tipo* 158 Voiturette in 1938 and in April 1939 the Maserati company's new *Tipo* 4CL Voiturette with 16-valve four-cylinder engine appeared. In May 1939 the Tripoli Grand Prix was duly run to 1,500cc supercharged rules and the field comprised a strong entry of Alfa Romeos and Maseratis, plus two new Mercedes-Benz W 165 V12 1.5-litre cars. Driven by Hermann Lang and Rudolf Caracciola, the W 165 cars trounced the Italian entries and took the first two places.

The W 165s were raced only that once and never appeared in post-war days. The outbreak of war prevented the introduction of the new Formula for 1940 and instead it was introduced for 1947, the first year in which motor tracing returned to relative normality. This lasted officially until the end of 1953. Thus evolved the Formula to which the V16 BRM was built.

▶ This is the engine of the very fast, very powerful Maserati Tipo V4 4-litre 'Sedici Cilindri' (16 cylinders) with two 8C-2000 engines on a common crankcase. The V5 version had two 8C-2500 engines. *(Author's collection)*

◀ Built for the Grand Prix formula of 1938 onwards, the Mercedes-Benz W 154 had this 3,000cc V12 supercharged engine developing about 425bhp at 7,000rpm. *(Daimler)*

▶ Although Auto Union struggled in the early part of 1938 to make their V12 D-type cars competitive, they became a serious opponent for Mercedes-Benz and defeated them several times. *(Author's collection)*

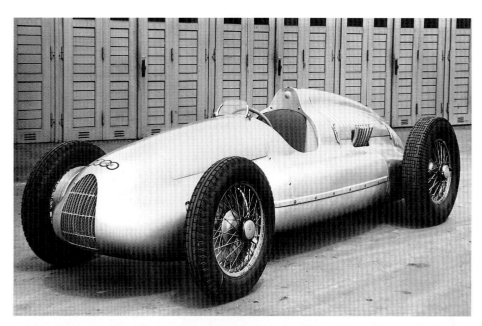

▼ The 1939 version of the 3-litre Mercedes-Benz, which was powered by the twin-stage supercharged W 163 engine with an increased power output of 480bhp at 8,000rpm. Aspects of the design influenced the BRM V16, the only completely new Grand Prix car to appear during the years 1945–50. *(Daimler)*.

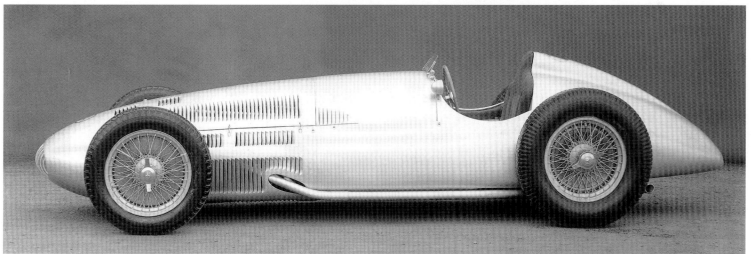

◀ One of the cars with the greatest influence on the design of the V16 BRM was the unraced Alfa Romeo Tipo 162 with 3-litre twin-stage supercharged V16 engine that had the cylinders at an angle of 135°. It was largely the work of Alfa's Technical director, Spaniard Wifredo Ricart. While he was designing this car, he consulted British expert Harry Ricardo and this similarity of names caused endless confusion as to who actually designed this Alfa Romeo. The cylinder layout was one of many features of the Tipo 162 copied on the BRM. Here, in this very poor photograph (believed to be the only one that exists of the completed car), is the Tipo 162 with Ricart at the wheel during the first road test in June 1940. *(Centro di Documentazione Storica Alfa Romeo)*

Chapter 3

The BRM V16 in detail

The concept of a 'National Grand Prix Car'

Raymond Mays and Peter Berthon had conceived
an unrealistically ambitious plan to build a new
Grand Prix contender and for this to be financed by
the British motor industry. While Mays whipped
up financial support from the industry, and was
astonishingly successful at it, Berthon laid down the
basic specification. Harry Mundy became, in effect,
chief engineer and the outline specification was
for a V16 engine layout, a centrifugal supercharger
developed and built by Rolls-Royce Limited,
and Porsche-type trailing link independent front
suspension.

A company known as Automobile Developments
Limited was set up to build the car, and the British
Motor Racing Research Trust was formed to
manage the finances. The Trust had a distinguished
membership of persons, firms, and corporate bodies
that had subscribed or promised to subscribe not less
than £100 to the funds of the Trust.

The car was designed during the period 1945–47,
and it was based essentially on 1939 German racing
technology, together with information gained
about Wifredo Ricart's unraced Tipo 162 Grand
Prix car. The original V16 cars were known as

◀ A front view of the BRM engine with the
carburettor removed. This photograph demonstrates
well the very wide 135° degree 'V'. It also shows very
clearly the ignition distributors, the supercharger, and
the induction manifold. *(LAT Photographic)*

Ken Richardson

Born 21 August 1911, died 27 June 1997

Born and brought up in the village of Bourne, Lincolnshire, William Kenneth Richardson became very enthusiastic about Raymond Mays' motorsport activities and after the setting up of ERA he was able to obtain a job as a mechanic with the team. Later he became head mechanic to Mays when he was racing R4D. He was conscripted into the army during the war, and afterwards returned to Bourne to work for Mays.

In 1949 Mays agreed to drive Tony Vandervell's 1.5-litre V12 Ferrari in the British Grand Prix at Silverstone. Richardson was nominated as co-driver – a fact that beggars belief as he had no racing experience whatsoever! This early Ferrari was a complete nightmare to drive, with power that came in suddenly rather than smoothly, inadequate performance and twitchy, unpredictable handling. Mays was frightened of the car and during the race he decided to hand over to Richardson. After a very short spell at the wheel, Richardson lost control at Abbey Curve and spun into part of the crowd, causing five spectators to suffer minor injuries.

Once the BRM V16 had become a reality and development started, Richardson became the main test driver and it can be argued that no one knew the foibles and virtues of the car better than Richardson. BRM's concept of testing was for Richardson to lap the Folkingham test circuit as quickly as possible, and the cars did not test on any other circuits – Monza apart – and nor was any testing done where times of Formula 1 rivals could be used for comparison and evaluation purposes.

Mays rated Richardson's ability as a driver very highly and when BRM entered the 1951 Italian Grand Prix he wanted Richardson to be one of the drivers. It was a pretty stupid idea because Richardson lacked a full international competition licence and the Royal Automobile Club, the then governing board of British motorsport, would not support him in his application to drive in the Italian race. He quite simply lacked racing experience. The BRM team, of course, failed to start at Monza because of gearbox problems.

When the Owen Organisation took over BRM, Richardson's services were dispensed with. Just after the 1952 Earls Court Show the Standard-Triumph company invited him to test-drive the new prototype Triumph TR sports car. He tested the car on the service roads of Standard's Banner Lane, Coventry factory, and is supposed to have called it 'a bloody death trap'. As a result he was invited to join the company as development engineer in charge of the TR project.

The result was a virtual redesign of the car, including a new and much stiffer chassis, substantial modifications to the engine and restyled rear bodywork. Rival manufacturer Rootes Group had introduced a two-seater sports car known as the Alpine and with Sheila van Damm at the wheel one of these cars had exceeded 120mph (193kph) on the Jabbeke stretch of motorway in Belgium. Standard-Triumph wanted to match that performance. In May 1953, on the same stretch of road, Richardson drove a Triumph TR2 with metal tonneau cover, valances over the rear wheels, full-length undershield, non-standard gearing and overdrive, and he exceeded 124mph (200kph) for the flying mile.

In 1954 Richardson was instructed to set up a professional competitions department at Banner Lane. He and Maurice Gatsonides drove a TR2 to 27th place overall in that year's Mille Miglia. Thereafter under Richardson's management Triumphs competed regularly in races and rallies during the period 1954–58. Later the competition department raced special twin-cam TRS cars and rallied TR4s. Leyland acquired Standard-Triumph in 1961 and after that year's Le Mans race, Richardson was peremptorily dismissed. Until he retired he continued to work in the motor industry as a freelance consultant.

▼ Although Ken Richardson always seemed a man of little substance while he worked for Raymond Mays, during his time as head of the Triumph competition team he emerged as a different man, as he guided the Triumph TRs to both racing and rallying success. He is seen here talking to journalist Edward Eves, who is sitting at the wheel of one of the Le Mans Triumph sports cars. *(LAT Photographic)*

the Type 15 and were built for a new Grand Prix formula that came into force for 1947 (although its implementation had been planned before the Second World War) for cars of up to 1,500cc supercharged or 4,500cc unsupercharged.

For what it is worth, one of the cars was timed at 186mph (300kph) at Barcelona in 1950 and under ideal conditions they must have been capable of at least 200mph (322kph). *The Motor* magazine commented: 'Theoretically, this car should be capable of beating all European circuit records, and it carries with it the high hopes of every English racing enthusiast.'

Engine

The V16 engine was an exceptionally complex but basically orthodox design. Had it been a Ferrari engine and not a BRM one, it would have been described as 'jewel-like', for all the components were small (as evidenced in the photograph of the man holding engine components in one hand) and the capacity of each cylinder was only 92.1cc, although in external appearance the engine was nevertheless big and bulky, as was the car as a whole.

The twin-stage centrifugal supercharger was developed and built by Rolls-Royce. Twin overhead camshafts per bank of cylinders were driven by gears from the centre of the crankshaft. There are no clear or certain figures for engine power and, although much higher figures have been mentioned, in the V16's later days, when it was running with reasonable reliability, a genuine 485bhp at 12,000rpm is credible.

Based on the published cylinder dimensions of 49.53mm (bore) and 47.8mm (stroke) my calculation of the engine's capacity is 1,473.58cc (for the method of calculation see page 7). This assumes, of course, that the usual quoted dimensions for bore and stroke are accurate.

The two banks of cylinders were set at an included angle of 135°. The cylinders were cast in blocks of four, with the cylinders and crankcase in RR50 aluminium-alloy. There were four cylinder heads, one for each block of cylinders and these were cast in RR53 aluminium-alloy. Bridge clamps were used as holding-down studs to distribute the pressure between internally cast struts leading directly to the combustion chambers, thereby minimising the risk of head distortion.

The combustion chambers were hemispherical, with the valves at an included angle of 87.5° and seated on NMC (nickel, manganese, chromium) inserts. On the exhaust side of the engine the valves were sodium-filled and the valve guides were in direct contact with the water in the cooling system to achieve maximum heat dissipation.

Double hairpin valve springs were used. The camshafts ran in roller bearings and each pair was driven by a train of single-spur gears mounted in a light alloy housing, which could be withdrawn as a unit from the centre of the cylinder block. A Pesco fuel pump was driven from the rear end of one camshaft, and the four distributors for the ignition from the front ends of each camshaft.

These distributors had been developed by Lucas and each had three contacts: the first broke the primary current; the second closed the circuit again; and the third, which could be switched into action again by a manual control, carried a retarded setting for use when starting.

Coil ignition was used as the high rpm that the engine attained precluded the use of magnetos because there was insufficient time for the magnetic flux to build up in the windings. There were separate coils and the current was provided by a small-capacity lightweight battery mounted at the rear of the chassis. There was a single plug per cylinder and each was mounted centrally in the cylinder.

Cast in groups of four, the cylinders and the crankcase were in RR50 aluminium-alloy. The Nitralloy steel crankshaft ran in ten main bearings. The bearings were Vandervell Thin Wall with the bearing caps bolted laterally into the main bearing casting in addition to the usual vertical securing studs. The bearing caps were located longitudinally by round dowels and were not dependent on the studs for location. The individual cylinder liners were cast in high-tensile iron and they were held down by the detachable cylinder heads against a flange towards the top of each liner, and Neoprene sealing rings were used to maintain a watertight joint at the base of the linings.

A system of increasing gears also took the drive from the centre of the crankshaft to the two-stage Rolls-Royce centrifugal supercharger. The shortness of the stroke meant that the engine could attain very high revs, and it was designed to operate between 6,000rpm and peak engine speed which, even in 1951, was 12,000rpm (at which the piston speed was only 3,800ft/min).

The cylinder linings proved to be a major defect and they led to unreliability and major failures. Although the very short stroke resulted in very short cylinder liners, they were in compression by their top and bottom flanges. It proved impossible to secure eight of these per bank of cylinders absolutely square and to maintain an equal 'nip' at the cylinder head gasket over a wide range of temperatures. The result of this was water leaking into the cylinders, hydraulic locks being formed and the liners disintegrating with disastrous results. At the time the failures were wrongly attributed to sparks induced between the ignition leads.

The aluminium-alloy pistons were machined from Y-alloy forgings, and the connecting rods were nickel-chrome steel. The big-end bearings were like the mains, of the Thin Wall-type. The cylinders were arranged so as to permit drive at approximately half-speed from the centre of the crankshaft to the clutch. An output shaft with duplex driving gears was housed in the lower half of the crankcase, which was cast in magnesium alloy. These gears also provided the drive for the centrifugal water pump, together with the pressure and scavenge oil pumps on either side of the engine, and the supercharger mounted at the front.

Although the engine was designed to be used with a fuel-injection system, this was fitted for a brief period only during the early development of the V16. Throughout the remainder of the life of the V16 the engine relied on two 2.5in diameter SU carburettors that were considerably smaller than the original single throttle proposed for fuel injection. The supercharger was designed to run at 3.25 times engine speed, but because of engine breathing restrictions, this was later increased to 4.0 times engine speed.

That the breathing restrictions had a marked adverse effect on engine performance is illustrated by the fact that although the original estimated power output of the engine with 3.25 blower ratio was 600bhp at 12,000rpm, the maximum achieved in practice was 485bhp at 10,000rpm with the higher blower ratio of 4.0:1. The greatest restriction in breathing, however, was the valve gear, but after an original design error in the geometry had been rectified, this proved very satisfactory.

However, by restricting maximum valve acceleration to 52,000ft/sec^2, the lift was only 0.25in, and this throttling effect explained why the gains of power achieved when the supercharging speed was increased were small. If the engine breathing had matched supercharger performance, then the problem of poor torque in the middle engine speed range – about which drivers constantly complained – would have been resolved.

An even greater problem from which the V16 suffered during its racing career was the continuously rising torque curve, with its peak at the point of maximum power. The result of this was when the driver accelerated thorough a fast corner the limit of tyre adhesion could be quickly reached, accompanied by the car sliding sideways through loss of adhesion. If the original Rolls-Royce power estimates had been reached, this would have been substantially reduced by the use of supercharger vortex throttling.

Vortex throttles had been designed and made, but they were never fitted. They would have regulated the boost pressure above a predetermined speed, so that an optimum degree of supercharge pressure could have been achieved without excessive boost above 10,000rpm. This was never realised because of the poor engine breathing.

A vast range of power outputs have been quoted for the V16, but the most reliable figures seem to be 430bhp at 11,000rpm in original form and 485bhp at 12,000rpm for the Mk II. The point has to be made very clearly that although components of the V16 suffered from a great number of different problems, the most frequent and persistent failures and shortcomings related to the engine.

Transmission

Transmission was by a triple-plate clutch and a five-speed and reverse gearbox mounted transversely at the rear, with a ZF limited-slip differential.

The clutch was a 7.5in (190mm) diameter dry multi-plate design manufactured by Borg & Beck with Ferodo linings secured by Redux cement and rivets. The spring pressure was centrifugally augmented by the use of bob-weights on the withdrawal. The complete clutch assembly weighed only 30lb (13.6kg).

From the clutch the drive was taken by a jointed prop-shaft to the final drive unit, which incorporated the five-speed gearbox. The gearbox was of the countershaft type with the drive taken through one pair of dog-engaged constant-mesh gears (there was no direct drive) and the shafts lay transversely across the car, with the drive entering the gearbox through a pair of bevel gears on the left side. Inside the gearbox was an oil pump that provided lubrication for the complete gearbox, and this directed jets of oil to surfaces that were under load. All gears were of case-hardened nickel-chrome steel.

The drive was taken through a pair of large spur gears in the centre of the layshaft, and the final drive incorporated a ZF limited-slip differential. There was available a range of gears for the input bevels and the final drive gears. These gave a range of 13mph (21kph) to 17mph (27kph) per 1,000rpm top gear according to the circuit.

With the highest ratios the maximum speed in the lower gears was said to be approximately, 1st, 95mph (153kph); 2nd, 115mph (185kph); 3rd, 130mph (209kph); and 4th, 165mph (265kph). Subject to circuit conditions, the speed equivalent to peak rpm in top gear would be just over 200mph (322kph). There was a sliding block-type universal joint on either side of the final drive unit, and from these the drive was taken through short shafts ending in Hooke-type universal joints inboard of the rear hub carriers.

Harry Mundy

Born 1915, died 1988

Harry Mundy was a great motor racing enthusiast and a great automobile engineer. He was educated at King Henry VIII School in Coventry and thereafter served an apprenticeship with the Alvis company at Holyhead Road in Coventry. On completing his apprenticeship he went to work for ERA in Bourne as a draughtsman. It was at ERA that he met Wally Hassan, who had previously been with the old Bentley company, and they became lifelong friends.

When ERA was folding in 1939 Mundy returned to Coventry and joined Morris Engines, but as an RAF reservist he was soon in the RAF. He rose to the rank of Wing Commander and during the last year of the war he was on the technical development staff of Air Commodore F.R. Banks, Director of Engine Research and Development at the Air Ministry. Banks's illustrious career included formulating the aviation fuels used in Schneider Trophy-winning aircraft.

Mundy had stayed in contact with his colleagues from ERA days and he was one of the first to learn about the BRM project. At an early stage Berthon asked Mundy to help with design of the BRM V16 engine. Following VJ Day in August 1945, Mundy received the consent of Banks to spend the afternoons at Berthon's home in London where a drawing office had been set up.

Here Mundy became Chief Designer of the V16 and he worked on initial layout drawings. At this early stage, while Berthon was hooked completely by the concept of a V16 and Eric Richter favoured a V12, Mundy thought that a V8 would be completely adequate. Mundy moved to Bourne in 1946 and he worked on the V16 BRM until 1950, by which time there was no further demand for design work as such and everything was concentrated on development.

That year Mundy moved to Coventry Climax, builders of fork-lift trucks, fire pumps and engines. Here he worked on the FWA engine originally intended for use with a portable fire pump, but redeveloped in 1,098cc form for use in competition sports cars. In a significant change of direction he joined *The Autocar* as Technical Editor.

While he was working at *The Autocar* Colin Chapman persuaded him to design a twin overhead camshaft conversion for the Ford Cortina engine and this powered the Lotus Elan (and many other Lotus models) from 1961 onwards. Ever since the Lotus twin-cam engine appeared, the story has been told that Mundy did the drawings for the Lotus engine 'over a weekend for a fiver in cash'. Make of it what you will, but it must be apocryphal.

After Jaguar bought the Coventry Climax company in 1963, Wally Hassan persuaded Mundy to return to pure engineering. Mundy joined his friend at Jaguar and together they designed the Jaguar V12 engine. Mundy retired in 1980, but he continued to undertake some consultancy work until his death in 1988.

▼ Harry Mundy was a great engineer whose talent was confined by the precepts laid down by Berthon. Perhaps his greatest work lay in his role in the design of the Jaguar V12 engine. *(LAT Photographic)*

Tony Rudd

Born 8 March 1923, died 22 August 2003

In the 1930s, Anthony Cyril Rudd started his connection with motor racing by helping out with the White Mouse Racing Team which Prince Chula Chakrabongse of Siam (as it was then known) set up to prepare, enter and manage racing cars for his cousin Prince Birabongse Bhanubandh. As a result of his experience with the White Mouse team, he chose to train as an engineer in an apprenticeship with Rolls-Royce. He was forced to break off his apprenticeship by the Second World War and he was conscripted into the Royal Air Force, where he flew Avro Lancaster bombers after training as a pilot. After hostilities ceased, he resumed his apprenticeship at Rolls-Royce.

In 1951 Rolls-Royce seconded Rudd to BRM to assist with development of the centrifugal supercharger, which was produced by Rolls-Royce. Rudd stayed with BRM and never returned to Rolls-Royce, remaining with BRM for 18 years. During that time he was involved in continuing development of the V16 engine and he was responsible for the design and construction of the Mk II version of the car. He later worked on development of the four-cylinder 2.5-litre cars raced from late 1955 onwards. In 1962, following the sacking of Mays and Berthon, he took on full technical control of the team.

After the failure of the H16 BRM of 1966–67 and the abysmal season that the team endured in 1969, Rudd left BRM and joined Lotus. He had no involvement in racing, but worked on the production cars and in due course became Engineering Director of that division of the company. His brief included improving production quality and the development of Lotus's own twin-cam engine.

Following the death of Colin Chapman in 1982 he played a major role in the management of Lotus and at the request of the Chapman family he headed the Formula 1 team in 1989 following the conviction of Fred Bushell for his involvement in the DeLorean financial irregularities. When the Formula 1 team was sold in 1990, he resigned from Lotus and became a freelance consulting engineer. His autobiography *It Was Fun!*, published in 1993, is an outstanding motor racing book.

◀ During his long career in motor racing, Rudd tolerated some of the most difficult personalities, not just Mays and Berthon, but also, during his later days at Lotus, Colin Chapman. *(LAT Photographic)*

Chassis

The original chassis frame was a simple affair typical of 1930s practice, albeit with a reasonable degree of stiffness. It was based on two 2.5in (63.5mm) tubes each side, with a pierced sheet-steel plate welded on each side to form one unit. At the front a large-diameter cross-tube provided support for the front suspension, and towards the rear there was a cross-tube (of similar construction to that of the side members) running under the driving seat, and two tubular cross-members. To achieve a low seating position the engine and propshaft were set at an angle in the chassis.

At the front, the independent suspension was by Porsche-type trailing links, the pivots of which were carried in light alloy housings bolted to the chassis frame at the point where the front cross-tube ran. There were ball-joints on the links in place of the normal kingpins. The actual suspension units, front and rear, were Lockheed pneumatic struts containing compressed air and incorporating hydraulic dampers. These struts, which proved completely trouble-free, were very light and compact (they weighed only 4lb/1.8kg each). At the front they were actuated by small levers on the inner ends of the pivot pins of the upper trailing links.

There was a de Dion rear axle, and the hub carriers were joined by the tube running behind the light alloy final drive. Lateral location was by a ball-pivoted block sliding vertically in the casing of the final drive, and fore and aft location, together with brake torque, was taken by folded channel-section radius rods (later replaced by tubular rods), pivoted at their forward end to the chassis members. A rotating joint was incorporated in the centre of the de Dion tube to permit the necessary relative movement at each end when one side of the axle rose and the other fell.

The suspension of the BRMs was not without its problems – not in reliability, but in performance. At the Pedralbes race in October 1950 the BRMs were slower in and out of the corners than the Ferrari opposition. Almost a year later at Monza in practice for the Italian Grand Prix (in which the team failed to start) they were still slower in and out of corners than the Italian opposition.

The steering box was of the worm and nut type and was mounted forward on the left-hand side, with a horizontal rearward-facing drop arm, and with a similar arm pivoted in the equivalent position on the right-hand side; thus the steering arm was in three sections. The steering column incorporated three universal joints passing down the centre of the 'V' of the engine and only just clearing the induction manifold. There were 2¼ turns of the steering wheel lock-to-lock.

Girling was responsible for both the original drum brakes and the disc brakes first adopted in 1952. The drum brakes had three leading light alloy shoes on each wheel; the 14in (356mm) brake drums were of chromium-iron construction with magnesium-alloy backplates. There was servo-assistance by an engine-driven Pesco gear pump, and this circulated brake fluid through a circuit connected to the front brakes.

Pressure on the brake pedal closed a valve and built up pressure in the system; this applied the front brakes directly, and the fluid pressure supplemented the pedal pressure on the master cylinder for the rear brakes, which had their separate closed hydraulic line. Both systems drew their fluid from a common fluid tank mounted on the central cross-member.

The Girling disc brakes were hydraulically operated with a diameter of 13.5in (343mm) at the front and 13in (330mm) at the rear. They were initially far from trouble-free and two British National races were lost because the brakes grabbed and BRM drivers, leading the race, spun away their lead. Dunlop centre-lock wire-spoked wheels with light alloy rims, Rudge-splined hubs, and twin-eared spinners were fitted.

To assist in achieving a low bonnet line, the radiator header tank was mounted at the rear of the engine, and only the radiator matrix was positioned in the nose of the car. Separate water off-take pipes ran from each cylinder into two large pipes leading to the header tank. From this a single pipe led down to the radiator and then low down on each side to the water pumps. The whole system was sealed and ran at low pressure.

Behind and below the main water radiator was a shallow oil radiator, and the supply of oil for the dry sump lubrication system was carried in a tank mounted level with the engine on the left side of the chassis. There were two aluminium-alloy fuel tanks: the larger with a capacity of 25 gallons was fitted in the scuttle over the driver's legs, while the smaller tank, with a capacity of 15 gallons, occupied the front part of the tail. Capacity was subsequently increased to 50 gallons in total by installing a larger tank in the tail, and for long races fuel tank capacity could be increased to a maximum of 78 gallons (354.6 litres).

Behind the fuel tank in the tail was a small tank containing the oil supply for the gearbox, and this was mounted on a tubular structure above the battery. By carrying much of the fuel in the scuttle tank, the variation in weight distribution as fuel was consumed was kept to a minimum. The body was panelled in aluminium-alloy and, as can be seen from the pages of this book, the original smooth, uncluttered shape lost its good looks through enlargement of the radiator, together with the addition of ducts and a profusion of louvres. The height to the top of the scuttle was only 2ft 6in (762mm).

The cockpit was roomy with a wide, comfortably upholstered seat. The throttle was the furthest right of the foot pedals in contrast to the Italian style of having a central throttle. There were only two instruments in the cockpit, a strip-type tachometer, which had been developed by a company called Speciality Instruments of Norwich, and on the left side of the cockpit, a round instrument that combined three functions: oil pressure, oil temperature, and water temperature.

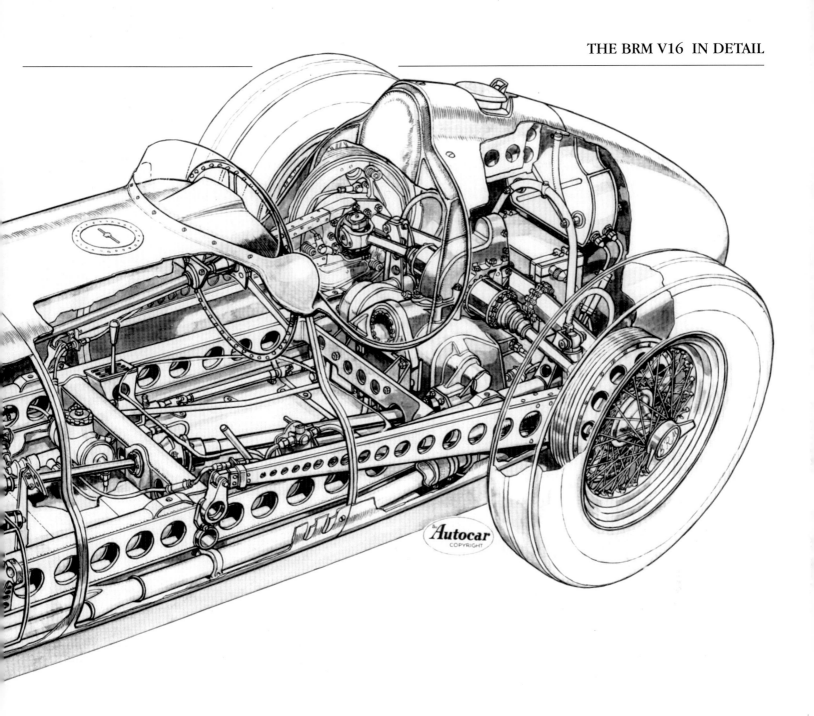

▲ This magnificent cutaway drawing of the original BRM by the great Max Millar shows very clearly how the engine and transmission line are angled in the chassis, enabling the driver to sit alongside the transmission rather than above, and thus reduce the overall height of the car. Also clearly featured and visible are the front trailing arm suspension, the rear de Dion axle, and the five-speed gearbox in unit with the final drive. (LAT Photographic)

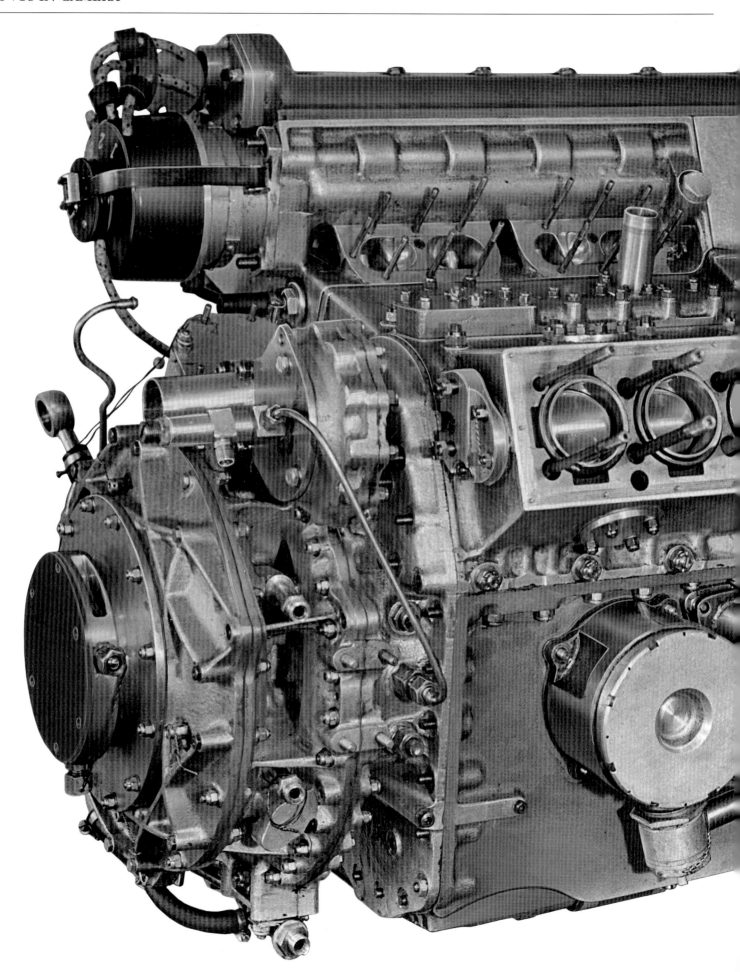

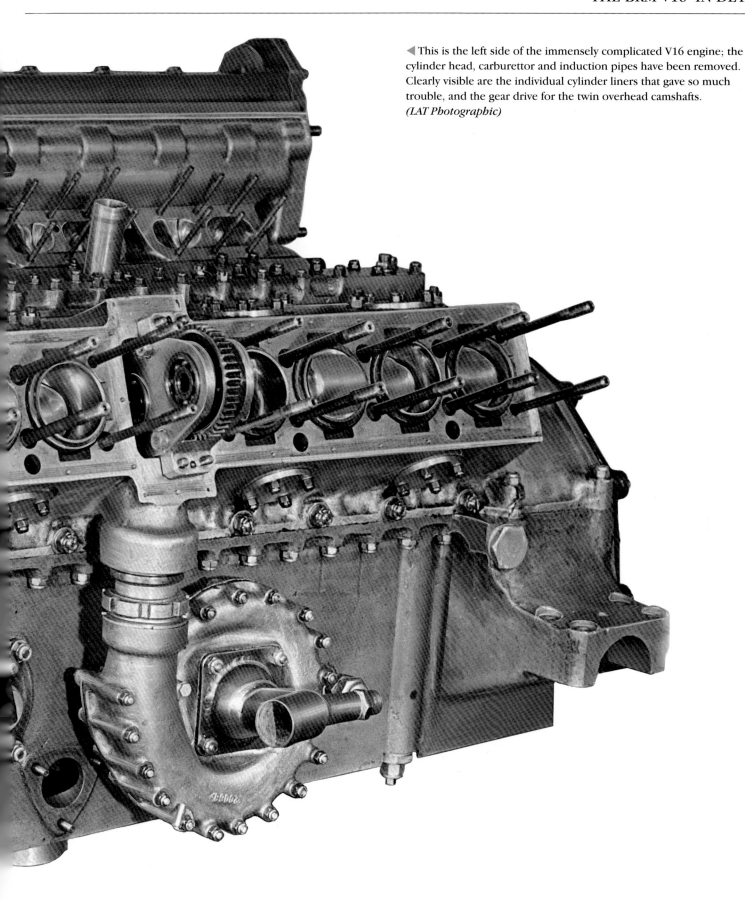

◀ This is the left side of the immensely complicated V16 engine; the cylinder head, carburettor and induction pipes have been removed. Clearly visible are the individual cylinder liners that gave so much trouble, and the gear drive for the twin overhead camshafts. *(LAT Photographic)*

▲ The V16 engine on the dynamometer. Some experts, notably the late Geoff Richardson of ERA-powered RRA Special fame, challenged its accuracy. *(Grand Prix Library)*

▼ This is the Nitralloy crankshaft of the V16 engine. It was made in two pieces and the joint was centrally placed between the two main drive gears. *(LAT Photographic)*

◢ A hand, holding in its palm a connecting rod, piston, and gudgeon pin, illustrating the diminutive size of the engine components. *(LAT Photographic)*

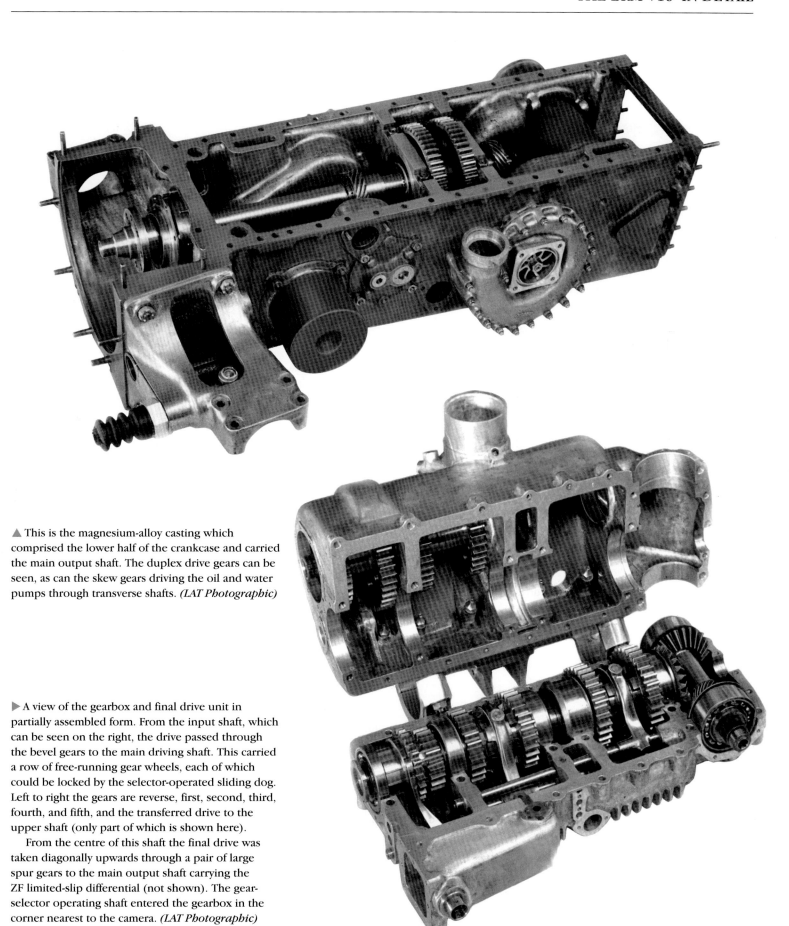

▲ This is the magnesium-alloy casting which comprised the lower half of the crankcase and carried the main output shaft. The duplex drive gears can be seen, as can the skew gears driving the oil and water pumps through transverse shafts. *(LAT Photographic)*

▶ A view of the gearbox and final drive unit in partially assembled form. From the input shaft, which can be seen on the right, the drive passed through the bevel gears to the main driving shaft. This carried a row of free-running gear wheels, each of which could be locked by the selector-operated sliding dog. Left to right the gears are reverse, first, second, third, fourth, and fifth, and the transferred drive to the upper shaft (only part of which is shown here).

From the centre of this shaft the final drive was taken diagonally upwards through a pair of large spur gears to the main output shaft carrying the ZF limited-slip differential (not shown). The gear-selector operating shaft entered the gearbox in the corner nearest to the camera. *(LAT Photographic)*

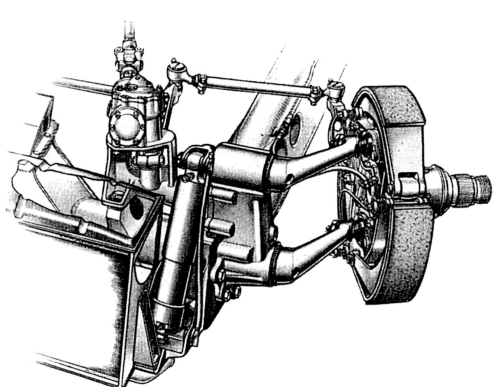

▲ In this drawing the front
suspension, steering, and the
three leading-shoe brakes are all
visible, as are the steering box,
suspension pillar mountings,
and the suspension strut.
(LAT Photographic)

▶ Seen here as raced in the 1951
British Grand Prix, the V16 is
posing for *The Autocar*'s camera
at Folkingham. Although the large
air intake (an essential change that
was made for 1951 to improve
cooling) rather spoils the smooth
and uncluttered appearance of the
V16, it essentially remained a very
handsome car. *(LAT Photographic)*

◀ The cockpit of the 1951 BRM. The view is dominated by the wood-rimmed steering wheel (it had domed studs on the underside). The ribbon-type tachometer is mounted at the top of the scuttle – at this time competition cars vibrated severely and it seems highly unlikely that drivers could read this instrument clearly when the car was travelling at speed. Badly positioned and incorporating three functions (oil pressure, oil temperature, and water temperature), the small dial to the left of the steering wheel must have been quite impossible to read at speed. The gear lever for the five-speed gearbox, the top of which can be seen on the right of the cockpit, operated in an open gate. *(LAT Photographic)*

◀ Another view of the cockpit, taken at the 1951 British Grand Prix. It shows rather more clearly the lever for the five-speed and reverse gearbox operating in an open gate with a hinged flap that was flicked up to engage first and reverse gears. Note the scrutineer's tag attached to the steering wheel. *(Guy Griffiths Collection)*

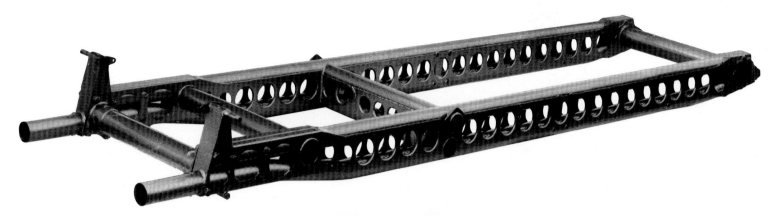

▲ In this photograph the rear of the BRM chassis is nearer the camera. The original chassis frame of the Type 15 was a very simple but reasonably stiff ladder-type structure composed of two longitudinal tubes, to which pierced sheet-steel spacers were welded on between them. There was a large-diameter cross-tube at the front to locate the suspension, a cross-member of the same construction as the longitudinal members at the scuttle and, behind it, two cross-tubes, one of which located the rear suspension.
(LAT Photographic)

▲ By the standards of the time the BRM V16 was low-built, as is obvious from this photograph. Apart from the front suspension, clearly visible is the hole at the top of the radiator where the portable electric starter was inserted.
(LAT Photographic)

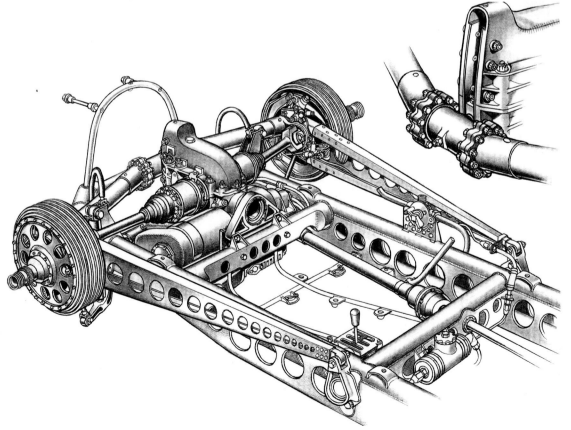

◀ In this detailed drawing the rear suspension and the combined gearbox and final drive unit can be easily examined (at this time the term 'trans-axle' did not exist). Also clearly visible are the original folded metal radius arms, the gear lever moving in an open gate and the hydraulic brake reservoir. On the chassis side-member further away can be seen the control taps for the fuel supply system. The drawing inset shows the lateral location of the de Dion tube.
(LAT Photographic)

▲ For the 1952 season the V16 was fitted with Girling disc brakes with disc diameters of 13in (330mm) at the front and 13.5in (345mm) at the rear. Like all disc brakes in their early days, they were far from perfect and had a tendency to grab. *(Guy Griffiths Collection)*

▶ A very keen supporter of BRM in its early days, Tony Vandervell (of the Vandervell Thin Wall Bearing company) imported a succession of Ferraris to provide opposition to BRM when they were raced. The first of these cars was this green-painted standard short-chassis Tipo 125 Grand Prix car; it was one of the cars that had made Ferrari's Formula 1 debut in the Italian Grand Prix in September 1948. Raymond Mays, seen here at the wheel during the British Grand Prix in May, handed it over towards the end of the race to his head mechanic Ken Richardson. Richardson, who had never driven in a race before, spun off into a spectator enclosure and injured a number of people, fortunately none seriously. The Ferrari was returned to its maker. *(Guy Griffiths Collection)*

'The Conspirators'. In this publicity photograph, Peter Berthon points out something of alleged significance to Raymond Mays on one of the drawings for the V16. (LAT Photographic)

This is an early photograph released some time before the official launch in 1949 to show how the V16 would look. The air intake, which was reminiscent of aviation practice, was rather large. Mainly because of the large wheels fitted, the tops of the tyres were higher than the nose. (LAT Photographic)

Clearly visible in this photograph is the substantial de Dion tube. It is also possible to see the slim rods that connected the hubs to the suspension, and the gaiters on the lower ends of the suspension struts. Underneath the car were the exhaust pipes and outlets for cooling air. (LAT Photographic)

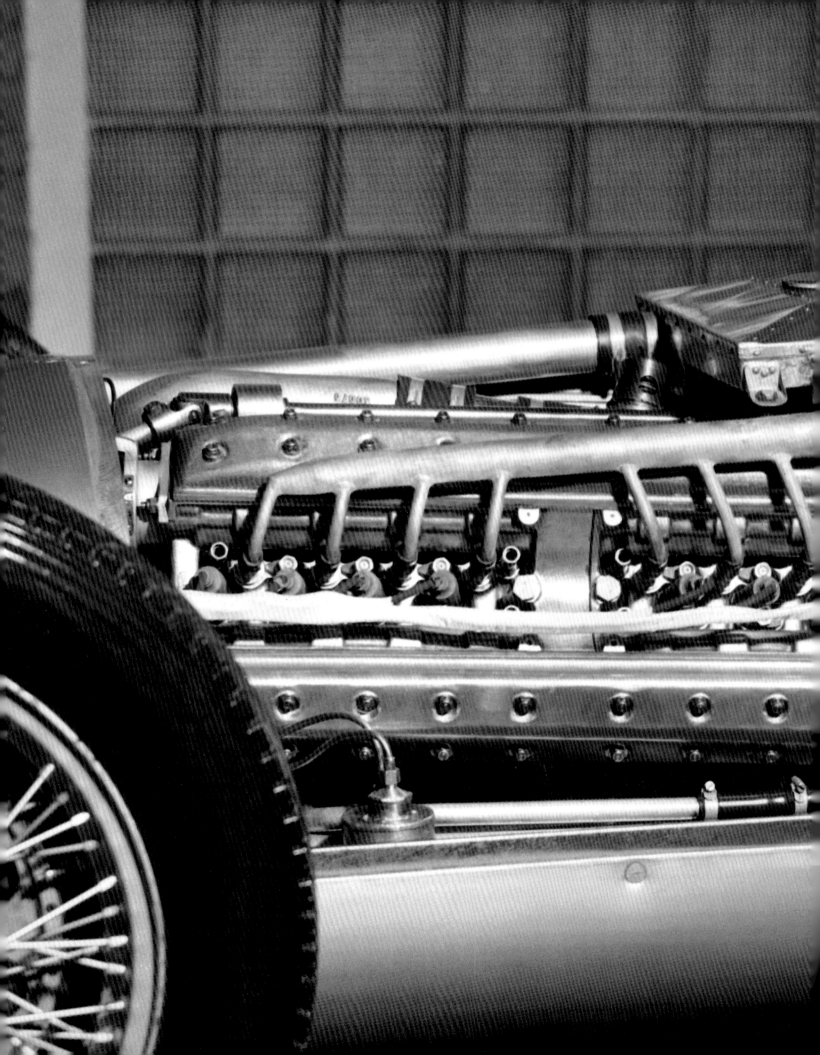

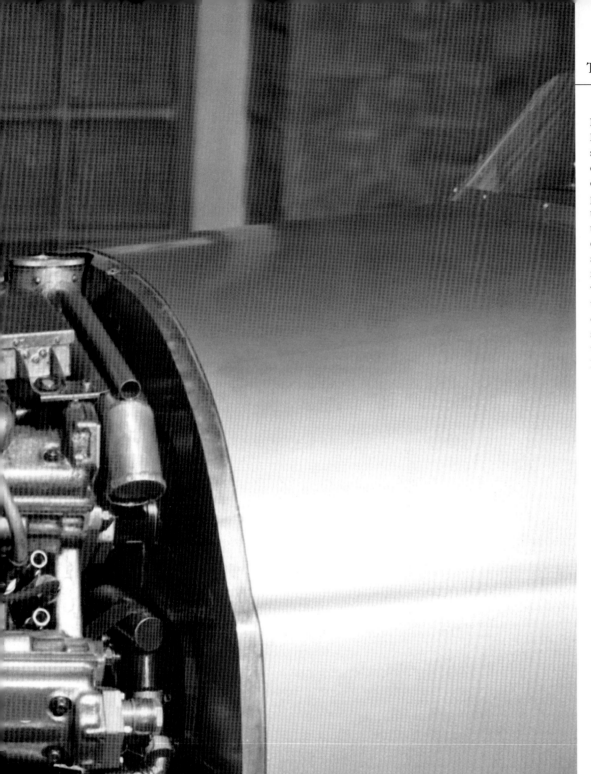

PREVIOUS SPREAD
Lucas Industries, a leading
supporter of the BRM project,
commissioned Louis Klemantaski,
one of the greatest motor racing
photographers of all time, to take
the photographs to be released
to the press. 'Klem' enjoyed
commissions of this sort, which
allowed him to exercise artistic
flair without the pressure under
which racing photographs were
taken. This is one of several views
of the V16 taken in the dark with
spot lighting. Behind the car is
the glass wall of the test house at
Bourne. *(LAT Photographic)*

◄ Klemantaski's photograph of the
immensely complex V16 engine.
This view is dominated by the
radiator header tank mounted
over the rear of the engine and
with riser pipes connected to the
head of each cylinder. On the
scuttle, the oil for the oil tank and
the vent pipe can be seen. The
jointed steering column passes
over the top of the engine close to
the pipe that connects the header
tank with the radiator. Alongside
it, just visible, is the main inlet
pipe from the supercharger.
(LAT Photographic)

◄ The presentation of the V16 BRM on 15 December 1949 was held in the former Crew Briefing Room at Folkingham Aerodrome. Speaking is Donald McCullough, Chairman of the Trustees. *(LAT Photographic)*

▼ The dustsheet has been removed and now Raymond Mays, suffering from influenza and a high temperature, makes his address. The ropes possess a peculiar stiffness and it has been suggested that this was because of the extreme cold. It seems more likely to the writer that the ropes were brand-new and previously unused. *(LAT Photographic)*

▶ Another view of the launch of the BRM on 15 December 1949. The project was backed by great optimism, but there was no serious appreciation of the immense problems in developing a car of this complexity into a race winner. Seated behind the car is Donald McCulloch (Chairman of the British Motor Racing Research Trust who, technically, owned the project), with on his left the Duke of Richmond and Gordon and Peter Berthon. On McCulloch's right is Earl Howe and, standing, Raymond Mays. *(Tom March Collection)*

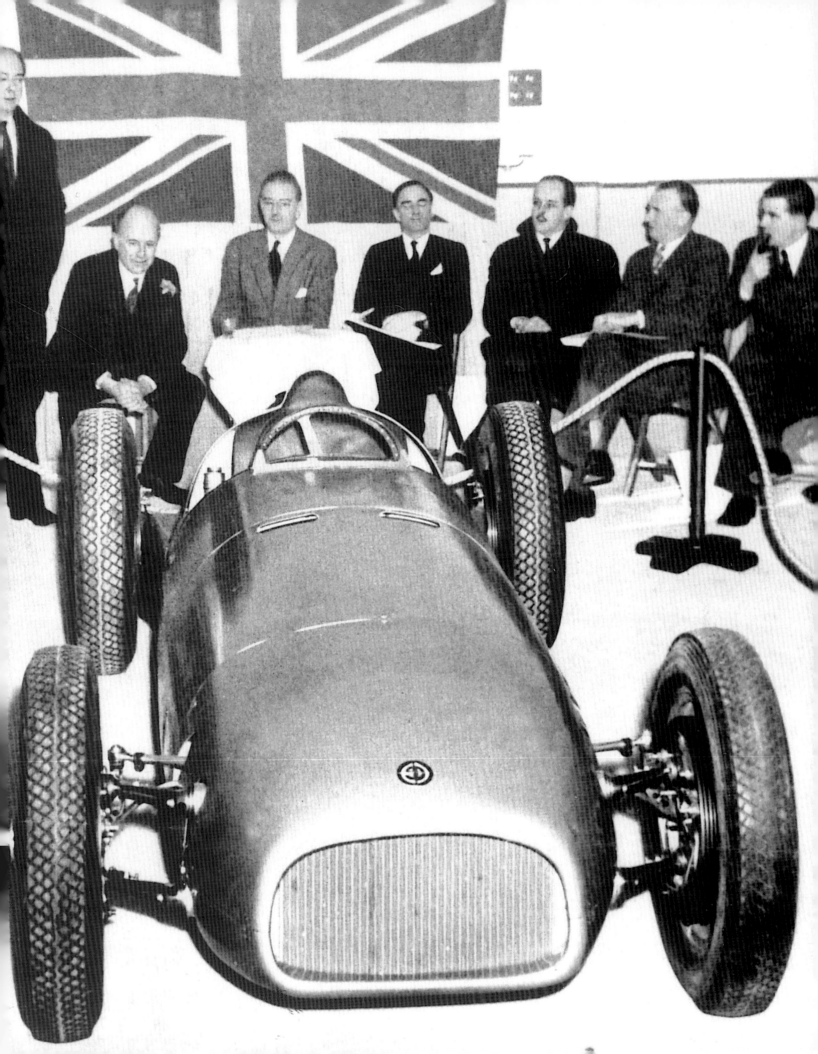

◀ After the presentation, the car was wheeled out on to the circuit by mechanics dressed in white overalls. The tail of the V16 in its original form was particularly shapely, and was reminiscent of that of the E-Type ERA. *(LAT Photographic)*

▲ Before the V16 was fired up, this posed photograph of people involved in the project was taken; Raymond Mays is at the wheel; Peter Berthon is on the left of the photograph close to Mays; Head Mechanic Ken Richardson is close to the car on the right of the photograph. At the back are the principal members of the design team: Eric Richter, in spectacles behind Frank May, and, Harry Mundy in dark coat. *(LAT Photographic)*

▶ Looking rather forlorn, the V16 sits on the concrete of the Folkingham runway waiting for Raymond Mays to demonstrate it to the press. Of the styling of the BRM V16 in its original form *The Autocar* said, 'From the first sight the car creates a good impression. Its lines are crisp, clean and businesslike. It looks lower built than anything seen hitherto and at the front is an air intake of simple but distinctive outline…' *(LAT Photographic)*

◀ Compared with the very elegant tail, the nose of the BRM V16 was blunt and ugly. At this stage the hole for the insertion of the electric starter was absent. *(LAT Photographic)*

OVERLEAF From the rear three-quarter view, the BRM V16 was a very handsome motor car. *(LAT Photographic)*

▶ In contrast, from the front
three-quarter view the V16 was
not a pretty car – the lines were
too heavy. Note how the bodywork
covers the rear suspension, a
feature that was soon changed.
The car is painted in the original
light green chosen by Mays.
(LAT Photographic)

After the press had been given the chance to take photographs of the V16 from various angles, Raymond Mays climbed into the car for further pictures to be taken. *(LAT Photographic)*

In this side view of the V16 with Raymond Mays at the wheel, the car looks superb and the styling matches that of any of the Continental opposition. It is only the frontal treatment that looked wrong. Over the years the body was to be much modified, mainly to improve air flow or cooling. *(LAT Photographic)*

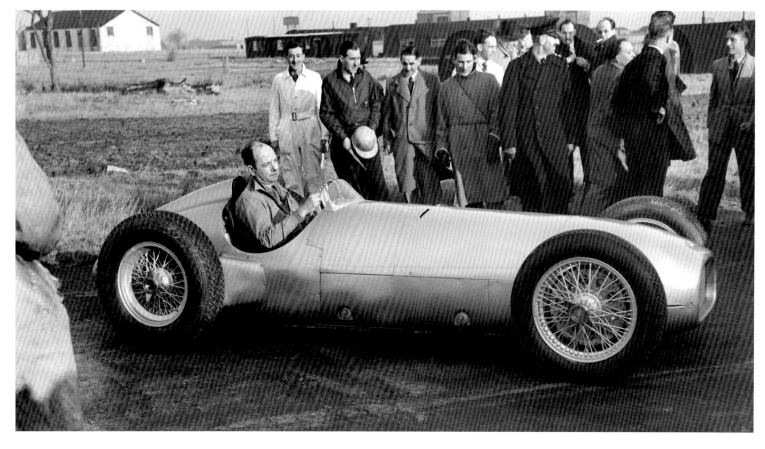

▶ Anxious not to be seen to hog all the limelight, Raymond Mays arranged for a photograph to be taken showing him with the representatives of the BRM's principal supporters.
(LAT Photographic)

▼ Then it was time for Raymond Mays to take the V16 out for some high-speed runs on Folkingham Aerodrome. Those who had not heard the V16 engine run before were staggered by the incredibly high noise level.
(LAT Photographic)

◀Although no great speeds were attained, and both Raymond Mays and Peter Berthon felt pressured into having the launch before they were ready, clearly the day at Folkingham was a great success and any doubts about the project were silenced. *(LAT Photographic)*

◀Handed out to the press generally was this rather blurry photograph that gives the impression that the car is travelling at considerable speed. Although the BRM was already well behind schedule when the launch at Folkingham took place, the car was a great white hope and it was reckoned that it would transform Britain into a true and very great power in motor racing. If told of the traumas, disasters and mistakes ahead, no one would have believed it. *(LAT Photographic)*

Chapter 4

The 1950 season

A faltering start

Raymond Mays demonstrated the V16 at the British Grand Prix at Silverstone in May 1950. That year the race was also given the title of European Grand Prix. It was the first round of the newly inaugurated World Championship for Drivers. The works Alfa Romeo 158s took the first three places in the order Giuseppe Farina, Luigi Fagioli and guest driver Reg Parnell. If the BRM V16 was to succeed, the Alfa Romeo 158 was the car that it had to beat.

Alfa Romeo had introduced the Tipo 158 Alfetta in 1938, and in pre-war days and 1946 these cars ran in the Voiturette category for cars up to 1,500cc supercharged. Italy entered the war in June 1940 on the Axis side, and because of Allied bombing of Milan in December 1942 Alfa Romeo moved all special projects, together with Design and Experimental personnel, to Lago d'Orto north of Milan and close to Lago Maggiore. This included the Tipo 158s, together with the sensational rear-engined Tipo 512 Voiturettes designed by Wifredo Ricart. The Tipo 162 Grand Prix car remained at the factory in the Portello suburb of Milan and was destroyed by bombing.

◀ The first overseas foray for the BRM V16s was to Barcelona for the Penya Rhin Grand Prix in October 1950. Ferraris dominated the race, Alberto Ascari winning, but the two BRMs were at least able to achieve higher straight-line speeds than the Italian entries before having to retire. This view of Peter Walker sweeping through a fast curve emphasises the lack of crowd protection (with large numbers of spectators standing on the outside of the corner) and the considerable width of the road. *(LAT Photographic)*

The Portello company returned to racing with the 158s in the St Cloud Grand Prix held in a suburb of Paris in June 1946, but the two cars entered failed to finish because on both of them the sleeve holding the disc pressure bearing of the clutch overheated. Thereafter the Alfettas won their next three races. On the introduction of the new Grand Prix Formula for 1947 the Alfettas changed overnight on 31 December 1946 from Voiturettes to Grand Prix cars, and they dominated Grand Prix racing until 1951.

They won every race entered, except the International Trophy at Silverstone in May 1951 when they were defeated by a tremendous downpour of rain and a flooded track that caused the race to be abandoned after six laps. The Alfettas won a total of 24 races before being beaten by Ferrari in the British Grand Prix, and thereafter winning another four races before withdrawing from racing at the end of the year. Alfa Romeo was a team of immense power and superb organisation and they had the world's best drivers. Defeat of the Alfa Romeos was BRM's goal, but it was never to be achieved or, even remotely, approached.

European Grand Prix

Silverstone, 13 May 1950

Originally, the plan had been to enter the Grand Prix at Silverstone in May, but this was dropped when it became increasingly obvious that the V16 was insufficiently developed to be competitive. The race was to be attended by His Majesty King George VI, Queen Elizabeth, and other members of the Royal Family, including the Princesses Elizabeth and Margaret. This prompted the Trustees to insist that Mays demonstrate the car in front of the Royal family and a crowd that was expected to number at least 120,000.

Mays lapped the circuit twice at medium speeds, and the whole effort was surprisingly free from problems. The crowd roared their approval and the Royal Family seemed suitably impressed. The outcome was that the Trustees, the press, and the public wanted the V16 to be raced immediately. This was not unreasonable, bearing in mind how long the car had been under development.

▶ The BRM V16 first appeared at a race meeting when Raymond Mays demonstrated it before the European Grand Prix at Silverstone in May 1950. Here the car accelerates past the pits, which were rough-and-ready, temporary structures. With the benefit of hindsight it is sad to see just how many people at all levels, from uninformed members of the public to experts, were convinced that the V16 would be a winner. *(LAT Photographic)*

◀ The Royal family arrived at Silverstone in a special Thrupp & Maberley-bodied Humber Pullman and it then drove them round the circuit to a private stand specially constructed from scaffolding from which they watched the racing. In the background are two Mark V saloons made available by Jaguar for other distinguished visitors. *(Tom March Collection)*

▼ Clearly visible on the stand are, from right, HRH Princess Margaret, His Majesty King George VI and Her Majesty Queen Elizabeth. *(Tom March Collection)*

After the European Grand Prix, development work continued on the V16 and this largely consisted of flogging the car round and round Folkingham until something broke, repairing it, and then continuing with the lapping. The people involved in the BRM never understood the futility of doing the same thing over and over again and expecting a different result.

The Folkingham circuit was not fast enough to provide good times, and most of the driving was undertaken by head mechanic Ken Richardson, whose only Formula 1 race experience was at the wheel of Vandervell's Ferrari Thin Wall Special, a standard short-wheelbase, single-cam-per-bank Tipo 125 which he drove for a few laps before crashing in the 1949 British Grand Prix. There could be no comparisons with other Formula 1 cars and no adequate monitoring of performance improvement. It was all rather pointless and no real progress was made. In addition a new problem had appeared. The engine would bend a connecting rod and

shatter a piston without warning. The problem was recognised by water pouring out of the exhausts or out of a plughole when a spark plug was removed. Mays and Berthon did not want to race the cars until this problem was solved, but the Trustees were proving intransigent and insisted that two cars should run in the International Trophy race at Silverstone on 26 August.

▼ In its earliest form the pale green V16 had smooth and uncluttered lines, but it was a big and excessively bulky car. Compared with its original form first seen in 1949, the car's appearance was now improved by the fitting for the demonstration of a more aerodynamic nose section with smaller air intake, together with a small hole above the intake to accept an electric starter; there was also a BRM badge in transfer form on the nose. That the BRM was not yet ready to race is emphasised by the lack of rear-view mirrors. *(LAT Photographic)*

▲ Raymond Sommer is seen after completing the specially sanctioned laps that the RAC stewards required to permit the BRM to take part in the race. *(Guy Griffiths Collection)*

◄ Raymond Mays was able to show the car and discuss it with Their Majesties King George VI and Queen Elizabeth. With them is Princess Margaret. *(Author's collection)*

▲ The winner of the 1950 British Grand Prix – and the first World Championship for drivers – Giuseppe Farina, at the wheel of his Alfa Romeo 158, heads towards the chequered flag. If BRM was to be successful, it had to beat the Alfa Romeos. With the benefit of hindsight it could never have done that. (Tom March Collection)

▶ By 1950 the BRM was not the only British-made Grand Prix car. Geoffrey Taylor's small company based at Tolworth in Surrey had also built three Grand Prix cars with twin overhead camshaft four-cylinder 1,490cc (78 x 78mm) engines. The first two cars had single-stage supercharging, but twin-stage supercharging giving 230bhp was adopted on the third car. This is the first car owned by George Abecassis, seen on its debut in the British Empire Trophy on the Isle of Man in May 1945. (Guy Griffiths Collection)

BRDC International Trophy

Silverstone, 26 August 1950

The V16s were entered in the International Trophy at Silverstone for French driver Raymond Sommer and for Reg Parnell. The choice of a French driver ('perfidious frog') was unpopular. Raymond Sommer was, however, very enthusiastic and had paid his own expenses to travel to Bourne to try the V16. Although, as already mentioned, the roads on the Folkingham airfield circuit were not long enough for full testing of the car, but he was satisfied with his impressions and he accepted an invitation to drive the BRM.

The offer to Sommer was, apparently, made to reciprocate the invitation made by Antony Lago to Raymond Mays to drive the new Monoposto Talbot in the 1939 French Grand Prix at Reims. The point should perhaps be made that Sommer was quite elderly by racing driver standards at almost 44 and well past his prime.

Two days before the race one of the V16s had engine failure with water pouring out of a plughole because of a bent con-rod and cylinder failure. Berthon concluded that there was insufficient time to remove the engine and fit another, so one entry, the car to be driven by Parnell, had to be scratched. The team concentrated in getting the other car to Silverstone in time for the last day's practice on the Friday, the day before the race. At 8.30 that morning the surviving car cracked a cylinder liner.

Initially Mays and Berthon considered that there was no alternative but to withdraw the entry, and they informed the Trustees of their views that the team should give up any intention to run in the race. Notification was given to the race organisers, the British Racing Drivers' Club (BRDC) and their sponsors the *Daily Express*. Only then was it appreciated that the whole of the pre-race publicity had centred on the race debut of the V16 BRM and that some 120,000 spectators were expected.

Although Mays believed that to run at Silverstone and fail could mean the premature end of the BRM V16, the team had no alternative but to accept the necessity of making every endeavour to field one car. There was a circular argument from which there was no escape. The BRM had been under development for 5½ years and was still not raceworthy (and not competitive, although no one really knew that for a fact) and, in reality, it never would be. If they raced the car now and failed, then the project was quite possibly doomed; so the team should wait to race the car until it was raceworthy and this still could result in the project being doomed.

The RAC stewards agreed to allow the BRM to start without taking part in official practice (it was on the Friday when these discussions took place) provided that the car arrived at the circuit on the race day, the Saturday, before 10am and that Sommer completed three fast laps. The team's engine builder David Turner had built up the two engines for the Silverstone race and then taken his wife on holiday to Skegness where they stayed on a caravan site.

Turner responded to a message over the Tannoy system at the site and was summoned back to Folkingham by telephone. While he was driving back, the exhausted mechanics were roused at their homes and lodgings and dragged to the workshops for their fifth successive 'all-nighter'.

After a cross-county drive to Folkingham, Turner built up an engine from the two broken ones and with new connecting rod and piston. At 4.30am the shattering bark of the V16 engine could be heard across the Lincolnshire countryside as the car was fired up and ran smoothly.

One of the team's Austin Lodestar lorries and Mays at the wheel of his Bentley Mk VI set off for Bicester airfield (the nearest to Silverstone), while another of the Austin Lodestars took the V16 the ten miles or thereabouts to RAF Cranwell where a Bristol 170 Freighter of Silver City Airways, chartered by the *Daily Express,* flew it to Bicester.

At Bicester airfield the V16 was loaded on to the Lodestar and driven to Silverstone. After it had been fired up on the electric starter, Mays completed a warming-up lap and then Sommer took the wheel for his three laps. His speeds were 78.78mph (126.76kph), 81.24mph (130.72kph) and 79.99mph (128.70kph).

The International Trophy was run in two 15-lap qualifying heats and a 30-lap final. Giuseppe Farina won the first heat with his Alfa Romeo 158. Then came the ten-lap race for 500cc cars, and in this Sommer finished second with a Cooper-Norton loaned by the works to Moss with another Cooper-Norton.

Sommer then drove a works DB2 Aston Martin, one of a team of three, in the One-hour Production Sports Car race for cars over 2,000cc and he finished second in the class. The overall results were dominated by Jaguar XK 120s, and the 3,000cc class was won by Duncan Hamilton at the wheel of an overdriven Healey Silverstone – all round the circuit it sounded as though the Riley engine of the Healey was about to break.

Then the cars came out for the second heat of the Trophy race. Sommer started from the back row of the grid because of the lack of official practice. When the flag fell, Sommer fed in the clutch, the BRM jerked forward and stopped. A driveshaft had broken.

▲ After the team's Austin Lodestar had collected the BRM at Bicester Airfield and delivered it to Silverstone, the mechanics carefully roll the car down the ramps of the Austin. *(LAT Photographic)*

Both Sommer and the team were completely stunned, and BRM never fully recovered from the damage to its public image. Although, on both occasions, Sommer was blameless, the matter was not helped by the fact that the same thing had happened to him at the wheel of the CTA-Arsenal, the French National racing car, at the start of the French Grand Prix at Lyon in 1947.

Press and public alike poured scorn and derision on the BRM, and although the general thrust was fair, much of the detail was distorted in the newspapers. Tales of how members of the public threw coins into the cockpit of the BRM are untrue. For many months the *Daily Express* withheld starting money for the BRM, claiming that the car had not moved. It was, however, eventually paid. Poor Sommer was killed at

the wheel of his Cooper 500 in a race at Cadours in the Haute-Garonne later in the year.

There was a great deal of discussion and argument about the failure of the driveshaft at Silverstone, but at the end of the day it has to be concluded that the specification issued by BRM for the component resulted in a driveshaft of inadequate strength. It was, of course, the first time that any driver had tried to take the V16 off the line in anger, and Sommer's acceleration may well have hastened an inevitable failure.

◀ The BRM mechanics then pushed the BRM from the paddock to the pits where it was fired up on the electric starter. (LAT Photographic)

▲ In accordance with the requirements of the RAC stewards, Raymond Sommer drove three laps of the circuit early in the day's proceedings. Sommer found that the track was damp and slippery this early in the day and he was content to cover the laps at, or slightly less than, 80mph (just under 130kph). It was fast enough to satisfy the stewards. (Guy Griffiths Collection)

▶ AND OVERLEAF After Sommer's three laps, Raymond Mays then drove the BRM from the pits back to the paddock. It was still quite early in the day and the grandstand in the background was empty, emphasising the fact that few of the large number of spectators who came to Silverstone that day to see the BRM actually did so. The BRM back in the paddock, with Mays at the wheel. From the front the BRM looked very impressive. Compared with the BRM's previous appearance at Silverstone, three months earlier, cooling louvres had now been cut into the bonnet. (LAT Photographic)

◀ Raymond Sommer, on the right in linen helmet, seen before the 1950 International Trophy race with Franco-American driver Harry Schell, who usually drove Maseratis and turned in stalwart, gutsy performances for Vanwall in 1955–56. Sommer's performance was impeccable, but he was much maligned when the BRM broke a driveshaft, because a similar failure had occurred on the French SEFAC Grand Prix car with Sommer at the wheel at the start of the 1947 French Grand Prix at Lyon. *(Guy Griffiths Collection)*

▶ This photograph and those that follow show the terrible debacle unfolding. Here Raymond Sommer, looking relaxed, talks to Raymond Mays before the BRM is pushed out to the starting grid, while the head mechanic does up the bonnet catches. The louvres on the bonnet and sides permitted the exit of under-bonnet heat and were added after the car's appearance at the British Grand Prix. The bonnet strap was also an addition after the Grand Prix and, even in 1950, was inappropriate on a Formula 1 car. *(Guy Griffiths Collection)*

▼ Raymond Mays gives instructions (something he was rather too good at), while mechanics have attached the electric starter and are about to fire up the engine. *(Guy Griffiths Collection)*

◀ Because of some delay, the mechanics have held off from starting the car for the time being, and Sommer stands up in the cockpit to see what is going on. Peter Berthon, on the right, is also alert to the situation. *(Guy Griffiths Collection)*

▼ Now the electric starter is being applied and Raymond Sommer watches the instruments as the engine is about to fire. The moment of the infamous driveshaft failure draws closer… *(Guy Griffiths Collection)*

Mays' sprint car

Apart from the V16, there was another development at Bourne. Mays had decided to build a sprint car powered by a 2-litre ERA engine with a chassis incorporating V16 components. He claimed that this was for test purposes, but some members of the BRM Trust considered that it was an undesirable diversion of effort from the development of the V16, and others saw it as the scam that it was.

There were BRM Lockheed air strut suspension units, and the transmission incorporated a cross-shaft at the rear, which carried sprockets and drove forward to the rear wheels by chains. For reasons that are none too clear, the design of the car proved fundamentally flawed and it was abandoned without being used in competition.

▶ Raymond Mays' sprint car built in 1950 was neat and well built, but for whatever reasons the design was flawed and it was abandoned. *(Tom March Collection)*

BARC International Meeting

Goodwood, 30 September 1950

Following the unhappy race debut at Silverstone, testing resumed and was generally trouble-free. In mid-September the cars were lapping Folkingham satisfactorily, and the decision was taken to enter one car for Parnell to drive at the BARC's International meeting, sponsored by the *Daily Graphic*, to be held at Goodwood on 30 September. On 19 September an entry was sent by telex for a car to run in two races driven by Reg Parnell.

This meeting failed to attract much in the way of overseas entries, apart from Baron Emmanuel de Graffenried and Prince Bira, both at the wheel of 4CLT/48 San Remo Maseratis. The programme consisted of a number of very short races. If the BRM started, it had a good chance of finishing. In the week before the race the BRM team practised at the circuit. In unofficial practice on the day before the race meeting Parnell lapped the Goodwood circuit in 1min 40.8sec.

Parnell held the circuit record with his obsolescent 4CLT/48 Maserati in 1min 40.0sec, so he was clearly not trying his hardest. Two cars had been prepared and Parnell drove the car entered for Sommer at Silverstone. In official practice Parnell lapped in 1min 37.6sec, and second fastest was Brian Shawe-Taylor (ERA) in 1min 40.8sec. Race day started with an overcast sky; it then began to drizzle, and after that heavy rain set in for the day.

Woodcote Cup, Formule Libre

At this meeting the positions on the starting grid were settled by ballot. This was always a stupid arrangement as it could mean the fastest cars having to fight their way through from the back of the grid. It was not too bad on this occasion as there were only a few starters for this five-lap race, and Parnell drew second place on the front row alongside Peter Whitehead (ERA). A morose-looking Mays, dressed in his habitual but now very damp overcoat, watched the race from under a blue umbrella.

At the fall of the flag, Parnell, determined to drive a very cautious race, moved off the line gently to avoid a repetition of the Silverstone incident. Whitehead and de Graffenried went ahead, but by Madgwick, the first

BARC WOODCOTE CUP, FORMULE LIBRE		
30 September, Goodwood, 2.4-mile (3.86km) circuit, 5 laps, 12 miles (19.3km)		
1st	**Reg Parnell (BRM Type 15)**	**9m 10.0s, 78.50mph (126.31kph)**
2nd	'B. Bira' (Maserati 4CLT/48)	9m 11.6s
3rd	Emmanuel de Graffenried (Maserati 4CLT/48)	–
Fastest lap: R. Parnell, 82.01mph (131.95kph)		

◀ For reasons that are unclear, at Goodwood the BRM team was housed in the scrutineering bay and not the paddock. This stopped enthusiasts from inspecting the cars. The mechanics are working on the car before the race. The large figure on the left wearing a hat with his back to the camera is Tony Vandervell. *(LAT Photographic)*

▼ Here the V16 is seen before practice at Goodwood. Head mechanic Ken Richardson is in control of the jack at the rear of the car, and behind him stands Tony Vandervell. *(Author's collection)*

OVERLEAF In this photograph the mechanics can be seen pushing the car from the scrutineering bay to the starting grid where it was fired up on the electric starter. *(LAT Photographic)*

corner, the BRM was in the lead and Parnell was now in full control, driving no faster than necessary to stay in front of the opposition by a small margin.

Whitehead retired and de Graffenried dropped back, while Bira closed up on the BRM, but as he did so Parnell accelerated, but by only enough to just stay ahead. Parnell led Bira across the line by a margin of 1.6sec and in achieving the BRM's first race win he had averaged 78.50mph (126.31kph).

Daily Graphic Goodwood Trophy, Formula 1

The field for the 12-lap Formula 1 race was much the same and Parnell drew a position on the second row of the starting grid. The rain continued unabated at the start and became even heavier during the race. Again Parnell made a very gentle start, Bira forged ahead off the line, but the British driver accelerated into the lead with the BRM as the leaders came out of Madgwick.

Although Parnell stayed in front for the rest of the race, the conditions were such that he never got into top gear, and there were handling problems exacerbated by the very wet and slippery track; the BRM was snaking under acceleration and the front end lacked adhesion. When Parnell braked for corners, Bira closed right up with his Maserati, but the British driver accelerated clear and as the race progressed he gradually extended his lead. Parnell took the chequered flag 12.4sec ahead of the Siamese driver.

This did not stop Bira complaining to his pit staff that Parnell had baulked him and nearly had him off the track several times. It was a remarkable exaggeration by a man noted for his serious and gentlemanly attitude, but it may have arisen from sheer frustration at not being able to get to grips with the BRM. After the race Parnell was presented with the Goodwood Trophy filled with champagne, and he immediately passed it to Mays for him to drink first.

BARC GOODWOOD TROPHY, FORMULA 1

30 September, 2.4-mile (3.86km) circuit, 12 laps, 28.8 miles (46.3km)

1st	Reg Parnell (BRM Type 15 '151')	20m 58.4s, 82.48mph (132.71kph)
2nd	'B. Bira' (Maserati 4CLT/48)	21m 10.8s
3rd	Bob Gerard (ERA B-type)	21m 39.4s
4th	Emmanuel de Graffenried (Maserati 4CLT/48)	21m 39.8s
5th	Brian Shawe-Taylor (ERA B-type)	21m 41.0s
6th	Graham Whitehead (ERA B-type)	21m 52.0s

Fastest lap: Reg Parnell, 84.95mph (136.68kph)

◀Reg Parnell, a Derbyshire pig farmer, very experienced racing driver, and the most successful British driver in early post-war years, was selected to handle the BRM, and he is seen here at the wheel before the racing started. Ken Richardson is on the left of the photograph and Raymond Mays is behind the car, understandably looking nervous. *(Guy Griffiths Collection)*

▼ The V16 eventually started its racing career when it ran in the wet meeting at Goodwood in September 1950. Reg Parnell is seen here, and this very brave driver won two short races against weak opposition. We have no idea what he is indicating. As the BRM bore the same racing number in both races, it is difficult to identify in which event he is running, but it is probably the five-lap Formule Libre Woodcote Cup race. *(LAT Photographic)*

▲ Here, Reg Parnell is driving a very difficult car in very wet conditions in the 12-lap (28.8-mile/46.3km) Goodwood Trophy, which he won from Bira (Maserati) and Bob Gerard (ERA). *(Guy Griffiths Collection)*

▶ Another view of Parnell on his way to the second of his two wins at Goodwood. *(Guy Griffiths Collection)*

Penya Rhin Grand Prix

Pedralbes (Spain), 29 October 1950

The failure at Silverstone could have left BRM reluctant, psychologically, to race again in 1950, but instead they had bounced back very rapidly, and the two minor victories at Goodwood raised the team's spirits and hopes. On top of this Peter Berthon was satisfied, 'that the cars had reached a stage of overall reasonable reliability and performance without vices'. It was now very late in the season and only a limited number of races were left to choose from. The decision was made to enter cars for Reg Parnell and Peter Walker in the 195.8-mile (315km) Penya Rhin Grand Prix on the fast but bumpy Pedralbes street circuit in Barcelona.

The entry was, of course, accepted and the organisers agreed to pay starting money and expenses. To all intents and purposes the race was the Spanish Grand Prix. The Penya Rhin (or Peña Rhin) was in effect a Catalan businessmen's club and it had been organising the race since 1946. In 1951 the Spanish Grand Prix was revived for the first time since the Spanish Civil War. It was not held again until 1954, and then the Penya Rhin Cup was a supporting race for sports cars.

The procession that left Folkingham consisted of team manager Peter Haynes, the Lucas competitions manager, successor to Jack Emmott whose brief career had ended when he had resigned after the International Trophy race, nine mechanics, the team's Commer mobile workshop, and two of the Austin Lodestar trucks, each of which carried one car. They drove to Dover and their ferry docked at Dunkirk at 4am the next morning.

The slow-moving procession had to cover 900 miles (1,450km) to reach the circuit. What slowed it down was the heavily-loaded Commer, which was underpowered and a bad hill-climber. On the straight, foot to the floorboards, it could attain close to 70mph (113kph), but its comfortable cruising speed was much lower.

On the first night the team reached Avalon, the second night was spent at Montpelier, and on the following day the team arrived in Barcelona. Parnell and Walker had already arrived in the latter's Jaguar XK 120, and they had been using this to learn the circuit. The team's headquarters were in the premises of Fernandez Mercedes-Benz, the Barcelona agents for the German make.

Alfa Romeo missed the race, but there was a strong entry of unblown Ferraris, 4.5-litre cars

◀ In this photograph of Parnell in the wet at Goodwood the BRM looks very skittish and the cockpit is obviously cramped. *(LAT Photographic)*

driven by Ascari and Serafini, while Taruffi had an earlier 4.1-litre Tipo 340. For Ferrari the race was an opportunity to consolidate their performance in the Italian Grand Prix at Monza where Ascari took over Serafini's car to finish second to Farina's Alfa Romeo.

The circuit had a length of 3.9 miles (6.28km) and it ran through the streets of Barcelona, taking in 1.72 miles (2.77km) of the very wide Avenida Generalissimo Franco that was a main thoroughfare running east–west through the centre of the city. In practice Peter Walker lost time in learning the circuit because Ken Richardson, who was reserve driver, insisted on hogging the car, and when Walker did get his hands on it he spun the car while working out braking distances into corners. The writer remembers Walker as a fast and fearless driver, but at Barcelona, two of the trustees, David Brown and Tony Vandervell, thought his approach was too cautious and tentative.

There were some problems with the cars in practice and both needed quite a lot of work on the carburettors before they would run cleanly. In addition, a low-pressure oil pipe fractured on Walker's car and practice time was lost while it was replaced. For BRM it was an important test – a good performance would give the team much-needed encouragement for 1951, but practice soon revealed that, although the BRMs were very fast in a straight line, they had quite serious handling problems.

In practice the 4.5-litre Ferraris were fastest and Ascari and Taruffi lapped in 2min 23.8sec, 98.20mph (158.00kph), while Serafini's fastest lap with the 4.1-litre Ferrari was 2min 26.4sec. Parnell lapped in 2min 30.4sec, 94.90mph (152.72kph) and Walker in 2min 31.8sec, about 94mph (151kph). De Graffenried was fastest of the Maserati drivers in 2min 32.2sec, while Louis Rosier (Talbot-Lago) achieved 2min 33.6sec.

Parnell was timed fastest of the entire entry at 186mph (299kph) over a timed kilometre of the 1.72-mile (2.77km) straight, slightly downhill at the start, along the Avenida Generalissimo Franco. Although the BRMs were faster than the Ferraris in a straight line, the handling was distinctly inferior.

At the start Parnell struggled to get away and lost a lot of ground, while Walker stalled. Parnell passed 16 cars on that first lap and he came past the pits in fourth place behind the Ferraris, but he retired because of supercharger drive failure on the second lap. Although Walker's engine was misfiring and all too obviously down on power, he kept going steadily and was heading for fourth place when he retired at two-thirds distance because an external oil pipe to the gearbox broke. Criticisms of his driving seem to have been misplaced. The Ferraris of Ascari, Serafini, and Taruffi took the first three places.

Some journalists and some of the people associated directly with BRM regarded the outcome at Pedralbes

as 'a fiasco' or something similar. This writer disagrees, and he considers that the 1950 season as a whole was encouraging. The first car had not appeared until the European Grand Prix in May, and Sommer's failure to start the International Trophy at Silverstone seemed a fiasco, but in fact was simply unfortunate; the September Goodwood meeting had resulted in real achievement; and the Pedralbes race, despite the retirements, was very encouraging for the team, its technicians, and it supporters.

This race was the team's first long-distance event; failures were to be expected and the causes of retirement at Barcelona were easily cured. The deficiency in roadholding was more serious, but there was the whole of the winter to sort it out. BRM seemed to be on the up and up, and supporters could expect, at a minimum, reasonably good results in 1951. Instead, however, Pedralbes proved to be one of the V16's two best performances before the existing Formula 1 came to an effective end.

The attitude surrounding the team at the time was not one of encouragement and the carping and criticism by Trustees that had been going on all season reached a peak. Members of the Trust who attended the race criticised everything and everybody, notably Peter Walker. Although the criticisms were intended to be positive and helpful, in reality they were anything but. One of the worst critics was Tony Vandervell. He obviously thought that he knew better than anyone else, but when he parted company with the team to prove it, it took him five years to develop a much simpler concept into a race winner.

There were at this time a number of proposals for changing the team's fortunes, and these included transferring the team to a base in the Midlands where it would be in much closer contact with the British motor industry, and appointing an independent controller of the company. Neither of these proposals was implemented. It was of course very difficult to cut BRM loose from its founding fathers, Mays and Berthon, and it bumbled along in the same incompetent, inchoate way even after it was sold to Alfred Owen's Owen Organisation two years later.

▶ This scene is in the rather gloomy BRM garage at Pedralbes. Ken Richardson is at the wheel about to go out for a few laps. Willie Southcott tightens the bonnet strap as Arthur Ambrose watches. *(Grand Prix Library)*

PENYA RHIN GRAND PRIX (BARCELONA CUP), FORMULA 1

29 October, Pedralbes, 3.9-mile (6.25km) street circuit, 50 laps, 194.2 miles (312.5km)

1st	Alberto Ascari (Ferrari Tipo 375)	2hr 5m 14.8s, 93.80mph (150.92kph)
2nd	Dorino Serafini (Ferrari Tipo 375)	2hr 6m 55.4s
3rd	Piero Taruffi (Ferrari Tipo 375 '340')	48 laps
4th	Philippe Étancelin (Talbot Type 26)	47 laps
5th	Emmanuel de Graffenried (Maserati 4CLT/48)	47 laps
6th	Yves Giraud-Cabantous (Talbot Type 26)	46 laps
Rtd	**Peter Walker (BRM Type 15)**	**33 laps (broken gearbox oil pipe)**
Rtd	**Reg Parnell (BRM Type 15)**	**2 laps (sheared supercharger drive)**

Fastest lap: Reg Parnell, 84.95mph (136.68kph)

▲ The flag has just dropped for the start of the Penya Rhin Grand Prix and Reg Parnell has accelerated through to a position alongside the Ferraris that occupied the first three places on the starting grid. *(LAT Photographic)*

◀ Peter Walker at the wheel of his BRM in the Barcelona race; he was much slower than Parnell, partly because his car's engine was down on power. Otherwise all seemed well with Walker's car, but the rear axle was leaking oil and this resulted in the car's retirement. *(LAT Photographic)*

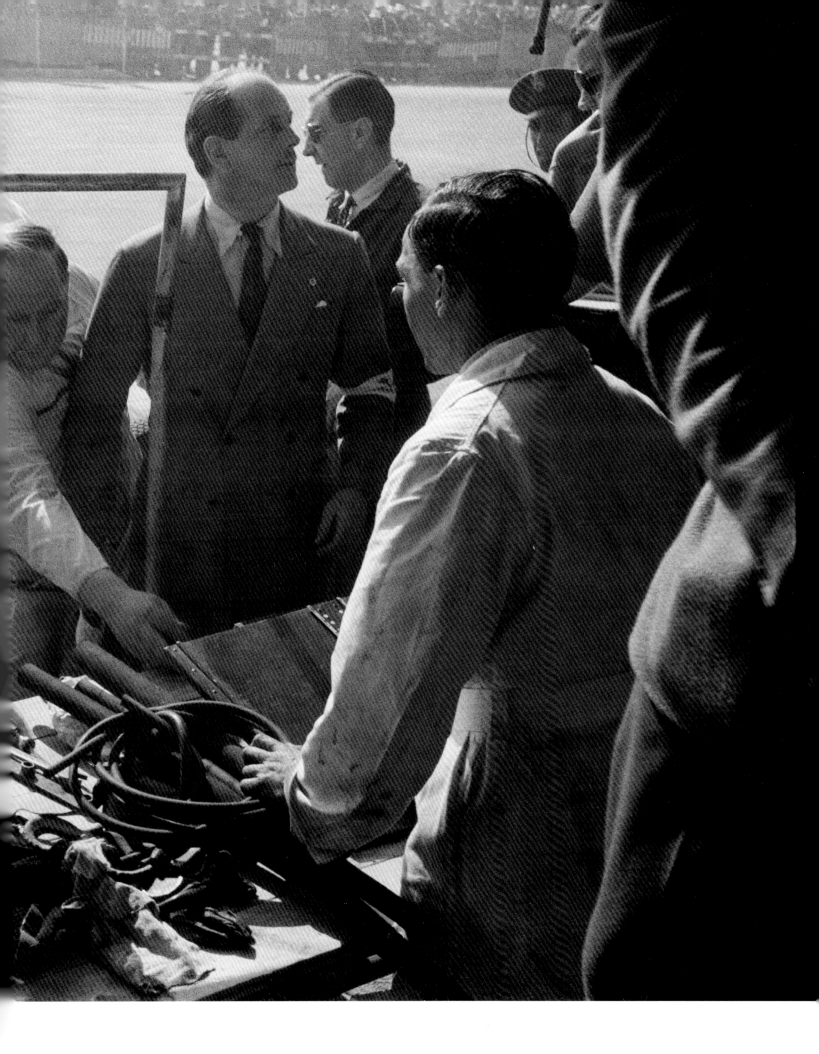

PREVIOUS SPREAD Peter Walker is in the pits at Barcelona during his refuelling stop; head mechanic Ken Richardson is partially hidden by the stanchion supporting the pits canopy. Willie Southcott is handling the fuel hose, while Reg Parnell, who retired early in the race, reaches round Peter Berthon for an item on the pit counter. *(Klemantaski Collection)*

◀ After only two laps the supercharger drive failed on Reg Parnell's car and he is seen, having removed his helmet, crawling back to the pits to retire. The cars in this race ran with different numbers, painted white in practice and black in the race. *(LAT Photographic)*

▶ ▼ Two views of Peter Walker on the same stretch of the circuit. In the second photograph he is crawling back to the pits, helmet on lap, as the rear axle had begun to seize up. At this time Spain was very much a peasant country and the race was held on a Sunday, so most of the male spectators turned up wearing suits. *(LAT Photographic)*

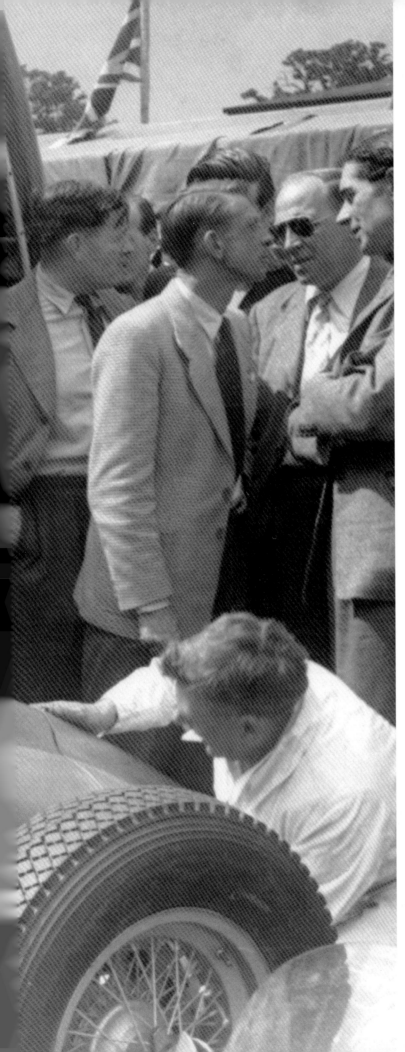

Chapter 5
The 1951 season

The problems continue

The early days of BRM had resembled the opening scenes of a Greek tragedy: burgeoning hope and amour propre turning to dust and despair, and although there was to be an encouraging performances in 1951, it was attributable to the sheer guts of the drivers.

The 1951 Grand Prix season witnessed the end of the battle between Alfa Romeo and Ferrari – a battle between old technology and new. Ferrari had entered Grand Prix racing in 1948 with 1,500cc supercharged cars, but these proved to be uncompetitive, so Maranello's chief engineer Aurelio Lampredi developed an unblown Grand Prix car, and the 4,500cc Tipo 375 version finally beat the Alfa Romeos for the first time in the British Grand Prix and then went on to win the German and Italian races.

◀ This fascinating photograph was taken at the 1951 British Grand Prix. From left: José Froilán González (Argentinian works Ferrari driver who won the race); Peter Berthon; Squadron-Leader Dickie Stoop (private Frazer Nash and, later, Porsche driver who was notorious for 'ear-wigging' on other people's conversations); Ken Richardson; Reg Parnell (in sunglasses); and Peter Walker. Hidden behind González is Onofre Marimon, a friend and compatriot of González and later a works Maserati driver who was killed in practice for the 1954 German Grand Prix at the Nürburgring. *(Guy Griffiths Collection)*

Early-season disaster

The Trust was already conscious that the existing Formula 1 could be abandoned at the end of 1951, and if BRM were to continue it would be necessary to design and build a new car from scratch. Only if the BRMs were raced frequently and successfully could the team be confident of the continuation of the existing Grand Prix Formula. As the Trust was already struggling to raise sufficient funds for a season of selected events at an all-told cost of around £80,000, the building of a new car was totally out of the question.

In summary, the team had been developing the V16 for over six years and, ignoring the International Trophy fiasco, it had raced only twice. The argument above applies again, and with the benefit of hindsight it is blatantly obvious that more generous support from British industry and British organisations would only be forthcoming if the cars were raced frequently and successfully.

There were, however, still many major shortcomings, most of them emanating from inherent design faults. The cars were not inadequately powerful, but the full potential of the engine had never been exploited. The power output was constantly being increased, and as the power rose so the flaws in the design were exposed, and components failed with the greater stress put on them.

Negotiations opened for two BRMs to compete in the Swiss Grand Prix held on the magnificent Bremgarten circuit at Bern, which in 1951 was to be on 27 May. The Automobile Club Suisse, organisers of the race, offered excellent starting money. At a meeting of the Trustees on 19 April it was agreed that the team's immediate aim was to prepare two cars to run in the Swiss race.

At this time two new developments were offered to BRM. Rolls-Royce had devised a vortex throttling system, and SU had produced a fuel injection system (which ultimately proved unsuccessful against the later German Bosch and British Lucas systems). Both required considerable further development to suit the needs of BRM, and Berthon decided that the team could not afford them.

In late 1950 Berthon had decided to adopt specially made SU twin-choke carburettors, which had both a horizontal air intake and horizontal dash-pot pistons. As Laurence Pomeroy, Technical Editor of *The Motor*, commented, these carburettors combined all the problems of a downdraught carburettor with the disadvantages of a horizontal carburettor. They had a magnesium mounting, low in weight but lacking stiffness, so they vibrated badly. The float chambers were prone to flooding, and the carburettor needles came out of their jets – although,

for a very long time, the team was unaware of all these shortcomings.

A major engine problem was plug-fouling, and there were different ideas as to the cause and the solution. Rejecting more sophisticated solutions, Berthon insisted on fitting a motorcycle-type oil feed restrictor, thereby minimising oil flow into the supercharger.

The team travelled to Silverstone for a testing session on 14 May – less than a fortnight before the Swiss race – and the drivers were Reg Parnell and Prince Bira, both of whom had testing contracts. A supercharger quill shaft broke and the test had to be abandoned.

A new stronger quill shaft was made in time for the Silverstone test to be resumed on 17 May. Parnell and Bira were joined by Peter Walker. While Walker was at the wheel there were two loud blow-backs

from the engine and, obviously, Walker stopped immediately. The car was returned to Bourne for the engine to be stripped and examined. The examination revealed that a connecting rod had broken and damaged the crankcase. No second engine was available because of delays in supercharger deliveries caused by problems with bearings and seals.

The final straw came when Bira was testing the sole running V16 at Bourne. The car developed a gearbox oil leak because the aluminium-alloy casting that acted as a front gearbox mounting broke. Oil dripping on to the exhaust pipe caused a conflagration. Bira made clear his feelings by pulling out of his contract shortly afterwards. The entry in the Swiss race was scratched. It was the first in a dismal succession of disasters that brought the V16's Formula 1 career to an end.

Now the team set its sights on the French Grand Prix (that year given the additional title of European Grand Prix) to be held at Reims on 1 July. The

engine failure experienced when Walker was at the wheel was traced to a cylinder ring joint failure. There was no way that the BRMs could be raced before they were fitted with new rings. Supercharger problems had been solved by Rolls-Royce, but these latest items could not be supplied by the end of the month, and the entry for the Reims race had to be scratched. Now the team's efforts were concentrated on running in the British Grand Prix at Silverstone on 14 July.

▼ This publicity photograph was released to the press early in 1951. In the background the runway of Folkingham airfield can be seen. It formed the main straight of BRM's test circuit. On the left is the Commer travelling workshop that had been donated to the team by the Midlands Automobile Club, operators of Shelsley Walsh hill-climb, and on the right the Hillman Minx van presented by the Rootes Group. Raymond Mays is at the wheel of the BRM in its latest form. The original paler green had been abandoned in favour of a light metallic green *(Author's collection)*

British Grand Prix

Silverstone, 14 July 1951

During the week prior to the Silverstone race the team's problems continued. Because of a hastily assembled engine, when the mechanics were under extreme pressure following an earlier engine failure, the feed valve to the low-pressure oil system was in the off position, and a camshaft seized. The supercharger had to be changed as a precaution as it was fed from the system and may have been damaged by oil starvation.

There were other continuing problems; at high engine speeds the cars were chucking out oil from the crankcase breathers and the twin-choke carburettors were flooding their float chambers because of vibration, and the result was the flooding of the engines by straight fuel. At dusk on the eve of the race one car was test-driven by Parnell and Walker. Assembly of the second car was still being carried out when the electricity supply to the racing workshop failed. Assembly was completed in the light of the headlamps of the transporters, which had been parked up against the windows.

The cars missed practice and started from the back of the grid. While the Alfa Romeos and the Ferraris were battling for victory at the head of the field, Parnell and Walker had worked up ahead of the tail-enders, the old Maseratis and Talbot-Lagos, and were holding seventh and ninth places, but trailing fuel spray caused by venting of unburnt fuel. When they made their first refuelling stops, Parnell came in first; he was groggy and in immense pain, complaining of being burnt. When one of the BRM crew touched the inside of the cockpit, the heat burnt his hands.

Walker then made his pit stop; he was even groggier than Parnell, and the cockpit of his car even hotter, but again he was sent back into the race. In the pits the mechanics prepared dressings of wads of cotton wool soaked in Aquaflavine ointment for soothing burns. There were problems with the team's motorcycle-engine-powered refuelling equipment, and after the cars had left the pits it was discovered that only 50 gallons had been put into each car, instead of the 60 gallons needed to complete the race, and they would have to make second refuelling stops.

The team pointed the refuelling flag at Parnell to call him in, but he and Walker were lapping together and both came into the pits. The mechanics managed to wave Walker on. Walker then came into the pits and his car was refuelled, but it was obvious that he was in a terrible state and the car should have been withdrawn. Parnell

completed the race in fifth place, five laps behind the winner, and Walker took seventh place, six laps in arrears.

The cause of the drivers' burns was inadequate insulation of the exhaust system from the bodywork, and it is almost incredible that such a basic fault should still have existed after so many years' development. It was far from clear why the fault did not manifest itself at Barcelona the previous year. Both drivers had displayed tremendous bravery in protecting the interests of BRM and, especially, the reputations of Mays and Berthon. Parnell and Walker also had such high reputations that they would not have been criticised – outside of the team – if they had pulled out of the race. For some obscure reason the Trustees believed that Walker did not give of his best – this went back to his performance in the Spanish race the previous year – and the Le Mans winner was never to drive for the team again.

It is very difficult to be objective about the performance of the V16s at Silverstone. The drivers were heroic, far more so than BRM deserved, and their having to suffer burns because of the problems with the exhaust systems was disgraceful and reflected gross negligence. However, even allowing for the fact that the drivers, within only a few laps of the start, were incapable of giving their best, it was obvious beyond doubt that the cars were still not competitive at an international level.

After the Silverstone race the drivers submitted lengthy and detailed reports about the cars, and there were post-mortems, together with recommendations and decisions for the future. There was neither the time nor the money for further development before the racing season ended. If BRM was to survive, then it had to race in the last World Championship race of the year at Monza on Sunday 16 September. Two cars were entered in this race, but from this point onwards virtually nothing went right for the team.

▶ Plans for a full season in 1951 fell apart because of continuing development problems, and the V16 cars started in only one race, the British Grand Prix at Silverstone in July when they were driven by Reg Parnell and Peter Walker. The cars missed official practice, but they were allowed to start from the back of the grid. This is Parnell's car seen in the pits before the race. Despite the sheer bulk of the V16, it was a very handsome machine before its body was cut into to create louvres, ducts, and additional intakes. *(Guy Griffiths Collection)*

◢ In the pits at the British Grand Prix, John Cooper (no relation to the John Cooper of Cooper Cars), discusses prospects with Raymond Mays. Cooper was Sports Editor of *The Autocar* and he was also responsible for the design of the Martin 500cc car that Stirling Moss raced in 1951, and which acted as the prototype of the production Kieft. Later he designed the completely unsuccessful Formula 2 car built for Stirling Moss in 1953, the Cooper-Alta, which incorporated many Cooper of Surbiton parts. John Cooper of *The Autocar* was killed in a road accident with a road test Frazer Nash in 1953, and it has always been believed that the cause of the accident was structural failure. *(Guy Griffiths Collection)*

BRITISH GRAND PRIX		
14 July, Silverstone, 2.889-mile (4.63km) circuit, 90 laps, 260 miles (418km)		
1st	José Froilán González (Ferrari Tipo 375)	2hr 42m 18.2s, 96.11mph (154.64kph)
2nd	Juan Manuel Fangio (Alfa Romeo Tipo 159)	2hr 43m 9.2s, 95.61mph (153.84kph)
3rd	Luigi Villoresi (Ferrari Tipo 375)	88 laps, 93.39mph (150.26kph)
4th	Felice Bonetto (Alfa Romeo Tipo 159)	87 laps, 92.44mph (148.74kph)
5th	**Reg Parnell (BRM Type 15)**	**85 laps, 90.50mph (145.61kph)**
6th	Consalvo Sanesi (Alfa Romeo 159)	84 laps, 89.50mph (144.01kph)
7th	**Peter D. C. Walker (BRM Type 15)**	**84 laps**
Fastest lap: Giuseppe Farina (Alfa Romeo 159), 99.99mph (160.88kph)		

▲ To work on a car in such crowded conditions must have been very difficult. This is the car that Peter Walker drove in the Grand Prix. It was common for boxes such as those shown to contain an array of spark plugs of different grades. Racing cars of the period were plagued by spark plug failure and if a car came into the pits with an engine problem, the first thing that the mechanics did was to change the plugs. *(Guy Griffiths Collection)*

◄ The great interest generated by the presence of the BRMs in the Silverstone race resulted in large crowds in the team's pit, which made working on the cars very difficult. *(LAT Photographic)*

▲ Tony Vandervell supported
BRM, and he bought Ferraris
from Maranello, partly for design
study purposes and to provide
opposition for the BRMs in British
races. But it was not long before
he became disillusioned by the
incompetence and failure of the
Bourne organisation, and after
developing the Ferrari Thin Wall
Special into the most potent
4½-litre unsupercharged racing
car of all time, he developed and
raced his Vanwall cars that later
gained immense success. Here, on
the left of the photograph, with
Peter Berthon, he examines the
engine bay of one of the cars.
(Guy Griffiths Collection)

▶ Another view of Tony Vandervell
and Peter Berthon in the pits at
the British Grand Prix. On the left
of the photograph in conversation
with Raymond Mays is Leslie
Johnson, Jaguar driver and owner
of ERA, who would be racing their
own unsuccessful Bristol-powered
Formula 2 car in 1952.
(Guy Griffiths Collection)

◀ Many drivers tried the cockpit of the BRMs. Here, race-winner Argentinian Froilán González, a great hulk of a man known familiarly as the 'Pampas Bull', sits in the cockpit. From left are Onofre Marimon, Mays, Parnell, and Walker. *(LAT Photographic)*

▶ Another conversation in the pits. From left, Peter Walker, Ken Richardson, engineer Eric Richter, Mays and Owen Organisation PRO Rivers Fletcher.
(LAT Photographic)

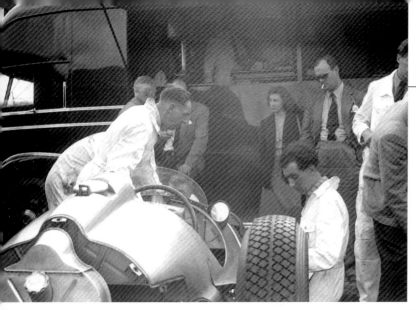

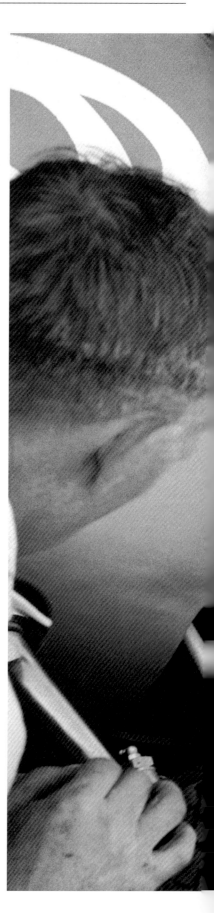

◀ There was something slightly feverish in the way the mechanics are working on Reg Parnell's BRM. Peter Berthon, hidden by the mechanic left centre, is leaning against the side of the team's Commer transporter, deep in conversation. *(Guy Griffiths Collection)*

◀ A further view of the mechanics working on the V16s in the paddock at Silverstone. It is as if a phoney optimism masks an expectancy of failure. *(Guy Griffiths Collection)*

◣ This view of the rear end of the V16 shows clearly the very hefty de Dion tube. Throughout its development and racing life the V16's rear suspension was largely free of problems. The tank is the oil reservoir for the final drive. *(Guy Griffiths Collection)*

▶ A plug change in the pits for Reg Parnell's car, with a box containing different grades of plugs placed on the top of the engine. The practice with the V16s was to warm up the cars on soft plugs, and once warmed to replace them with hard racing plugs. One of the problems facing all mechanics at this time with cars of 12 or more cylinders was that they had quite likely cooled down before the soft plugs could be removed and the hard plugs fitted. *(LAT Photographic)*

▶ Another view of the mechanics working in the pits on Peter Walker's car, with the engine cover sitting loose on the engine (it saved looking for somewhere to safely prop it up). This photograph gives an excellent view of the massive radiator and the independent front suspension with Lockheed pneumatic struts. *(LAT Photographic)*

▲ BRM had the Commer mobile workshop seen here, and the Austin Motor Company also supplied the team on long-term loan three of their Lodestar lorry chassis with van bodies. The Commer had boards mounted on its sides with the name and address in raised silver lettering, together with the team's badge. *(Guy Griffiths Collection)*

▶ Because the BRMs had arrived too late at the circuit and missed practice, the cars started from the back of the grid. Peter Walker's car is on the left of the photograph, Reg Parnell's on the right, and Peter Berthon stands in the centre, between the two cars. *(LAT Photographic)*

◀ Reg Parnell sits at the wheel of his V16 on the starting grid. With him is head mechanic Ken Richardson. *(LAT Photographic)*

▶ Early in the race Peter Walker was struggling to achieve good lap times. Here he is about to be lapped by Juan Manuel Fangio, who at this stage was locked into a fierce battle for the lead with José Froilán González. *(Guy Griffiths Collection)*

▼ Early in the British Grand Prix the BRM of Parnell leads one of the old unsupercharged Talbot-Lagos. *(Tom March Collection)*

◀Reg Parnell with his V16 BRM on the way to fifth place and one World Championship point in the 1951 British Grand Prix. Because both Parnell and Walker still had faith in the project, and believed that the BRM would be a world-beater, they were prepared to suffer terrible burns from the exhaust system to bring the cars to the finish. The results at Silverstone were the only finishes by the V16s in a World Championship race. The cars were still uncompetitive, mainly because of the lack of controllability of the power and the inability to get it on to the road. *(Tom March Collection)*

▼ Early in the 1951 British race Alberto Ascari (Ferrari Tipo 375 on the right) laps Peter Walker's BRM. At this time the bodywork of the V16 was still very smooth and uncluttered. In this race the cars appeared with larger radiators and air intakes. *(Tom March Collection)*

▲ The BRMs suffered from badly overheated cockpits, caused mainly by heat from the exhausts that ran very close along the sides of the car. Despite burns, both drivers bravely struggled to the finish, their efforts completely overshadowed by the battle between Alfa Romeo and Ferrari. BRM neither earned nor deserved such selfless behaviour from its drivers. Seen here is Reg Parnell, who finished fifth, five laps behind the winner of this 90-lap race. *(Guy Griffiths Collection)*

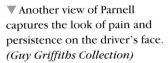◀ The mechanics swarm over the BRM of Peter Walker during his refuelling stop. While Peter Berthon leans over to speak to Walker, Tony Rudd burns his hands on the inside of the cockpit, and Mays watches the opposition pass. *(LAT Photographic)*

▶ Peter Walker's car finished seventh, six laps behind the winner. Walker, in agony in the closing stages of the race from his burns, was lapping in a haze of pain and confusion, and driving totally on 'auto-pilot'. *(Tom March Collection)*

▼ Another view of Parnell captures the look of pain and persistence on the driver's face. *(Guy Griffiths Collection)*

◀ With this single-plug Ferrari (the other members of the Ferrari team had the latest and more powerful twin-plug engine) Argentinian José Froilán González defeated the works Alfa Romeos for the first time since 1946. Alberto Ascari then won the German and Italian Grands Prix for Ferrari, but in the Spanish race in October the Ferraris suffered from tyre troubles, and by finishing fourth Ascari missed out on a win in the World Championship and took second place with 25 points net (28 gross). The Ferrari should have been the leading car for two more seasons, but because of BRM's incompetence the existing Formula 1 was to all intents and purposes scratched. (*Tom March Collection*)

◀ At Silverstone this Alfa Romeo Tipo 159 was driven into second place by Juan Manuel Fangio. He had already won the Swiss and French Grands Prix, but after defeats at Silverstone, the Nürburgring, and Monza, he won the Spanish race and clinched the Drivers' World Championship with 31 points net (37 gross). (*Tom March Collection*)

▶ In this photo, taken late in the race, Peter Walker looks very groggy and barely in control; he was fortunate to finish the race without an accident. This angle shows the superb lines in profile of the V16. (*LAT Photographic*)

Italian Grand Prix

Monza, 16 September 1951

As at Silverstone the drivers were to be Parnell and Walker, but the race clashed with the Tourist Trophy at Dundrod, and Walker was due to be there as a member of the Jaguar team. Initially it was proposed that Leslie Johnson should take his place, but instead Mays nominated head mechanic Ken Richardson to drive alongside Parnell. Mays was apparently fully aware that Richardson lacked the necessary experience to be granted a full international licence.

Then team manager Peter Haynes had to drop out because one of his children was seriously ill. Tony Rudd assumed that he would step in to take Haynes' place for this race, but Berthon vetoed this because he thought that Rudd was too friendly with the mechanics and so would be unable to enforce discipline. So it was decided by way of compromise that Rudd would be in charge on the journey to Monza; Richardson would take over responsibility for race preparation, and then Rudd would be pit manager.

The team departed in a convoy consisting of the Commer mobile workshop and two of the Lodestars, while Mays, accompanied by Richardson, travelled separately in a Ford Zephyr. The main party embarked at Dover, but when the cross-Channel ferry arrived at Dunkirk it was unable to enter the harbour because the sea lock gates had jammed. The ferry returned to Dover and the team had to split up into two for the crossing back to France. Some 15 hours had been lost by the time the convoy once more set off for Milan.

The journey was long and weary: the team drove over the Alps and through the Simplon tunnel. At high altitudes the Commer boiled its petrol, and at many of the hairpin bends it had to take several bites to get round corners, while the Austins suffered from overheated radiators. There were problems with Italian customs because the carnets had not been properly stamped at Calais, but eventually the team reached the destination, the Hotel Marchese at Villasanta, opposite the gates to the Royal Park and the other side of the park from the Autodromo.

A special unofficial practice session had been arranged for the BRMs on the Thursday before the race. This was to enable BRM to reach a decision about gear ratios, and for an official observation of Richardson's driving, following which a report was telegraphed to the RAC in London. The axle ratios were too high and lower ratios were to be fitted to both cars. During Friday's practice Parnell's car developed engine trouble, which proved to be incipient big-end

failure, while Richardson had gear-selector problems and spun into the straw bales at Lesmo.

The results of Richardson's crash included a damaged radiator, steering arm, and brake back-plate, together with crumpled nose cowling. Repairs were carried out with the assistance of Count 'Johnny' Lurani and the Alfa Romeo factory. At 10pm on the Saturday, the eve of the race, the organisers telephoned the team to arrange an immediate meeting about Richardson's licence. Not surprisingly the RAC had declined to sanction him to drive. BRM proposed withdrawing Richardson's car, but the organisers were anxious that both BRMs should start the race.

The race committee suggested that Austrian driver Hans Stuck, who knew the Monza circuit well and was present at the circuit, should be invited to drive Richardson's car. It seems, in retrospect an odd choice, and it is remarkable that the organisers did not propose an Italian driver who lived near the circuit. Stuck was contacted in the very early hours of race day and he said that he would be delighted to drive the BRM.

The organisers arranged a special practice session for 7am. Parnell's car had now been fitted with the spare engine and Richardson took this out at 6am with a view to running in the new engine, but the new engine developed problems just as Stuck was about to practice in the ex-Richardson car. Stuck made an exploratory run in the ex-Richardson car, revving wildly as he accelerated away to the accompaniment of a cloud of smoke and the smell of burning clutch lining.

Initially, the team believed it to be supercharger trouble and both cars returned to the BRM garage for a full examination to be made. In fact it proved to be big-end bearing failure. While Stuck's car was being pushed away, there was a noise from the back axle – the car was stiff to push and the gearbox seemed to be very hot. The trouble was diagnosed as a bearing failure on second and third gears. Berthon concluded that there was a severe risk of the gearbox seizing up altogether.

There was insufficient time left to remove the gearbox from Parnell's car and fit it to Richardson's for Parnell to drive, and it was reluctantly decided to withdraw from the race. As there had been no gearbox problems on the cars at Silverstone, it was concluded that the problem resulted from the much higher speeds attained on the Monza circuit. It was another devastating blow, and when the withdrawal was announced the Italian spectators hissed and booed the team.

▶ Grim-faced mechanics push one of the BRMs through the paddock for the Italian Grand Prix at Monza; the mechanic on the left is pulling the portable electric starter. The cars at this race had new air intake grilles with ten horizontal bars. *(LAT Photographic)*

▼ Hope is still alive as one of the V16s is pushed out to practice at Monza. *(Grand Prix Library)*

Testing at Monza

BRM decided to remain at the circuit for testing. During this time one of the V16s was driven for 12 laps by Piero Taruffi, a member of the Ferrari team. His main criticism was the lack of steering precision, and he indicated that the inability to position the car accurately at speed was costing time. He apparently lapped in 2min 0.0sec compared with the best Ferrari time by Ascari in practice for the race of 1min 55.1sec.

Stirling Moss responded to a request to test the car and he reached the circuit on 4 October and drove the V16 regularly over the next four days. His best lap was timed at 1min 58sec compared with the official lap record of 1min 56.7sec set by Fangio with the Alfa Romeo 159M in the Grand Prix. Moss would have undoubtedly lapped faster if the V16 had not run out of revs above 10,500rpm. He had attained 11,400rpm on the straights during his fifth day at the circuit, but the engine started to misfire at high rpm.

BRM spent ten weeks at Monza, but winter weather set in and eventually brought the testing to an end. Moss had returned to continue testing, but the whole area became blanketed in fog and this, coupled with the failure of the team's last engine on 12 November, brought testing to an effective end and the team set out for home on 14 November.

While BRM was always hampered by financial difficulties, it was unfortunate that they had not previously conducted a thorough testing session on a circuit where lap times could be compared with those of other teams, and where drivers of wide experience could drive the cars and give feedback on handling, steering and braking.

It was especially useful that Italian Grand Prix drivers like Taruffi, with experience of the fastest contemporary cars, had the chance to evaluate the V16. There were many lessons to be learned from the long test session at Monza, but unfortunately, partly for cost reasons, there was little attempt to apply these lessons in the development of the cars over the winter months.

◀ This photograph shows the V16 in the form in which it was tested at Monza in the autumn of 1951. The photograph was, however, taken after the cars had returned to Folkingham. *(LAT Photographic)*

▼ An interesting cockpit shot of the V16 in late 1951 form. It shows the ribbon-type tachometer, and there were only two other instruments, one of which was multi-functional and almost impossible to read at speed. Again, this photograph shows just how cramped was the cockpit of the V16. *(LAT Photographic)*

Chapter 6
The 1952 season

The beginning of the end – a season of non-championship racing

Between 2 and 4 October 1951 the Commission Sportive Internationale held a meeting at the Grand Palais, while the Paris Salon motor show was being held there, for the purpose of discussing the future of Formula 1. The current Formula 1 had, as mentioned earlier, come into force for 1947 after being delayed by the outbreak of the Second World War and there was no fixed date for when it would be replaced.

Already there were doubts about the likely level of competitiveness in the current formula. The Alfa Romeo 159 (the 1951 version of the Tipo 158 Alfetta first seen in 1938) had reached the end of its development; the Alfa Romeo team had already indicated that it was considering whether or not to continue racing; the Maserati 4CLTs and the Talbot-Lagos were obsolete; the V12 OSCA-powered cars of B. Bira and Franco Rol, introduced in1951, had performed disappointingly; only the V12 4.5-litre Ferraris and the BRMs were likely to provide competition (and there were obvious doubts about BRM).

On the other hand the Formula 2 for 2,000cc unsupercharged/500cc supercharged cars was flourishing (no one had built a serious blown 500cc contender). Many delegates saw Formula 2 as a basis in modified form for a new Formula 1. Despite vigorous

◀ Ken Wharton has his V16 nicely set up and balanced for his line through St Mary's in the *Daily Graphic* Trophy race at Goodwood. Wharton was a notoriously hard driver, and he ruffled a few feathers amongst fellow drivers. He and Roy Salvadori detested each other. *(Guy Griffiths Collection)*

opposition from the British delegate, Earl Howe, and his German counterpart, Alfred Neubauer (it is possible the Daimler-Benz company was considering racing a modern, revised version of the W 165), there was overwhelming agreement that the existing Formula 1 should cease at the end of 1953 and be replaced by a new formula of 2,500cc unsupercharged and 750cc supercharged. This meant that within two years the BRM V16 would be obsolete.

Very soon, however, there were more pressing causes for concern. After showing some ambivalence about the company's future role in racing, Alfa Romeo announced early in 1952 that they were withdrawing from Grand Prix racing altogether. The company planned to enter sports car racing, but the 2-litre and 3-litre Disco Volante (Flying Saucer) cars developed in conjunction with the Touring company were not raced in 1952 because of problems with the aerodynamic stability, while the 6C 34 3.4-litre versions with Colli coupé bodies that were entered in major endurance races in 1953 proved to be mechanically unreliable.

It seemed that Grand Prix racing would be completely dominated by the unblown 4½-litre Ferraris, for there was no likely serious contender, unless of course the BRM team could prove that the V16s were raceworthy – which meant fast and reliable. The general consensus was forming that the best course of action was to adopt Formula 2 for 2,000cc cars, as there were many makes racing in this category and even if none could match the power and speed of the works F2 Ferraris, at least race organisers were assured of large fields. Furthermore, this category, which would also officially come to an end in 1953, formed a basis from which cars complying with the new 2,500cc Grand Prix formula could be developed.

The situation was not completely hopeless, although it was unpromising. Not all organisers of World Championship events had committed themselves to holding their Grand Prix to Formula 2 rules. There was a slim chance of persuading these organisers to retain the status quo for their races. Although Mays wrote to all the organisers who were not yet committed to running their races to F2 regulations, and guaranteed BRM entries if their races were held to the existing formula, his word was no longer trusted, especially since the debacle at Monza.

As if oblivious to the reality of the situation, Mays released a statement to the press, part of which (edited for grammatical accuracy) read as follows:

BRM Limited announces that it is its intention to compete with a team of cars in all Grand Prix races, including the British, and in any international Formula 1 events that can be fitted in. With reference to recent conjecture and proposals about adopting Formula 2, BRM had no official notification of any such negotiations.

In the autumn of 1951 BRM had adopted Girling disc brakes and these are described in some detail in Chapter 5. Steady development, as far as finances permitted, had continued. The team had aimed to enter the 1952 season on a much more formidable basis with a complement consisting of six cars, together with the availability of eight engines and seven gearboxes.

This would have enabled BRM to undertake a full Formula 1 season; while one team of cars was away racing, a second team would be prepared at the works for the next race. It was how the Mercedes-Benz team raced in pre-war days and how they would do so again in 1954–55. It never happened because of BRM's financial situation, and in any event it was not necessary once it had been confirmed that all the important races in 1952 would be held to Formula 2 regulations.

At a meeting of the Trust on 8 February the decision was reached to limit the team to the three cars that had been built, plus sufficient parts that in theory at least represented the means to build up another two cars – but in practice would be used as a spares bank. It was announced that the 156.5-mile (251km) Valentino Grand Prix was to be held in Valentino Park, Turin on 6 April as a Formula 1 race before the first round in the World Championship, the Swiss Grand Prix at Bremgarten on 18 May.

The Turin race was shorter than a full-length Grand Prix, but it would have given the BRMs the chance to take on the works F1 Ferraris in a straight fight. If the BRMs performed well, which meant at least battling it out with the Ferraris for the lead if not actually beating them, it would have probably ensured the continuation of F1 for another season on at least a far less limited basis.

In the meanwhile BRM went testing at Monza with one car running on drum brakes and another with disc brakes. The tests started on Monday 17 March and the drivers included Stirling Moss and Ken Wharton; Peter Walker's contract had not been renewed. Testing at Monza was very successful, and while they were in Italy negotiations were conducted with the organisers of the Turin race for at least one V16 to run. The AC Torino offered BRM £1,500 per car, which was not to be sneezed at.

On 6 April the Turin Grand Prix was held without the BRMs. Instead of sending cars to compete in Valentino Park, Mays committed what amounted to suicide on BRM's behalf by missing the race and returning to England because Fangio had agreed to test the V16 and, if satisfied, to race the cars. Mays held Fangio in awe and he was almost desperate to get him to sign for the team. Negotiations had been going on for some time with Eric Forrest Greene (ex-Pat Argentinian importer of British cars that included Aston Martin, Bentley and Rolls-Royce) and

▲ Stirling Moss tested with the team again at Monza in March 1952 and he is seen at the wheel of the latest disc-braked BRM on the porphyry blocks at the double corner known before the rebuilding of the circuit in 1954–55 as the Vedano Curves. *(Author's Collection)*

▶ Another photograph taken during the testing at Monza in 1952 showing the prototype disc-braked car with Berthon at the wheel. Behind the BRM are Willie Southcott and Tony Rudd. *(Author's Collection)*

◀ Ken Wharton had the chance to extend his very limited experience of the V16 by driving it at Folkingham on 9 April before Fangio and González arrived at the test circuit. He is waiting for the mechanics to give him a push start. *(LAT Photographic)*

◀ A push-start for Ken Wharton at Folkingham on 9 April 1952. Wharton was the longest-serving of V16 drivers as he was with the team from 1952 to the end of the 1954 season. *(LAT Photographic)*

▶ Fangio is seated in the cockpit of the V16 at the test session at Folkingham 1952. *(Grand Prix Library)*

'Pancho' Borgonovo (secretary of the Automovil Club Argentina, sponsors of Fangio) acting as conduits.

It was admittedly a rare opportunity to sign up Fangio. He was available because of the withdrawal of Alfa Romeo and while he was committed to Maserati for Formula 2, there was considerable uncertainty as to if and when the new Modena cars would be ready to race. Fangio had indicated that he did not want to test the car at Monza as that was Alfa Romeo's home territory. Mays rejected the proposal that one car should run at Turin and then return to the UK as fast as possible after the race.

We shall never know quite how Mays' rather odd mind was working. It is most likely, however, that he was frightened that the car or cars would perform badly if they raced at Turin. With Fangio on board, however, the team would obtain massive publicity and that would certainly help to keep BRM alive. Mays, Berthon, and BRM were drowning and Fangio was their lifeline. Fangio was not aware of the dilemma facing BRM over the Turin race, and he later reassured the team that if he had known he would have willingly tested the V16 in Italy.

When he came to Britain, Fangio was accompanied by his compatriot and friend Froilán González. González's contract with Ferrari had not been renewed and he too was committed to drive the new Maserati if and when it was ready to race. Also with them were Forrest Greene, Borgonovo

and Senor d'Amico from the Argentine Embassy. The Argentinians first drove the disc-braked BRM on 8 April in torrential rain on a streamingly wet Silverstone circuit. Subsequently the same day González also drove the BRM in the wet.

Both drivers were very impressed with the V16 and agreed to race for the team. They were at Folkingham the following day for a meeting with the press. Ken Wharton was also at Folkingham, and early in the day he gained his further experience with the V16 after driving it only briefly at Monza. Fangio took the car out and on his first lap he failed to come round. Mays and others drove round the circuit to find him. He had taken a right-hand corner too fast, taken to the grass and hit a sleeper lying in the grass, which tore off the exhaust system.

BRM's season was restricted in the main to Formule Libre races, although the first two races, the Albi Grand Prix and the Tourist Trophy at Dundrod were both Non-Championship Formula 1 races. The principal opposition came from Tony Vandervell's Ferrari Thin Wall Special, an extensively modified 4,500cc F1 Ferrari that usually beat the BRM, together with works Tipo 375 Ferrari Indianapolis cars, with greater power and so-named because they had been designed with the prime purpose of competing in the 500-mile race. The BRMs were still very unreliable and they retired in their first four races in 1952, at Albi, Dundrod (the Ulster Trophy), Silverstone, and Boreham.

▼ This is an intriguing view of some of the people present at the BRM press conference on 9 April 1952. Mays holds court at the microphone; and clustered immediately round the car, from left, are Berthon, Dick Salmon, González, Fangio (all on Mays's right); and on Mays's left and seated on the car are the Argentinian brothers, Luis Elias Sojit and Manuel Sojit who travelled round the world with Fangio and reported his exploits for Argentinian radio. On the right of the photograph in dark glasses is the tall engine man Stuart Tresilian, and on his left Tony Rudd and Owen PRO, Rivers Fletcher. *(Tom March Collection)*

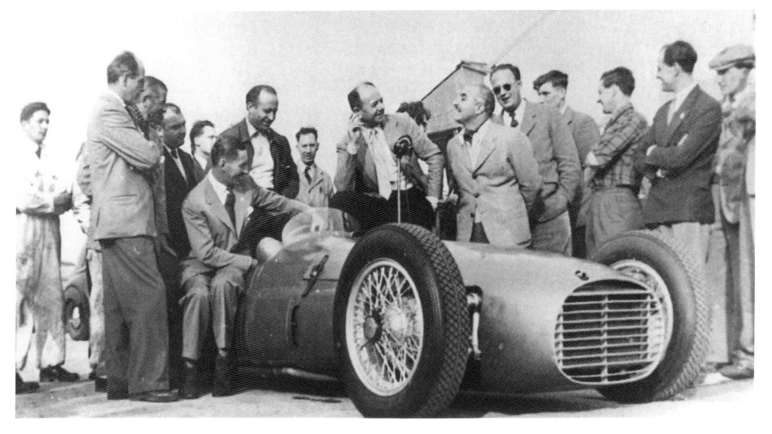

Albi Grand Prix

France, 1 June 1952

Modifications to the car that he was to drive had been at Fangio's request; a separate bucket seat was fitted and the driving position was raised higher than the propshaft to improve the driver's visibility; the position of the steering wheel was altered by redesigning the scuttle fuel tank. A new and simpler exhaust system had been adapted after Fangio had torn the exhaust off his car when he spun at Folkingham.

Two cars were entered at Albi for Fangio and González. Stirling Moss was driving a Jaguar on the day of the Albi race in the sports car Monaco Grand Prix, so Ken Wharton travelled with the team as reserve driver. Albi was a very fast and picturesque 5.56-mile (8.95km) road circuit famous for its narrow 1.0-mile (1.69km) straight, lined by plane trees.

The circuit record of 3min 6.7sec (102.17mph/164.39kph) had been set in the 1949 race by Fangio at the wheel of his Scuderia Argentina Maserati 4CLT/48. In this race the main opposition came from Louis Rosier and Brazilian Chico Landi with private Tipo 375 Ferraris. Otherwise there was just a miscellany of obsolete Maserati 4CLT/48s, Gordinis, and Talbot-Lagos.

There had been further engine problems before the cars left for the 900-mile (1,500km) road journey to Albi. The engines of the V16s had cylinder head retaining studs manufactured in 100-ton tensile strength steel. For no immediately apparent reason individual studs started to snap while the engine was stationary and cold.

The BRM machine shop hastily produced a batch of less-brittle 65/75-ton tensile strength studs manufactured in EN25V steel that had not been heat-treated. Because of an error made in the drawing office these studs were too short and another batch had to be made. The new studs were then fitted to the race engines.

The real panics started after the team had arrived at the circuit. When Tony Rudd was checking the engine fitted to the drum-braked car, he saw that water was seeping from one of the cylinder heads. It seemed that the stud had failed while it was cooling down after it had last been run. A full set of 65/75-ton studs was flown out. As the mechanics removed the old 100-ton studs, several broke and threads were stripped. Rudd was forced to conclude that some of the studs were too fragile to remove and they had to be left in place.

The weather was incredibly hot and when the drivers started practice, the cars were soon overheating. In the first practice session Fangio unofficially broke his own circuit record with a lap in 2min 55.0sec, 114.30mph (183.3kph). He soon

ALBI GRAND PRIX, FORMULA 1		
1 June, Circuit des Planques, 5.56-mile (8.95km) circuit, 34 laps, 189 miles (304km)		
1st	Louis Rosier (Ferrari Tipo 375)	1hr 50m 39s, 101.90mph (163.96kph)
2nd	Chico Landi (Ferrari Tipo 375)	1hr 50m 56.6s
3rd	Yves Giraud-Cabantous (Talbot-Lago Type 26)	1hr 51m 51.6s
4th	Alberto Crespo (Talbot-Lago Type 26)	1hr 53m 53.2s
5th	Peter Whitehead (Ferrari Tipo 125)	33 laps
6th	Rudi Fischer (Ferrari Tipo 212)	33 laps
Rtd	**José Froilán González (BRM Type 15)**	**6 laps (engine overheated)**
Rtd	**Juan Manuel Fangio (BRM Type 15)**	**16 laps (engine water leak caused by broken cylinder head studs)**

Fastest lap: José Froilán González, 106.99mph (172.18kph)

returned to the pits, however, because the car was overheating. Then González took out Fangio's car and lapped in 3min 2.4 sec before spinning, but he did no damage to the car.

Wharton was next allowed to take this car out for a few familiarisation laps, but it started to overheat again and he headed for the pits. This time the overheating had resulted in damaged cylinder heads. The team contacted Bourne and arrangements were made to fly out a replacement engine. In the meantime the team tackled the overheating problem by cutting louvres in the bonnet and bonnet sides.

The replacement engine arrived in a de Havilland

▼ During practice and the lead-up to the race, the BRM mechanics had to work furiously to get the cars to the start. González spent time with the mechanics in the garage, watching them work and giving encouragement. *(Grand Prix Library)*

DH89 Rapide twin-engined biplane; these pre-war aircraft of wood and fabric construction were still popular for air taxi work, but hardly suitable for freighting a bulky engine weighing around 500lb (226.75kg). The replacement engine was fitted with 100lb cylinder head studs, so before it was flown out the studs were re-torqued from the standard 450lb to 250lb torque and it arrived with instructions to re-torque before the race.

At dawn on race morning the mechanics started up the car to be driven by González in which the replacement engine had been installed. It immediately blew water out of the exhausts. Acting in considerable haste, Tony Rudd and the mechanics

started work on this engine; they fitted new flame rings and refaced all the joints before pressure-testing it.

The two BRMs started from the first two places on the grid and the race was destined to be yet another disaster for the team. At the drop of the tricolour Fangio accelerated into the lead, which he rapidly extended despite lapping some 16sec slower than his best practice lap. González made a very slow start, but was soon into his stride and hurtled through to hold second-place behind his teammate.

After only six laps González pulled into the pits to retire; the engine was sizzling and emitting clouds of smoke and steam; the cylinder heads were red hot and warped, although there was no stud failure, and a couple of pistons had failed.

For 14 laps Fangio led easily and the V16 sounded superb; then on lap 15 the Argentinian World Champion passed the pits with water pouring out of the exhausts, and on the next lap he pulled into the pits and retired; the BRM was only too obviously overheating and one of the 100lb cylinder head studs had broken. The Ferraris of Rosier and Landi took the first two places.

▼ The temperatures at Albi were very high, as can be expected in the Midi in early summer. It was not just the engines that were overheating, and large umbrellas were placed over the cockpits to keep them as cool as possible. The mechanics had cut louvres in the bonnet and bonnet sides in an attempt to stop the engines from overheating. *(Tom March Collection)*

▲ Fangio had set the official lap record at Albi in 1949 with a Maserati 4CLT/48. Here he is seen in the BRM during the 1952 race before his retirement because of a water leak from the engine. *(Grand Prix Library)*

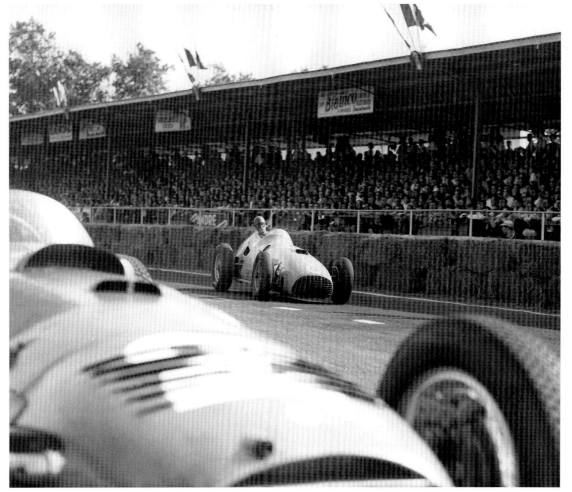

▶ After Fangio's BRM started to put water out of the exhausts, he made it back to the pits. Louis Rosier, the winner, passes the stationary BRM. *(Grand Prix Library)*

A recollection from Juan Manuel Fangio

In his autobiography *My Twenty Years of Racing*, written in collaboration with his manager Marcello Giambertone, Fangio recalled his races with BRM and described the circumstances leading up to his terrible accident at Monza:

I wasn't lucky in my first race with the BRM, the Grand Prix of Albi, on 1 June 1952. Mechanical troubles forced me to retire. The same thing happened six days later during the Ulster Trophy near Belfast. To get even with all that bad luck, I dashed to the nearest airfield to take a flight to Paris, as I had just received a telegram urging me to take part at the wheel of a Maserati in the Autodromo Grand Prix at Monza on June 8.

Bad weather and headwinds delayed us and we were late arriving at Le Bourget. Immediately I dashed to get a seat on the next flight leaving for Milan.

'I'm sorry, sir,' said the receptionist in a tone of professional regret. 'We have cancelled all flights to Italy because of bad weather.'

It was true and there was nothing to be done. Frantically I thought over the problem. The train perhaps? Railway timetables in hand, the receptionist showed me that I should arrive after the race.

'Tell me, then,' I asked, 'have I got time enough to drive there?' She looked at me politely but pityingly.

'Who do you think you are?' she said, 'Fangio?'

I didn't tell her. Instead I telephoned Rosier, knowing that he was in Paris, and explained my situation to him.

'Listen, Louis,' I said, 'have you got a fast enough car you could lend me?'

'But of course.'

Half an hour later he arrived with a Renault and handed me the keys.

'I filled her up,' he said, cutting short my thanks. 'You'd better get going or you'll be late.'

In my heart I knew I was making a mistake. No matter what anyone else thought or did, I had always maintained that one had to start a race completely rested. I had just driven in the Ulster Trophy at Belfast, I had dashed to Paris, and now I was setting out for Monza, some 500 miles (800km) away, with a lot of night driving.

Today I do not know if Rosier ever had any speed summonses from the French, Swiss or Italian highway police. As Giamba [Giambertone, his manager] said when I arrived at Monza two hours before the race was to start, the police probably didn't have time to read the number plate.

Not having practised, I should – according to the rules – have done five laps before the start. But the other drivers agreed to exempt me from doing so. Ascari, however, glanced at me and said, 'You look rather tired …'

'Oh, it's nothing.'

But, once again, I had the impression that I was doing something wrong. I tried to smother the feeling, reminding myself that I had not yet won one race since arriving in Europe that year. My pride was speaking, always a poor adviser. Although I was keeping up a relatively calm front, I felt I was just the same living on my nerves.

At 3pm 29 cars started the race. Naturally, I was in the back row as I had not practised. Even though I scarcely knew my six-cylinder Maserati, I was faced with passing all the other 28 cars. I immediately sensed that the Maserati was very different from the BRM that I had driven only 24 hours before.

Light, but very powerful, the Maserati had to be driven with close attention. While I was passing three or four cars I noticed that if I pushed hard on the accelerator, the rear end of the car had a tendency to weave, which did not bode well.

On the second lap I began to feel more confident and I closed up on the cars in front. Then, opening up on the Curva del Serraglio, I felt the rear end of the car skidding sideways. My right rear wheel hit the kerb. Scarcely had I heard the sound of it when I realised that, this time, I should not be able to avoid an accident.

Nine years have gone by since that moment, but every detail is still clear in my mind. My car started skidding across the road. I saw the bales of straw, which might, perhaps, soften the blow, although in fact they had been compressed as hard as rocks. I heard my tyres scream against the asphalt and I felt the car take off, leave the road and head for a confused mass of trees and shadows.

I clung to the wheel, but a jolt tore me from my seat and threw me forwards. At that instant I knew what it was like to die racing. The difference between life and death seemed banal, almost derisive. The whole incident probably didn't last for more than three or four seconds, but it felt as though it went on for ever.

In slow motion, I saw the branch of a forked tree coming towards me as though to pierce me. Then it brushed by with a hiss as I flew on towards an indistinct dark green spot. As I hit the ground, I realised that I no longer had my shoes on. If you have ever seen victims of a road accident you will know that they are often shoeless. Shock contracts one's feet, making them strangely small. Then the impact of the first blow slips off the shoes.

I landed in a shadowy patch of soft earth and grassy tufts. For an instant, as I was beginning to lose consciousness, I was aware of the smell of grass, of fresh damp earth which, Heaven knows why, reminded of the countryside near Balcarce and the faraway days when, as a little boy, I rolled in the fields.

Fangio fractured the vertebrae in his upper back and neck. He was put in a plaster cast right up his neck to his chin. Later in the year he flew back to Argentina and his first race after his accident was the Argentinian Grand Prix on 18 January 1953.

Ulster Trophy

Dundrod, 7 June 1952

There was a frantic rush to fly the cars to Belfast for the Ulster Trophy to be held on the Dundrod circuit only six days after the Albi race. One of BRM's Board of Trustees had promised the Prime Minister of Northern Ireland that BRM would enter three cars in this race. It was a difficult assurance to retract and it was also a race for Formula 1 cars. It will be recalled that Mays had promised that the team would run in 'any Formula 1 race that can be fitted in'. It could be argued that it could not be fitted in, but it would have run against the grain of everything the team was trying to achieve if they had elected not to compete in this race.

BRM fielded only the two Albi cars at Dundrod. So, immediately after the Albi race the mechanics removed the damaged engines from the cars and they were transported back to Folkingham by road. The mechanics then, together with the race cars, drove to Toulouse where they were loaded aboard a Bristol 170 Freighter, and they finally departed at 4.45am on the morning of Thursday, 5 June, only two days before the Ulster race. The Bristol flew via Bournemouth Hurn airport, where it refuelled, and it landed at Belfast at 11am.

As soon as they arrived, the long-suffering mechanics started work on the BRMs. The engine of Fangio's race car required only a replacement cylinder head stud, but while this was being extracted, a crankcase tapping was damaged. This car was used briefly in practice at Dundrod and then the undamaged cylinder heads were fitted to the engine used in practice at Albi.

At Bourne there remained an almost completed engine, and once the cylinder head studs had been replaced – which took a considerable amount of time, and with no opportunity to check it or run it on the dynamometer – it was transported as a matter of urgency to Dundrod. Garaged on the premises of an engineering company off Donegal Street in Belfast, the mechanics struggled to cure the overheating problems, but they were not successful.

Stirling Moss joined the team at this race and drove alongside Fangio. Both drivers started from the back of the grid and, because they were held for a long time waiting for the flag to fall, both stalled and had to be push-started.

Almost immediately Moss's engine started to overheat. He came into the pits after two laps, but he was told to keep going and he retired two laps later. Fangio survived for 25 laps, running third behind Taruffi (Thin Wall Special) and Hawthorn (Cooper-Bristol). Fangio's engine sounded very flat and would not rev above 9,000rpm.

ULSTER TROPHY, FORMULA 1		
7 June, Dundrod, 7.4-mile (11.91km) circuit, 34 laps, 252 miles (405km)		
1st	Piero Taruffi (Ferrari Thin Wall Special)	3hr 5m 47s, 81.43mph (131.02kph)
2nd	Mike Hawthorn (Cooper-Bristol)	3hr 9m 13.4s, 79.95mph (128.40kph)
3rd	Joe Kelly (Alta 1,500cc s/c)	3hr 12m 42s, 78.51mph (126.32kph)
4th	Louis Rosier (Ferrari Tipo 375)	3hr 14m 13.6s, 77.89mph (125.33kph)
5th	Philippe Étancelin (Talbot-Lago Type 26)	33 laps
6th	Oscar Moore (HWM-Jaguar 3.8-litre)	31 laps
Rtd	**Stirling Moss (BRM Type 15)**	**4 laps (engine overheating)**
Rtd	**Juan Manuel Fangio (BRM Type 15)**	**25 laps (fuel starvation caused by blocked fuel lines)**

Fastest lap: Piero Taruffi, 91.13mph (146.65kph)

Fangio came into the pits and it was obvious that his engine was suffering from fuel starvation, and the car was withdrawn. When the engine was stripped down, it was discovered that there was something in the fuel supplied by Esso that resembled cotton threads, and that this was jamming the whole fuel system. No satisfactorily explanation as to how it got there was ever arrived at.

▼ Although too old to race the BRM, Mays loved to be seen at the wheel. Here he delivers the V16 to the pits. *(Grand Prix Library)*

◀On race morning Stirling Moss drove his BRM V16 down to the start. His expression makes it clear how he felt about the car. *(Author's collection)*

Stirling Moss remembers Dundrod

Moss was thoroughly unhappy with his drive at Dundrod. The circuit consisted of narrow country roads and for much of its distance overtaking was difficult, if not impossible. Stirling found that the rather vague steering of the V16 was dangerous on such a narrow circuit, and what was tolerable on the wide expanses of Monza was intolerable on the narrow country roads of Dundrod.

That Moss was frightened by Dundrod was no reflection on his attitudes or abilities. He had already twice won the Tourist Trophy sports car race there with Jaguars, and co-driving with Fangio at the wheel of a Mercedes-Benz 300 SLR he won the Tourist Trophy there again in 1955.

There were two accidents with fatal results in the 1955 race and its licence was withdrawn by the RAC because it was so narrow and dangerous. Moss had much more to do with his life than race cars that he believed to be inadequately developed and dangerous. He withdrew from the team after the Northern Ireland race, and later wrote about his experience with BRM at Dundrod in his book, *My Cars, My Career*, an extract from which appears below:

Fangio and I lined up on the back of the grid, and it was raining again as the engines were started with two minutes to go. Then my engine stalled and had to be restarted, and as the starter held up the 30-second board I put the clutch out and selected first gear. With about 10 seconds to go, the clutch began to take up and the car began to creep ...

There was nothing I could do to stop it as I had the clutch right out. I had to heel-and-toe with my right foot on brake and accelerator together to keep the engine running, yet hold the car stationary. The clutch was taking up more and more, so I had to brake harder and harder, and of course just as the flag was about to fall the clutch burned out and the engine stalled.

I glanced across at Fangio and saw that he had stalled as well. So as the field roared away it left our two BRMs behind. The mechanics rushed out to push-start us, and we screamed off, Fangio first, and then me.

My clutch was slipping dreadfully, and he quickly lost me. Then I came to the left-hander before the hairpin and there he was facing back towards me, going down the road backwards, so the two V16s were nose-to-nose, careering down towards the hairpin in most unconventional style! He had taken avoiding action when 'Bira's' OSCA had flown through the hedge, and spun. He seemed to be going backwards faster than I was forwards.

He rolled beyond the hairpin and stopped, while I crawled round with the clutch slipping, and he then rejoined behind me. By the end of that first lap, apart from the bad clutch – which didn't matter too much as the gearbox really was so good – I couldn't get full revs and the engine was already boiling again.

On the second lap, after I'd passed some of the slower cars, the gear lever knob came off in my hand. I slung it at somebody as a souvenir.

By this time both Fangio and I were having trouble getting round the hairpin. We had to slip our clutches and with mine already practically burned-out this didn't help. The V16 was so high-revving, with such poor torque at low revs, that we had to keep it running between 10,000 and 12,000rpm to get results ... it would be like trying to hold an ordinary car at 4,000 and 5,000rpm in London traffic.

After the second lap I came into the pits with chronic overheating. They told me to keep it going. Frankly I wouldn't have minded if they'd called it off right then. As it was, I crawled round to complete four laps, then they pushed the car away. Fangio suffered persistent fuel starvation and kept stopping at the pits before finally calling it a day.

Ray issued a statement after the race, saying in part 'We are ashamed. But we had extremely bad luck. If the race had been a day or two later the result would have been different'.

BRM always wanted an extra day or two to make the result different; but their car was so complex and underdeveloped, and their organisation so chaotic, that they never got it ... and there are no 'ifs' in motor racing.

▶ In this photograph the mechanics relax after push-starting Stirling Moss's car from the pits so that he could motor down to the starting grid. He only completed four laps in total before retiring from the race. Although Moss had considerable affection for the Dundrod circuit, he drove insufficient distance in this race to adjust to the rather vague and uncertain steering characteristics of the V16 cars. *(Tom March Collection)*

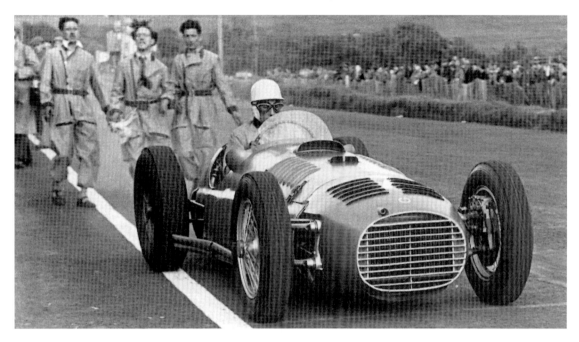

▼ Fangio had a real go with his V16 at Dundrod, even though it was suffering from fuel starvation. He was 25 laps at the wheel before he was forced to come into the pits to retire. *(Grand Prix Library)*

◄ Directional stability through corners was perhaps the most serious shortcoming of the V16 chassis. Engine failure was the biggest problem of all. The fuel blockage that caused Fangio's retirement was not the fault of the team and remains unexplained. *(Grand Prix Library)*

◄ Although he drove the V16s for the money, there is no doubt that Fangio was the only man of his generation capable of exploiting the full performance of the V16. But for his near-fatal accident at Monza it is obvious that the World Champion could have transformed the racing results for these cars. *(Author's collection)*

BRDC *Daily Express* Trophy

Silverstone, 19 July 1952

Following the race at Dundrod, Berthon modified the V16s further by fitting much larger radiators with blisters on the noses, together with the necessary larger water pumps and piping, although some members of the team considered that this was not the real answer to the overheating problem. The louvres cut in the bodies at Albi were retained and further louvres were made along the noses of the cars.

There had been considerable controversy about the BRDC switching the British Grand Prix to a Formula 2 race. In particular Peter Berthon thought that its secretary Desmond Scannell (responsible for the organisation of the Grand Prix) was knifing BRM in the back. He was of course heavily biased and most knowledgeable enthusiasts considered that the shambles that was BRM deserved no special consideration.

More objectively, however, if the British Grand Prix had been organised as a Formula 1 race it would have lost its World Championship status. There had been considerable pressure on the BRDC to include a Formule Libre race at the International Trophy meeting at Silverstone, now held in May, in which the BRMs could compete. There had not, however, been sufficient time to include this in the programme, but the pressure was maintained and so there was a Formule Libre race included in the programme at the British Grand Prix in July.

This Formule Libre race was to be the last occasion on which the cars ran in their light metallic green paintwork. In practice for the race the blisters on the noses of the cars in their new form were colour-coded for recognition purposes, yellow for González and red for Wharton, who was having his first race with the team.

The Silverstone race was over a distance of 35 laps and, apart from the BRMs, the main contenders were Piero Taruffi (with Vandervell's Ferrari Thin Wall Special), Luigi Villoresi (with a works Ferrari Tipo 375 of the latest 'Indianapolis' type), plus the older Tipo 375

Ferraris of Landi and Rosier. The field also included the two fastest ERAs, R4D with Ron Flockhart at the wheel and Bob Gerard driving R14B. González was fastest in practice in 1min 47.0sec, 98.48mph (158.45kph).

The front row of the grid, right to left, was González (BRM), Villoresi (Ferrari) 1min 49.0sec, Wharton (BRM) 1min 53.0sec, and Taruffi (Ferrari Thin Wall) 1min 53.0sec. The Thin Wall was the fastest in this race and, already, probably the fastest Formula 1 car in the world. Taruffi was suspiciously slow in practice and it may have been the case that there was some defect with the car.

At the fall of the flag the two Ferraris shot ahead, while both BRMs were slow away as usual and the Ferraris of Rosier and Landi swept past them, as did Bira with his V12 OSCA-powered Maserati. The Stewards had concluded that Taruffi had jumped the start, and in due course they notified Vandervell's pit of the decision to impose a one-minute penalty on the Italian. The pit succeeded in signalling this information to Taruffi, but it seems likely that none of the other drivers in the race was aware of the situation.

By lap five González was 4sec behind Taruffi on the road, but because of the penalty he was in fact 56sec ahead. The Argentinian was totally unaware of this and continued to press the Ferrari driver hard until lap eight when he entered Stowe corner too fast, lost control, and spun through the corner markers; a stake punctured the radiator and the steering was bent. The Pampas Bull cruised slowly back to the pits, pausing while marshals pulled the stake out of the steering.

Wharton, holding third place, had been instructed to come in and hand over to González if the Argentinian ran into problems. He saw what had happened, came into the pits immediately, and was waiting for González. The Pampas Bull hoisted his vast bulk out of one BRM and into the other and accelerated away swearing in Spanish. The change-over cost about 20sec. There were still 20 laps to go and as Taruffi set about making up the time penalty and moved into the lead, so González began to close up on Villoresi and seemed likely to catch and pass him before the finish. But just two laps from the chequered flag the BRM failed to come round.

The gearbox had failed, hastened by González's rough treatment, and when it was dismantled after the race it was discovered that the teeth on the input bevel had been stripped. Taruffi made up the penalty and was 50sec ahead of Villoresi on real time at the finish. No other drivers completed the full race distance and it was ironic that Flockhart and Gerard finished fifth and sixth. It was also ironic that the steadier Wharton, who was much more sympathetic to the mechanical state of his cars, would probably have finished third if he had been left in the car.

BRDC DAILY EXPRESS TROPHY, FORMULE LIBRE		
19 July, Silverstone, 2.927-mile (4.7km) circuit, 35 laps, 102.45 miles (164.84km)		
1st	Piero Taruffi (Ferrari Thin Wall Special)	1hr 6m 26.8s, 93.07mph (150.76kph)
2nd	Luigi Villoresi (Ferrari Tipo 375)	1hr 6m 17.0s
3rd	Chico Landi (Ferrari Tipo 375)	34 laps
4th	Tony Gaze (Maserati 4CLT/48)	33 laps
5th	Ron Flockhart (ERA D-type)	33 laps
6th	Bob Gerard (ERA B-type)	33 laps
Rtd	**José Froilán González (BRM Type 15)**	**7 laps (accident damage)**
Rtd	**Ken Wharton/J. F. González (BRM Type 15)**	**33 laps (gearbox failure)**

Fastest lap: José Froilán González (BRM Type 15) and Piero Taruffi (Ferrari Thin Wall Special), 1m 49.0s, 96.67mph (155.54kph)

▲ Raymond Mays is at the wheel of Ken Wharton's V16 in the pits before the start of the 100-mile (160km) race at Silverstone in July 1952. On the right of the photograph, watching with keen interest, is Eberan von Eberhorst, pre-war Auto Union race engineer, and at this time employed by Aston Martin. *(Tom March Collection)*

▼ Although Froilán González's command of English was almost non-existent and the team conversed through sign language, this pre-race photograph was obviously posed for the press. It seems that neither 'Pepe' nor Mays understood the difference between the Churchillian 'V for victory' and the vulgar 'two-fingered salute'. *(Getty Images)*

▶ The start of the Formule Libre race. Ron Flockhart (ERA R4D) heads the cars in this photograph, and Ken Wharton's BRM is very slow in getting away. Already out of sight are the Thin Wall Special, González's BRM, the Ferrari Tipo 375s of Rosier and Landi, and Bira's OSCA-powered Maserati. *(Guy Griffiths Collection)*

◀ On the day of the British Grand Prix meeting at Silverstone the BRM organisation entered two V16 cars in the Formule Libre race. To improve cooling the cars were now fitted with enlarged radiators that necessitated a 'blister' on top of the normal radiator grille. Extensive and continued testing had made the cars much more reliable. Here, Argentinian Froilán González is at the wheel, and he was chasing Piero Taruffi (driving Tony Vandervell's Ferrari Thin Wall Special) when he spun and damaged the radiator and steering. *(Tom March Collection)*

◀ This is Ken Wharton with the second V16 BRM at Silverstone. He was making steady progress up the field and holding fourth place when this photograph was taken. The fitting of larger radiators left insufficient room for the electric starter. From then onwards the cars were always push-started. *(Tom March Collection)*

▶ Froilán González was a highly emotional, very Latin character, and after crashing out of the race at Silverstone he looks forlorn and inconsolable. It has been suggested that he even shed tears after dropping out of the race. *(Getty Images)*

◀ When Froilán González spun off at Stowe Corner he hit the corner markers, damaging the front suspension; a stake holed the radiator and became lodged in the suspension. Here, in this somewhat indistinct photo, he is making his way slowly back to the pits to retire with the stake sticking out of the front of the car. He stopped at a marshals' station for it to be removed. *(LAT Photographic)*

◀ Another view of Ken Wharton in the Formule Libre race at Silverstone. He looks very relaxed, remarkably so bearing in mind the concentration and the physical effort required to drive these cars at competitive speeds. Viewed from the side the sheer bulk of the V16 is very apparent. *(Tom March Collection)*

▶ After Froilán González retired, Ken Wharton was brought into the pits in accordance with team instructions so that the Argentinian could take over his car. This was rather pointless when much of the race had been completed, but González climbed up through the field and was in third place when he was forced to retire because he broke the gearbox by using excessive force. Here he is back in the pits climbing out of the car, while Mays fiddles with the gear lever to satisfy himself that the 'box is broken. *(Getty Images)*

◀ The Formule Libre race at the British Grand Prix meeting was won by Piero Taruffi at the wheel of Tony Vandervell's highly developed Ferrari Tipo 375 known as the 'Thin Wall Special' (Vandervell Products manufactured the famed 'Thin Wall bearings'. Taruffi finished more than a minute ahead of second-place man Luigi Villoresi (works Ferrari) despite being penalised 60sec at the start for jumping the fall of the flag. *(Tom March Collection)*

Daily Mail International Trophy

Boreham, 2 August 1952

A very interesting motor race meeting in 1952 was the *Daily Mail*-sponsored event at Boreham in Essex on Saturday 2 August (a Bank Holiday weekend). The actual organisers were the very active West Essex Car Club. There were two exciting 100-mile sports car races, and the main event of the day was a 201-mile (320km) combined Formula 1 and 2 race, run for much of the distance in exceptionally wet conditions. In this race there were separate classes for each formula and separate results were published for each class.

BRM entered V16 cars for González and Wharton. Because the light metallic green colour used since 1951 showed every mark and was very time-consuming to keep clean, the cars were now painted a dark metallic green. For identification purposes, at this race only, the supercharger air intakes towards the back of the top of the bonnet were painted white on González's car and retained the old light metallic green colour on Wharton's. Both cars were fitted with Girling disc brakes.

In the same class as the BRMs there was a works Indianapolis-type Ferrari Tipo 375 for Villoresi (probably the same car as he drove at Silverstone), the older Ferrari Tipo 375s for Landi and Rosier, and several French-entered and driven Talbot-Lagos. Conspicuous by its absence was the Ferrari Thin Wall Special, not entered because Vandervell had not been able to agree starting money with the organisers.

On race day the weather was dismal and the sports car races were held under a lowering sky. By the start of the main event heavy rain was falling and it continued to rain for much of the race. At the fall of the flag Mike Hawthorn took the lead with his Cooper-Bristol and he stayed in front until late in the race when the rain had stopped and the circuit was drying out. Villoresi was then able to close up on Hawthorn and pass the Cooper-Bristol. This was how they finished, each driver winning his category.

It was another poor day for the BRM team and both cars were eliminated. As the cars accelerated off the line, González's car spun its wheels wildly when

DAILY MAIL INTERNATIONAL TROPHY, FORMULE LIBRE	
2 August, Boreham, 3-mile (4.8km) circuit, 67 laps, 201 miles (323km)	
1st Luigi Villoresi (Ferrari Tipo 375)	2hr 25m 36s, 82.83mph (133.27kph)
2nd Chico Landi (Ferrari Tipo 375)	2hr 25m 46s, 82.74mph (133.13kph)
3rd Philippe Étancelin (Talbot-Lago Type 26)	66 laps
4th Louis Rosier (Ferrari Tipo 375)	66 laps
5th Alberto Crespo (Talbot-Lago Type 26)	63 laps
6th Yves Giraud-Cabantous (Talbot-Lago Type 26)	62 laps
Rtd J. F. González (BRM Type 15)	**3 laps (accident damage)**
Rtd K. Wharton (BRM Type 15)	**58 laps (gearbox failure)**

Fastest lap: Luigi Villoresi, 1m 59.8s, 90.16mph (145.093kph)

Note: Race ran concurrently with Formula 2 event and separate results were issued.

he got away and he was well down the field. As he fought his way up to the front, he was sliding badly, this way and that. On only lap three he entered the corner known as Hangar Bend much too quickly, lost control, spun and slid backwards into the straw bales, throwing up a shower of straw and mud. The spectators scattered and the BRM's progress was halted when it collided with a parked car.

This was not the cool, calm, collected González who achieved the first victory over the Alfa Romeos at Silverstone in 1951 and who in 1954 was the stalwart of the Ferrari team in its battle with Mercedes-Benz. This performance in particular reinforces the writer's view about the reasons why both Fangio and González signed for the ill-favoured BRM team. Both were relatively poor men from a poor country and this writer believes that they were seduced by the money offered by BRM. Once they were driving for this shambles of a team, they became primarily interested in the money.

Wharton drove a slow, rather erratic race. He was unhappy in the wet, especially as his disc brakes were misbehaving and grabbing unexpectedly. He

was lapped twice by Hawthorn before the BRM succumbed to gearbox failure after 58 laps.

The racing at Boreham had been great, despite the terrible weather, but the gate money was poor because of the weather, the location of the circuit, and the fact that it was an airfield perimeter track. Efforts to match the success of the *Daily Express*-sponsored International Trophy at Silverstone failed and the circuit was abandoned for racing. It became a Ford test track.

Since the BRM was presented to the press at the end of 1949, the team had competed at eight race meetings. This statement includes the 1950 International Trophy at Silverstone and is phrased the way it is because Parnell drove the V16 in two short races at Goodwood that year. The cars retired at every circuit except Goodwood and it was quite simply an appalling record.

The way in which the mechanics had to carry out engine work at the circuits, often having to bodge repairs, resembled that of a badly organised amateur team, but BRM was supposedly a serious professional organisation. There could be no confidence whatsoever in the BRM team's ability to finish a race.

OVERLEAF Froilán González's car is seen in the paddock at Boreham before the *Daily Mail* Trophy race. As time passed, so the bodywork of the V16 BRM became less effete and increasingly butch. In this photograph the V16 exudes an aura of power. *(LAT Photographic)*

▼ Although the mechanic changing the plugs on Froilán González's car is not fully in view, his hands on the socket are clear. It is obvious that changing the plugs on the V16 was a thankless task. *(LAT Photographic)*

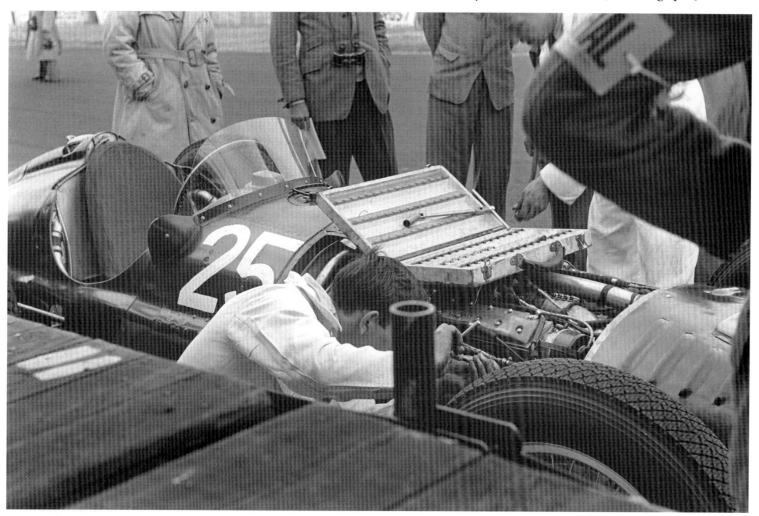

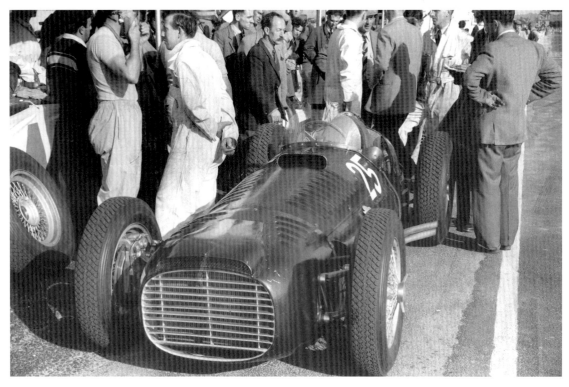

▲ Another view of Froilán González's car in the pits at Boreham. This photograph was taken shortly before the mechanics pushed the car out to practice. Practice took place in the dry. *(LAT Photographic)*

▼ Ken Wharton has just left the pits in practice and is about to accelerate away with a view to turning in a serious timed lap. *(LAT Photographic)*

▶ The BRM mechanics are push-starting Ken Wharton who is just about to go out to practice. *(LAT Photographic)*

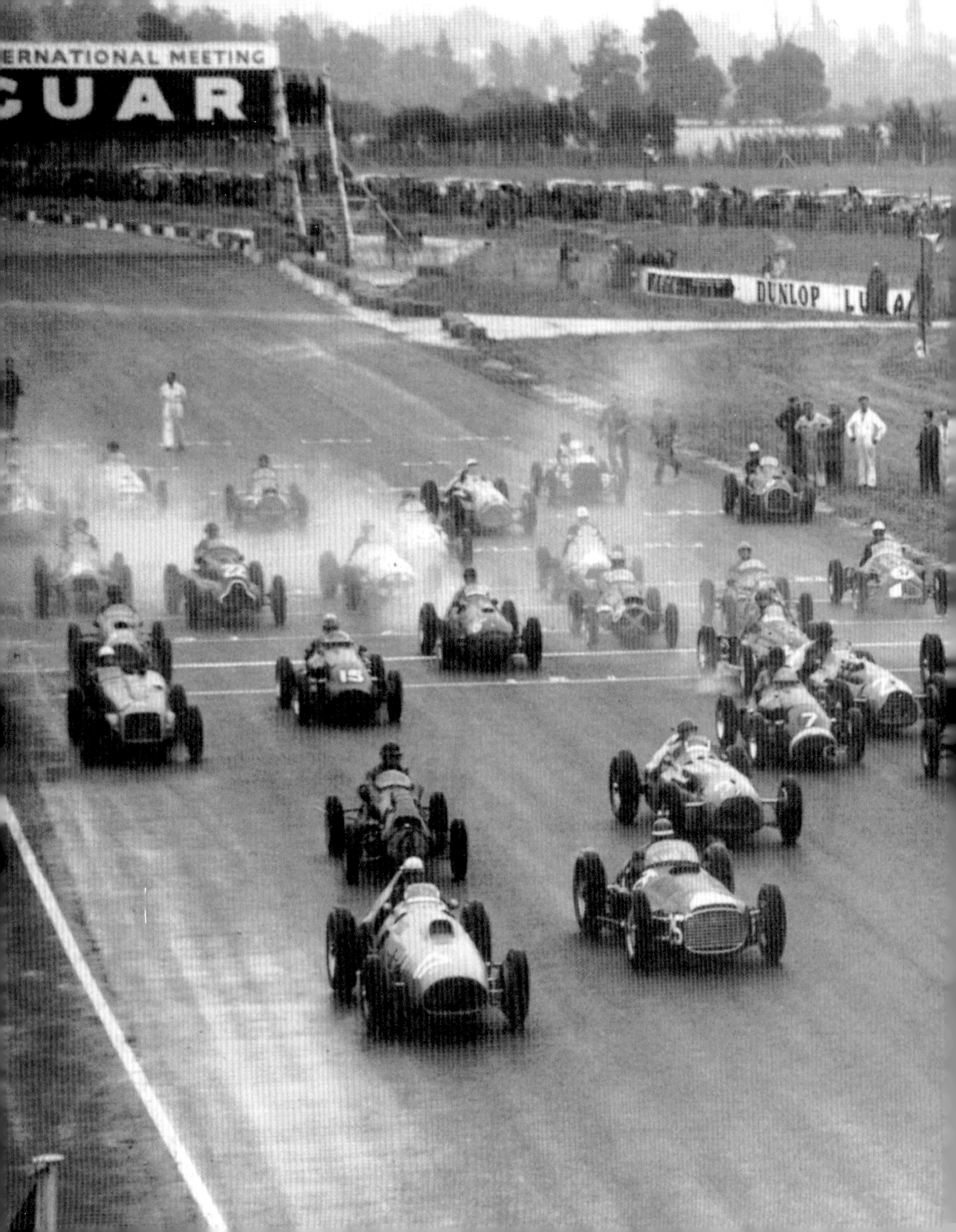
ERNATIONAL MEETING
CUAR
DUNLOP

◀ A magnificent view of the start at Boreham. Although the circuit is wet, rain has temporarily stopped falling, but soon it will start 'stair-rodding' and the drivers will be racing on an inundated circuit. Prominent in this view are number 29 (Ferrari) leading away; to Landi's left is Rosier with his Tipo 375; the BRMs, numbers 25 and 26, are in the centre; on the left of the photograph is Villoresi (works Ferrari Tipo 375), and behind him Mike Hawthorn (Cooper-Bristol). *(LAT Photographic)*

◀ Ken Wharton is seen in the wet at Boreham with his BRM. At this meeting the cars were painted a smoky dark green for the first time because of the difficulty in cleaning stains off the light green paintwork. Wharton has a handkerchief stuffed in his mouth to absorb some of the moisture. He drove a slow race and was lapped twice by Hawthorn (Cooper-Bristol) and he retired nine laps from the finish. *(Guy Griffiths Collection)*

▼ Another view of Ken Wharton in the *Daily Mail* Trophy. It shows very clearly the terrible conditions in which the race took place. *(LAT Photographic)*

Mike Hawthorn's thoughts on the BRM V16

The outstanding performances of Mike Hawthorn with his private Cooper-Bristol had come to everyone's attention and it was suggested to Mays that the BRM team should give him a test drive. He drove to Folkingham to drive the V16 and Mays was suitably impressed. It was suggested that he should drive one of the cars to be entered at Turnberry in Scotland later in August. Mike had also been offered a test drive in Vandervell's Thin Wall Special and he wanted to drive that car before he made a decision. Later Mike wrote about the BRM in the first volume of his autobiography, *Challenge Me the Race*. This is what he said:

Just before the Italian Grand Prix there was a race sponsored by the Scottish Daily Express *at Turnberry, Scotland, which is a disused aerodrome. Raymond Mays rang me up and asked if I would drive a BRM up there. At the same time Tony Vandervell rang me up and asked me if I would drive his 4½-litre Thin Wall there. I was obviously very keen on doing this, as my father did not want me to use my own car; he wanted to get it ready for the next race.*

I went up to Bourne to try the BRM first. I met Mays and

Berthon and got into the car; they pushed me off. But it was no use – it was incredibly quick, the acceleration was fantastic, but every time I came to a corner and went below 8,000 revs the power went right off. You would come out of the corner with the revs down and as you accelerated it would just fluff and burble; then, suddenly, as you reached the 8,000 mark the full power would come in with a bang and you had a job to hold the car straight.

At over 8,000 revs it really did motor, but the steering was nothing to write home about. I made the mistake of doing my first lap without ear plugs and that nearly shattered my ear drums – the noise was incredible. I told Mays that I had got to try the Thin Wall first and then I would let him know my decision as to which car I would drive later in the week.

I went to Silverstone and tried the Thin Wall. It was a beautiful car. I thoroughly enjoyed driving it and I believe that I unofficially broke the Silverstone course record, which was held by Farina in the same car. I was very pleased with it and I said that I would like to drive it at Turnberry. I told Mays that I had chosen the Thin Wall.

Scottish Daily Express National Trophy

Turnberry, 23 August 1952

The Turnberry race was a British National event, so González was not eligible to drive. Mays invited Reg Parnell to drive one of the cars, so he appeared alongside Wharton. Wharton drove car No. 52 with disc brakes, while Parnell was at the wheel of the newly-completed car No. 53 running on drum brakes.

The race was the *Scottish Daily Express* National Trophy over 20 laps of this short airfield circuit. Hawthorn with the Thin Wall Special was fastest in practice in 1min 16sec, 83.36mph (134.13kph), Wharton was a second slower and Parnell lapped in 1min 18sec. As the cars lined up on the grid, there was a panic when one of the high-pressure lines running across the engine on Parnell's car split.

Seeing the mechanics working away on Parnell's car, Hawthorn strolled across to find out what was going on and said, 'Don't worry. Hang on; take your time because we can hold the race back a bit till you get it fixed. It would be a pity to start without one of us – it'd spoil the race.' When the mechanics had finished working on Parnell's car, Mike said, 'All right, then, let's go racing.'

Ironically, when the flag fell for the start, the BRMs shot off and Hawthorn was left on the grid and retired immediately because of gear-selector problems. Parnell headed Wharton, until the gear knob came away in his hand. While Reg struggled to change gear with the lever, Wharton went ahead. On lap eight a steering ball-joint failed on Wharton's car and he succeeded in bringing the V16 to a halt safely. Parnell went on to win by a comfortable margin from Tony Gaze's Maserati 4CLT/48.

SCOTTISH EXPRESS NATIONAL TROPHY, FORMULE LIBRE		
23 August, Turnberry, 1.7-mile (2.74lkm) airfield circuit, 20 laps, 35 miles (55km)		
1st	**Reg Parnell (BRM Type 15)**	**26m 33s, 79.50mph (127.91kph)**
2nd	Tony Gaze (Maserati 4CLT/48)	26m 43s
3rd	Graham Whitehead (ERA B-Type)	No time published
4th	Geoff Richardson (RRA Special)	No time published
5th	Alastair Birrell (ERA A-Type)	No time published
6th	Bill Dobson (Ferrari Tipo 166)	No time published
Rtd	**Ken Wharton (BRM Type 15)**	**7 laps (steering failure)**
Fastest lap: Mike Hawthorn (Ferrari Thin Wall Special), 1m 16s, 83.36mph (134.15kph)		

◀ Despite the many problems faced by the team whenever they raced, the V16 cars – seen on the starting grid at Turnberry – were always smartly turned out and spotlessly clean. *(Graham Gauld)*

▶ While the two BRMs power off the line at Turnberry, each in its cloud of tyre smoke, Mike Hawthorn struggles – unsuccessfully – to find a gear in the Thin Wall Special's box. *(Bill Henderson Collection)*

◀Wharton at speed amid Turnberry's bleak expanses. His race was short-lived due to steering failure. *(Bill Henderson Collection)*

▼ Reg Parnell won the *Scottish Daily Express* Trophy after driving for much of the race with a gear lever that lacked its knob. Parnell had been brought back into the team after being dropped by Mays for publicly criticising the BRM. *(Bill Henderson Collection)*

▶ Congratulations at Turnberry for a truly deserving race winner. The BRM had now won three short races, and on each occasion Reg Parnell was at the wheel. *(Bill Henderson Collection)*

The sale of the team

An account by John Bolster of *Autosport*

By August 1952 it was known that the Trustees were contemplating winding-up the team and selling the assets. This prompted John Bolster, Technical Editor of *Autosport*, to write the following article headed 'Farewell to the BRM'. Not unexpectedly it proved controversial, with support and protest fairly evenly divided.

It is with a full sense of my responsibility that I write this article. It gives me no pleasure to do so, for, on the surface, it seems rather like kicking a man when he is down. I hope that I shall not be thought guilty of so despicable an act, but that is a risk that I must take, for my message must be given now.

Right from the start of the BRM project I was filled with misgivings. In the nature of things I am in receipt of much confidential information, which I shall certainly never make public. It soon became obvious that the publicity side of the venture had got completely out of control and it was then that the fatal mistake was made, which more than anything else, has done so much harm to our sport and has inflicted such damage on our industry.

The impression was allowed to be created that all the best brains, and all the biggest firms, in British engineering were to get together and produce a National car. It is easy for the lay press to build up such a story, but, as far as I know, no real attempt was made to deny this monstrous suggestion. In consequence, even at this very moment, every Continental race spectator believes that the machine was designed by a pool of Britain's finest engineers, and that it represents their idea of what the perfect racing car should be. One still even finds many Europeans who cannot be convinced that this is not a government-sponsored effort.

NOT a National Effort

It is much too late to explain that this is not, and never has been, a 'national' car, for we would not be believed. If we alleged that it was not designed by an engineer (or engineers) of the very highest qualifications, and that only a handful of private firms had provided the admittedly large 'kitty', polite laughter would be our reward. If we stated that the British Racing Drivers' Club had never been consulted, and that the first two drivers, Reg Parnell and Peter Walker, were not allowed to give any advice after the Barcelona fiasco, we would be branded as liars. It is, in fact, impossible to retrieve the deplorable impression that has been created.

Effect on Markets

What is the result of all this? I could give many examples, but two will suffice. The manufacturers of one of our best cars, who used to do a good trade in Belgium, have been informed by their agents that the demand has fallen right off, and that this is entirely due to the BRM. What is so unfair is that [this] particular factory has had nothing whatever to do with [the BRM], and would not, to be brutally frank, touch it with the end of a barge pole.

The other case concerns some irrefutable evidence that our hitherto excellent reputation for engineering products has been lowered in Scandinavia. It is pointless to multiply such instances, for many of our readers who have been among foreigners during one of the well-known farces know the type of ribaldry that is evoked at our expense.

It might seem that I am merely washing dirty linen, for the present [Grand Prix] formula is virtually dead, and the BRM can race no more [in World Championship events]. If that were so, I would never have written this unpleasant story, but there are now strong rumours that a new BRM will be dished up for the forthcoming formula [of 1954 onwards], and that is a really shattering thought.

If these stories are true – and they have been uttered by those who should know – the name must be changed to one that can have no national implications. The present title is associated irrevocably with an admittedly mythical combination of Britain's finest engineering brains and technique. The name of our country must never again be so used, and if these people do produce another car, it must have as simple a designation as the Formula 2 machines that are doing so much for our prestige.

Let them call it the 'Bourne Bombshell', or the 'Mays-Berthon Special', and we shall all wish them the best of luck in any race they may enter. Furthermore, if they can do it without newspaper headlines and the old ballyhoo, we shall like them all the better.

There remains the question of the propriety of collecting public subscriptions, and I am against this practice. I can well remember the begging for money that went on before the war for the E-type ERA and how little that achieved! I consider that the whole principle is wrong, and if a racing car cannot be built without resorting to such methods, I would rather it not built all.

To raise funds thus immediately gives rise to the danger that, once again, the device may be mistaken for a British national car. If the cash already subscribed is still intact, it might well be devoted to providing improved testing facilities for all our racing cars.

A Costly Lesson

I must make it perfectly clear that this contribution represents only my personal opinion, and it is not necessarily [the opinion] of this journal, or of any other body. I have not based my conclusions on mere surmise, for many of those who have driven the car, or have otherwise been associated with the project, are my friends.

I would rather not go into further detail, however, for what I have said needs no underlining. An expensive lesson has been learned, but if we profit by this mistake it will not all have been in vain. It is tragic that such an infinity of hard work must be written off completely, and it is with the deepest sorrow that I record this result.

In September it was announced that at an Extraordinary General Meeting of the British Motor Racing Research Trust, held at Stratford-upon-Avon, the Executive Council of the Trust had secured a unanimous vote in favour of the proposal to sell the business of British Racing Motors Limited as a going concern. Offers from British buyers only were to be considered, and the use of the title 'BRM' by any hypothetical purchaser would not be permitted.

The BMRRT's decision was compelled by the abandonment of the current Grand Prix Formula by the majority of European race-organising bodies two years ahead of schedule, and by the lack of financial support that had ensued. All season Mays had nurtured the hope that the decision to switch to Formula 2 would prove mistaken and that there would be a reversion to the old Formula 1 – but it was not to be.

In connection with the proposed sale, a firm of valuers based in Birmingham, Stephens, Champion & Slater, produced valuations which the BMRRT considered:

Plant and machinery at Bourne:	Going concern: £18,710 Forced sale: £14,110
Cars and spares:	Going concern: £30,500 Forced sale: £28,810

It is difficult to fathom the basis of these valuations and many would have suggested that the cars were worth only scrap value. The Trust's accountants calculated liabilities as amounting to £22,934.

On 14 October a meeting of the Trust Board was convened in the Owen Organisation board room at the company's headquarters at Darlaston in Staffordshire. The purpose of the meeting was to consider offers for BRM, and as the Owen Organisation was bidding, Alfred Owen resigned as Chairman of the Executive Council and as a Trustee.

There was one offer that bettered all others by a substantial margin and that came from the Owen Organisation. The offer was in the sum of £23,500 and it included the acceptance of all liabilities and responsibility for the service agreements of both Raymond Mays and Peter Berthon.

It was a remarkably generous offer, but Alfred Owen, Chief Executive of the Owen Organisation had been a firm and fervent supporter of BRM since day one, and his support and faith in the team had never wavered. Owen was a staunch Christian who would not attend races held on a Sunday.

An interesting point that is worth mentioning in passing is that the Sunday Observance Act, passed in 1780, made it illegal to charge admission to public entertainment or amusement events held on a Sunday in the United Kingdom, the day of the Lord. At the time the V16s were being raced, all professional football matches and all motor races were held on a Saturday. The Sunday Observance Act was not repealed until 1972.

The sale agreement took effect from 1 November 1952 and BRM became 'Engine Development Division – Bourne'. The long-term aim, apart from building a Grand Prix car complying with the new Formula that came into effect on 1 January 1954, was to develop, manufacture, and sell racing engines.

BARC International Meeting

Goodwood, 27 September 1952

Although the sale process was under way and the team had the sword of Damocles hanging over it, BRM entered all three cars on disc brakes at the autumn International Goodwood meeting on 27 September, and they were driven by González, Parnell, and Wharton.

Woodcote Cup, Formule Libre

The first of the two Formule Libre races was this five-lap event. The three BRMs faced the Ferrari Thin Wall Special. It was to have been driven by Mike Hawthorn, but he had crashed the Cooper-Bristol in practice for the Modena Grand Prix and was recuperating in hospital. So Giuseppe Farina flew over to drive the Thin Wall. For reasons explained on p182, Wharton's car failed to fire up and did not start the race.

Farina made a poor start with the Thin Wall, and this enabled González to accelerate into the lead and he won this 'sprint' from Farina and Parnell. As Farina accelerated out of the chicane on the last lap, the Thin Wall stripped its crown wheel and he coasted across the line. As a result the Thin Wall was a non-starter in the main Formule Libre race of the day.

WOODCOTE CUP, FORMULE LIBRE		
27 September, Goodwood, 2.4-mile (3.86km) airfield perimeter road, 5 laps, 12 miles (19.3km)		
1st	**José Froilán González (BRM Type 15)**	**8m 13s, 87.64mph (141.01kph)**
2nd	Giuseppe Farina (Ferrari Thin Wall Special)	8m 19.2s
3rd	**Reg Parnell (BRM Type 15)**	**8m 23.0s**
4th	Alan Brown (Cooper-Bristol)	8m 26.6s
5th	Louis Rosier (Ferrari Tipo 500)	no time published
6th	Roy Salvadori (Ferrari Tipo 500)	no time published
DNS	**Ken Wharton (BRM Type 15)**	**(fuel-feed problem)**
Fastest lap: José Froilán González, 1m 36.2s, 89.81mph (144.50kph)		

▲ In his younger days Raymond Mays had been a fine driver. Here he is is at the wheel of the BRM V16 that Reg Parnell drove to a second and a third place at the September Goodwood meeting in 1952. In his dealings with press, public and drivers Mays exuded the most wonderful sang froid, even though this very self-centred man suffered from torments every time the cars were raced. *(Guy Griffiths Collection)*

◄ BRM entered three cars at the September Goodwood meeting in 1952. Seen here in the cockpit, making himself as comfortable as possible on the starting grid for the very minor five-lap Woodcote Cup, is Froilán González, who won this race. Unfortunately we are unable to identify the gentleman in the beret who must have been very close to, or closely associated with, González to perch on the rear wheel like this. Visible behind the BRM is Chico Landi's Ferrari Tipo 375 4.5-litre car (No. 1), and half visible on the extreme right of the photograph is Alan Brown's Cooper-Bristol. *(Guy Griffiths Collection)*

▶ The start of the Woodcote Cup.
In clouds of tyre smoke, Froilán
González (No. 5) and Reg Parnell
(No. 6) accelerate away from
Giuseppe Farina (Ferrari Thin Wall
Special) and Alan Brown (Cooper-
Bristol). *(LAT Photographic)*

Thin Wall Special

FOR MAGNIFICENT MOTORING

▲ Ken Wharton's car would not fire up at the start of the Woodcote Cup, despite mechanics and others pushing it nearly all the way to the first corner, Madgwick, in an unsuccessful effort to bump-start it. In his book, *BRM* (Cassell & Co., 1962), written with Peter Roberts, Raymond Mays explained what happened to Wharton's car at Goodwood: 'The reason was exasperating. [Since the fuel filter clogging on Fangio's car at Dundrod, the team had installed a big fuel filter holding a gallon of fuel between pump and carburettor.] The driver had to switch off the fuel on the grid to avoid flooding, then switch on again before starting the engine. Unthinkingly, Wharton had switched off the fuel some distance before reaching the starting grid so that the engine cut out neatly by itself on the grid. Of course, this had emptied the fuel filter and it takes time to get a gallon of fuel back, pushing the car.' *(Guy Griffiths Collection)*

◄ From the start of the Woodcote Cup, Froilán González rocketed into the lead and went on to win with his BRM in 8min 13.0sec (87.64mph/141.01kph) – it was more of a short dash than a race as such. Initially Giuseppe Farina, with Tony Vandervell's Ferrari Thin Wall Special, had struggled to stay with him, but he had to give up the chase and he finished 6.2sec behind in second place, coasting across the finishing line because of a stripped crown wheel. *(Guy Griffiths Collection)*

▲ Reg Parnell finished third in the Woodcote Cup behind Giuseppe Farina who was in Vandervell's Ferrari Thin Wall Special. So many changes had been made to the BRM's body, with the addition of scoops, louvres, and a radiator much bigger than the original, that it is difficult to recognise it as the car introduced almost three years previously with such smooth, unbroken lines. *(Guy Griffiths Collection)*

Daily Graphic Goodwood Trophy, Formule Libre

In the closely fought battles between the BRMs and Vandervell's Ferrari Thin Wall Special it was the Ferrari from Park Royal (Vandervell's factory was situated on London's Western Avenue) that usually had the edge; the car handled better and was faster than the BRMs, and it was often better-driven. At Goodwood in 1952 the Thin Wall was unable to start the main race and it was a good opportunity for a grand slam. The V16s took the first three places and, in a race with a high level of attrition for the Formula 2 cars, Dennis Poore (Connaught A-series) and Stirling Moss (ERA G-Type) finished fourth and fifth. Obviously, the BRM team was delighted with the result, but it was a very hollow victory.

DAILY GRAPHIC GOODWOOD TROPHY, FORMULE LIBRE		
27 September, 2.4-mile (3.86km) airfield perimeter road, 15 laps, 36 miles (57.9km)		
1st	José Froilán González (BRM Type 15)	24m 30.6s, 88.13mph (141.80kph)
2nd	Reg Parnell (BRM Type 15)	24m 38.6s
3rd	Ken Wharton (BRM Type 15)	28m 48.8s
4th	Dennis Poore (Connaught A-series)	25m 18.0s
5th	Stirling Moss (ERA G-Type)	25m 27.2s
6th	Roy Salvadori (Ferrari Tipo 500)	25m 36.0s

Fastest lap: Reg Parnell, 1m 35.6s, 90.38mph (145.42kph), circuit record.

◀ Froilán González is seen here in the *Daily Graphic* Trophy at Goodwood. Giuseppe Farina non-started with the Thin Wall in this race, which was the main event of the day, so in the absence of serious opposition the BRMs took the first three places in the order González, Parnell, and Wharton. *(Guy Griffiths Collection)*

◀ Reg Parnell was a hard, stubborn driver, and here he is pressing on at the wheel of his V16 as he motors to third place in the *Daily Graphic* Trophy race. Parnell was also a very stylish driver, who had learned the laid-back, ostensibly relaxed, style from Giuseppe Farina. *(Guy Griffiths Collection)*

Charterhall International Meeting

Charterhall, 11 October 1952

The organisers of the meeting at Charterhall, which was just over the border north of Berwick-on-Tweed, had invited BRM to send three cars to run in the Formule Libre race at this meeting, but González had returned to Argentina, so two V16s were fielded for Wharton and Parnell. Heading opposition in this 40-lap race was Farina with the Thin Wall Special. Other entries included Peter Walker with his Cooper-ERA and 'Mr Bob' Gerard at the wheel of ERA R14B. The Cooper-ERA combined a lengthened Cooper Formula 2 chassis with a 2-litre ERA engine developed by special-builder Geoff Richardson.

Surprisingly, first away in the *Daily Record* Trophy was Walker with his promising new Cooper-ERA, but Gerard passed him at the first corner with R14B, and then Farina shot through into the lead. Next up were the BRMs that had made a slow start. Farina retired the Thin Wall because the gearbox broke and Parnell dropped out because of transmission problems.

The race then became a duel between Wharton and Gerard. Wharton was pursuing Gerard hard, and *Autosport* reported: 'Time and time again the snarling BRM closed up, only to fall back at the bends. Gerard was cornering at a remarkable pace … Eventually Wharton managed to edge past Gerard, but Gerard never let up and Wharton had to go all out to hold him off. Two laps from the finish, just when a BRM victory seemed likely, he spun off the road because of a grabbing front brake and the veteran ERA swept ahead and stayed there until the end. Wharton rejoined the race to finish second.

GLASGOW DAILY RECORD TROPHY, FORMULE LIBRE		
11 October, Charterhall, 2-mile (3.2km) airfield perimeter road, 40 laps, 80miles (129km)		
1st	Bob Gerard (ERA 2-litre B-Type)	58min 17.2sec, 82.40mph (132.58kph)
2nd	**Ken Wharton (BRM Type 15)**	**58min 22.6sec**
3rd	Louis Rosier (Ferrari Tipo 375)	58min 42.9sec
4th	Peter Walker (Cooper-ERA 2-litre)	39 laps
5th	Yves Giraud-Cabantous (Talbot T26C))	39 laps
6th	Mike Oliver (Connaught A-series)	39 laps
Rtd	**Reg Parnell (BRM Type 16)**	**5 laps (transmission)**

▼ The results of the Charterhall race were rather bizarre. Early in the race Reg Parnell, who retired because of transmission problems, leads Peter Walker (Cooper-ERA). *(LAT Photographic)*

▲ The nose of Ken Wharton's V16 is dipping under braking as he enters the hairpin leading on to the main straight at Charterhall, as a local policeman looks on. *(Graham Gauld)*

▶ A big crowd enjoys the sun while watching Reg Parnell at work in the early stages of the race. *(Bill Henderson Collection)*

Chapter 7
The 1953 season

The first year with the Owen Racing Organisation

Development of the V16 continued after the takeover by the Owen Racing Organisation, although the main focus was on development of a 2,500cc contender for the new Grand Prix formula. Tony Rudd was placed in charge of test and development of the V16s. Before and during the 1953 season considerable strides were taken in preventing cylinder stud problems.

The major engine failures which had been caused by deformation of the sealing ring between cylinder head and liner were largely solved by adopting the head-ring material used by Rolls-Royce on pre-war and early Second World War Merlin engines. The general design of the cylinder heads and liners was similar to that of early Merlin engines, but later Merlins were substantially different.

Following the adoption of these head-rings, if there was a failure it would occur when the engine was under maximum power, and the leak would pressurise the header tank and cause overheating, but it would be insufficient for water to blow into the bores against cylinder pressure. These and many other minor modifications resulted in a much higher level of engine reliability and consistent power outputs.

◀ A fine view of Ken Wharton on his way to winning the Formule Libre race at Castle Combe in August 1953. Although it was a short airfield circuit, the course itself was interesting and a couple of the corners were deceptive in that they looked rather faster than they really were. *(LAT Photographic)*

BARC International Meeting

Goodwood, Easter Monday, 6 April 1953

Chichester Cup, Formule Libre

In this short race, during which heavy rain fell, the two BRMs were driven by Wharton and Parnell. Emmanuel de Graffenried led away from the start in his works-loaned Formula 2 Maserati A6GCM. He stayed in front to win the race, although on the last lap Wharton made a near desperate attempt to pass him at the chicane. The V16 almost stood still because of wheelspin as Wharton accelerated hard at the exit and he finished four-fifths of a second behind the Swiss driver. Ron Flockhart finished third, three seconds behind, with ERA R4D. Poor Parnell's BRM sounded rough and woolly and he finished a poor fourth, unable to get to grips with the ERA.

▼ This lovely photograph shows Wharton squatting on the left rear wheel of his BRM before the start of the five-lap Chichester Cup race on Easter Monday. (*LAT Photographic*)

CHICHESTER CUP, FORMULE LIBRE

6 April, Goodwood, 2.4-mile (3.86km) airfield perimeter circuit, 5 laps, 12 miles (19km)

1st	Emmanuel de Graffenried (Maserati A6GCM)	9m 3.4s, 79.48mph (127.88kph)
2nd	**Ken Wharton (BRM Type 15)**	**9m 4.2s**
3rd	Ron Flockhart (ERA D-type)	9m 7.4s
4th	**Reg Parnell (BRM Type 15)**	**9m 15.0s**
5th	Tony Rolt (Connaught A-series)	9m 33.0s
6th	Ken McAlpine (Connaught A-series)	9m 39.4s

Fastest lap: Ken Wharton, 1m 46.2s, 81.36mph (130.91kph)

▼ In the wet Chichester Cup race at Goodwood on Easter Monday, Swiss driver Emmanuel de Graffenried, at the wheel of the latest version of the Formula 2 Maserati A6GCM, could put all the power down on the road, while Ken Wharton was battling with vicious wheelspin on the BRM. De Graffenried's Maserati was an interim model loaned by the factory, and the works cars were much streamlined. The Swiss privateer made a brilliant start to the season and his successes included a win in the Syracuse Grand Prix after the failure of the works Ferrari team. *(Guy Griffiths Collection)*

Richmond Trophy, Formule Libre

This 15-lap event was the main race of the Goodwood Easter Monday meeting and the opposition to the BRMs included Piero Taruffi with the Ferrari Thin Wall Special. Fast Formula 2 driver/car combinations included de Graffenried (Maserati), Salvadori (works Connaught), Tony Rolt (Rob Walker-entered Connaught), and Bob Gerard (Cooper-Bristol).

After making a really good start, Wharton led throughout on a drying track to win what was up until then Goodwood's fastest race at 90.47mph (145.57kph). During the race he broke the lap record five times and left it standing at 92.21mph (148.37kph). The Thin Wall was off form in this race, and Parnell retired his BRM because of a sheared supercharger quill-shaft.

RICHMOND TROPHY RACE (for the Glover Trophy), FORMULE LIBRE	
6 April, Goodwood, 2.4-mile (3.86km) airfield perimeter circuit, 15 laps, 36 miles (58km)	
1st Ken Wharton (BRM Type 15)	**23m 53.0s, 90.47mph (145.57kph)**
2nd Piero Taruffi (Ferrari Thin Wall Special)	23m 59.0s
3rd Emmanuel de Graffenried (Maserati A6GCM)	24m 15.8s
4th Roy Salvadori (Connaught A-series)	
5th Tony Rolt (Connaught A-series)	
6th Bob Gerard (Cooper-Bristol)	
Rtd Reg Parnell (BRM Type 15)	**(supercharger failure)**

Fastest lap: Ken Wharton, 1min 33.8sec, 92.21mph (148.37kph), circuit record

▼ The 15-lap Richmond Trophy race for the Glover Trophy was the main event of the day. Here Reg Parnell with his V16 BRM leads Roy Salvadori (Connaught) through the chicane that had been installed at Goodwood for the start of the 1952 season and first used at that year's Easter Monday meeting. It extended the length of the circuit from 2.38 miles (3.83km) to 2.4 miles (3.86km). Parnell retired because of supercharger failure and Wharton (BRM) won the race from Taruffi (Thin Wall Special), de Graffenried (Maserati) and Salvadori (Connaught). *(Guy Griffiths Collection)*

▶ Wharton made a brilliant start in the 15-lap Richmond Trophy and led throughout to score a rare victory over the Ferrari Thin Wall Special. *(Klemantaski Collection)*

▼ The Duke of Richmond and Gordon handed the Richmond Trophy filled with champagne to race-winner Ken Wharton, who took a gulp and then proffered the trophy back to His Grace. It was one of the great moments in Wharton's racing career. *(LAT Photographic)*

Charterhall International Meeting

Charterhall, 23 May 1953

Because the team' efforts were concentrated on preparation for the Albi race to be held the following weekend, BRM sent only a single V16 for Ken Wharton to drive in the 40-mile (64km) Formule Libre race at the Charterhall circuit near Kelso. The worthwhile opposition was limited to the ERAs of Ron Flockhart and Bob Gerard, and Peter Walker's Cooper-ERA.

On this short, very bumpy circuit laid out on the perimeter road of a Second World War airfield, the BRM was handicapped by the short straights and the inability to exploit the car's power and acceleration. In practice, Wharton lapped in 1min 24.8sec, an unofficial circuit record that he made official by matching it in the race.

At the fall of the flag the BRM made its usual slow start and Flockhart led away from Walker, Gerard, and Wharton in fourth place. The BRM quickly moved up to second place and closed up on Flockhart until Wharton spun because of a grabbing brake at a corner called Toft's Turn. He had difficulty in getting the car going again, and after rejoining in seventh place he came through to finish third behind the two ERAs.

GLASGOW DAILY RECORD TROPHY, FORMULE LIBRE		
23 May, Charterhall, 2-mile (3.2km) airfield perimeter circuit, 20 laps, 40 miles (64km)		
1st	Ron Flockhart (ERA D-type 2-litre)	81.40mph (130.97kph)
2nd	Bob Gerard (ERA B-type 2-litre)	
3rd	**Ken Wharton (BRM Type 15)**	
4th	Bobby Baird (Ferrari Tipo 500)	
5th	Tony Gaze (Maserati 8C-3000CM)	
6th	Peter Walker (Cooper-ERA 2-litre)	

Fastest lap: Ken Wharton, 1m 24.8s, 85.70mph (137.89kph), circuit record

▼ At the Charterhall meeting in May 1953 only a single BRM was entered and driven by Ken Wharton because the team's main efforts were concentrated on the Albi Grand Prix the following weekend. Wharton spun off because of a grabbing brake and rejoined to finish a poor third. *(Bill Henderson Collection)*

Albi Grand Prix

France, 31 May 1953

BRM made a three-car entry in the Albi Grand Prix held on 31 May 1953. Heading the opposition were three Ferraris: the works-entered Tipo 375 'Indianapolis' car with longer wheelbase; the Thin Wall Special driven by Giuseppe Farina; and the French racing blue 1951 car of Louis Rosier. Other entrants included Gordinis, old Talbot-Lagos, and Peter Whitehead with his Cooper-Alta.

The race was run on the famous high-speed Les Planques circuit in two 55.63 mile (89.51km) 10-lap heats for Formula 1 and Formula 2 cars respectively, with a 100.14-mile (161km) 18-lap final for the fastest 12 runners. It was a wonderful opportunity for the V16s to go some way towards redeeming themselves.

In the F1 heat Fangio set a tremendous pace and he won the heat. Wharton finished second. González's nearside rear tyre failed at around 150mph (240kph), with thrown treads smashing the exhaust and lashing forward, tearing off part of the small windscreen. After a wheel-change and a push-start, the Argentinian rejoined the heat to finish fifth.

The team's prospects in the final were destroyed by failures of the Dunlop tyres. Early in the final the BRMs moved into the first three places, but both González and Fangio had tyre failures. González rejoined the race after a wheel-change, but Fangio, whose blow-out was reckoned to have occurred at around 190mph (306kph) on the long narrow straight, had hit the bank damaging a hub while fighting for control, and the car had to be retired.

González had another tyre failure, but again rejoined the race to finish second behind Louis Rosier, plodding along with his 4.5-litre Ferrari. Wharton had taken the lead, but he had the most horrendous crash from which he was lucky to walk away almost unscathed. It really had been a race between the tortoise and the hare. Tyres apart, the BRMs, which were claimed to be developing 585bhp, had been at peak form and running so very beautifully. For BRM supporters who watched it had been a dream coming true that turned into a nightmare.

▲ At Albi the BRMs performed magnificently until their tyres failed. Fangio is seen here in the first heat, which he won easily. *(Grand Prix Library)*

ALBI GRAND PRIX, FORMULA 1 AND FORMULA 2

31 May, Circuit des Planques, 5.56-mile (8.95km) circuit, two 10-lap 55.63-mile (89.51km) qualifying heats and 18-lap 100.14-mile (161km) final

Formula 1 Heat

1st	**Juan Manuel Fangio (BRM Type 15)**	**29m 57.8s, 110.78mph (178.24kph)**
2nd	**Ken Wharton (BRM Type 15)**	**31m 9.3s**
3rd	L. Rosier (Ferrari Tipo 375)	32m 4.4s
4th	M. Trintignant (Gordini Type 16 2.5-litre)	32m 8.3s
5th	**J. F. González (BRM Type 15)**	**32m 50.3s**
6th	Yves Giraud-Cabantous (Talbot Type 26C)	

Fastest lap: Juan Manuel Fangio, 2m 52.2s, 115.59mph (186.01kph), circuit record

Final

1st	Louis Rosier (Ferrari Tipo 375)	56m 36.8s, 105.53mph (169.80kph)
2nd	**José Froilán González (BRM Type 15)**	**57m 7.8s**
3rd	Maurice Trintignant (Gordini Type 16 2.5-litre)	58m 30.6s
4th	Roberto Mieres (Gordini Type 16 2-litre)	17 laps
5th	Peter Whitehead (Cooper-Alta)	17 laps
6th	Johnny Claes (Connaught A-series)	17 laps
Rtd	**Juan Manuel Fangio (BRM Type 15)**	**9 laps (broken hub)**
Rtd	**Ken Wharton (BRM Type 15)**	**11 laps (tyre failure, accident)**

Fastest lap: Ken Wharton, 2m 52.3s, 115.58mph (185.97kph)

▲Before forming up on the grid for the first heat at Albi, the cars have been warmed up on soft plugs, and the mechanics are seen here fitting hard plugs for the race. Rivers-Fletcher, Maurice Dove and Dick Salmon (foreground) are visible. *(Grand Prix Library)*

▼ Although González had to stop for a wheel-change in the final of the Albi race, he kept going steadily to finish second behind Rosier (Ferrari). *(Grand Prix Library)*

▶ Taken shortly after the start of the final of the Albi race, this photograph shows Louis Rosier (private Ferrari Tipo 375) leading Fangio. After the BRMs ran into tyre problems, Rosier scored an unexpected victory for the second year in succession. *(LAT Photographic)*

◀ At Albi this BRM, driven by Fangio, won the first heat. He was leading the final when a rear tyre failed with the result seen below. *(Grand Prix Library)*

▼ In the final Fangio had the left rear tyre blow at an estimated 190mph (305kph), stripping it down to the canvas. He is seen crawling past the Thin Wall Special pit. After the BRM had been checked by the mechanics it had to be retired because of a damaged hub. *(LAT Photographic)*

▲ After Ken Wharton took the lead, he had the most terrible crash, as can be seen from this photograph. On a twisty section of the circuit, he went into a violent slide at about 140mph (225kph) when a tyre threw a tread. He battled for control, but the car went off the road backwards, hit a two-foot high bank, turned over (pitching Wharton into the ditch) and hit a brick wall, part of which was demolished. Upside-down, the car careered along the remaining stretch of wall, before ricocheting into the middle of the road where it came to rest, still upside-down. Incredibly, Wharton escaped with bad bruising, and he was terribly shocked. The car was, of course, a write-off. *(Grand Prix Library)*

BRDC British Empire Trophy

Douglas (Isle of Man), 18 June 1953

On 18 June the BRDC held this traditional sports car race on the Douglas road circuit on the Isle of Man. Reg Parnell drove the prototype Aston Martin DB3S to a victory, and Ken Wharton finished second at the wheel of the works development Frazer Nash Mk II Le Mans Replica. BRM sent over chassis 2 (the González car at Albi) and with this Parnell completed four demonstration laps.

▶ Reg Parnell demonstrating the BRM on the Douglas, Isle of Man, circuit in June 1953. *(LAT Photographic)*

British Grand Prix support race

Silverstone, 18 July 1953

It reflected the diminishing importance of both the V16 BRMs and the Ferrari Thin Wall Special that the length of this race had been halved since 1952. Because of the complete destruction at Albi of the first BRM to be built, the team could only field two V16s at Silverstone. Fangio drove one and Parnell stepped down to let Wharton drive the other. In practice the Argentinian unofficially broke the circuit record with a time of 1min 46sec, but it was a balls to the wall effort, arms and elbows flailing, as he fought to beat Farina.

The Italian champion was a very smooth second fastest in 1min 47sec at the wheel of the Thin Wall Special. It did not bode well for BRM. Wharton was third fastest, and alongside him and completing the front of the starting grid was Mike Hawthorn with a works Tipo 625 2,490cc car that was a prototype for the new Grand Prix formula coming into force for 1954.

After practice, Fangio's car needed major engine work and it was yet another overnighter for the mechanics. Quite unnecessarily, Mays indulged in a piece of showmanship and drove Fangio's car from the team's headquarters in Brackley to the circuit along the A43 main road from Northampton to Oxford.

At the fall of the Union flag Hawthorn nosed ahead, but Farina was alongside as they went under *The Motor* bridge across the circuit and was in the lead as he entered Stowe, the first corner. Farina led throughout, and as the race progressed he twice broke the circuit record. Fangio took second place from Hawthorn on the second lap.

Farina pulled away further and further into the lead, while Fangio held on to second place despite an engine that was running rough and down on power. Hawthorn retired because of an overheating engine. Wharton drove a steady but unspectacular race to take third place. Almost inevitably Ron Flockhart drove R4D extremely well and he was the only other driver to finish on the same lap as the winner.

▶ There were always hopes of really good battles between the V16 BRMs and the Ferrari Thin Wall Special, but only too frequently they petered out because one of the contenders non-started or the BRMs had mechanical problems during the race. Fangio is seen at the wheel of a V16 in the 50-mile Formule Libre race at Silverstone on the day of the British Grand Prix. There had been problems with this car in practice and the mechanics worked through the night before the race. It ran badly in the race and Fangio finished second to Giuseppe Farina's Thin Wall Special, with Ken Wharton, at the wheel of the other BRM, coming in third. After the race it was discovered that an exhausted mechanic had assembled two rings on one of the cylinder joints on Fangio's engine.
(Tom March Collection)

BRDC FORMULE LIBRE TROPHY

18 July, Silverstone, 2.927-mile (4.71km) airfield perimeter circuit, 17 laps, 49.76 miles (80.07km)

1st	Giuseppe Farina (Ferrari Thin Wall Special)	30m 50.8s, 96.79mph (155.74kph)
2nd	**Juan Manuel Fangio (BRM Type 15)**	**31m 2.0s, 96.20mph (154.79kph)**
3rd	**Ken Wharton (BRM Type 15)**	**31m 34.0s, 94.58mph (152.18kph)**
4th	Ron Flockhart (ERA D-type 2-litre)	32m 8.6s
5th	Geoff Richardson (RRA Special 1.7-litre S)	16 laps
6th	Graham Whitehead (ERA B-type)	16 laps

Fastest lap: Giuseppe Farina, 1m 45.2s, 100.16mph (161.19kph)

▲ The opposition in the Formule Libre race at Silverstone included Mike Hawthorn at the wheel of a 2,490cc 4-cylinder Tipo 625 Ferrari. This was the model that Ferrari relied on at the start of the 2,500cc Grand Prix Formula in 1954. On the front row of the starting grid at Silverstone, the positions, from left, were: Juan Fangio (BRM), Giuseppe Farina (Ferrari Thin Wall Special), Ken Wharton (BRM) and Mike Hawthorn. As they awaited the fall of the starter's flag and the drivers blipped the throttles of their cars, the noise of the BRMs was so shattering that Hawthorn put his hands over his ears in an attempt to block it out. *(Guy Griffiths Collection)*

◀ Giuseppe Farina completely dominated the Formule Libre race at the British Grand Prix meeting. By this time constant development work had made the Ferrari Thin Wall Special the fastest and most powerful of all the 4,500cc unsupercharged Formula 1 cars. *(Tom March Collection)*

▶ For this race Dunlop provided Fangio's BRM with special tyres that had only 4mm of tread (instead of 7mm) as it was considered that these would be less likely to cause problems. In this photograph the 'lucky' horseshoe from a wedding cake on the supplementary intake is clearly visible. There is no record of how or why this came to be on Fangio's car, but subsequently Wharton insisted on it being put on the BRM that he drove. *(Tom March Collection)*

▶ Ken Wharton drove a steady race in the Formule Libre race at Silverstone to finish third behind Farina (with Tony Vandervell's Ferrari Thin Wall Special) and Fangio. Wharton was a versatile driver who, as well as racing single-seaters and sports cars, drove in rallies and trials. *(Tom March Collection)*

USAF Trophy Meeting

Snetterton, 25 July 1953
There were two short Formule Libre races at this meeting held on 25 July, and BRM policy under the Owen Organisation ownership was to race the cars whenever possible. There was no serious opposition in either race.

AMOC Trophy, Formule Libre
A single V16 driven by Ken Wharton ran in the first race over 15 laps, and he set fastest lap in practice. Joining him on the front row of the grid were Ron Flockhart (R4D) and Tony Rolt (Connaught A-series entered by Rob Walker). Wharton led throughout, setting a new lap record of 1min 47.4sec, 90.50mph (145.64kph). At the chequered flag he was 20.8sec ahead of the ERA.

USA Invitation Race, Formule Libre
This ten-lap race at the end of the day was poorly supported because, by the time the runners had been nominated, many of those competing had already loaded up their trailers and transporters and departed for home. Wharton took the lead at the start and lapped closely followed by Flockhart until R4D went off song. Then Leslie Marr with his Connaught A-series slipped ahead of the ERA, and that was how they finished.

Aston Martin Owners' Club Trophy, Formule Libre

25 July, Snetterton, 2.71-mile (4.36km) airfield perimeter circuit, 15 laps, 40.65 miles (65.4km)

1st	Ken Wharton (BRM Type 15)	27m 23.8s, 88.79mph (142.89kph)
2nd	Ron Flockhart (ERA D-type)	27m 44.6s, 87.60mph (140.97kph)
3rd	Tony Rolt (Connaught A-series)	28m 24.4s, 85.55mph (137.68kph)
4th	Geoffrey Richardson (RRA)	28m 49.4s

Fastest lap: Ken Wharton, 1m 47.4s, 90.50mph (145.64kph), circuit record

USA INVITATION RACE, FORMULE LIBRE

25 July, Snetterton, 2.71-mile (4.36km) airfield perimeter circuit, 10 laps, 27.1 miles (43.6km)

1st	Ken Wharton (BRM Type 15)	18min 27.2sec, 87.79mph (141.28kph)
2nd	Leslie Marr (Connaught A-series)	19min 47.8sec, 81.83mph (131.69kph)
3rd	Ron Flockhart (ERA D-type 2-litre)	20min 23.4sec, 79.45mph (127.86kph)
4th	B. Wyatt (Frazer Nash)	9 laps

Fastest lap: Ken Wharton and Ron Flockhart, 1m 48s, 90.00mph (144.84kph)

▼ In the Aston Martin Owners' Club Formule Libre race, Ken Wharton leads Ron Flockhart. This was a very minor British national race meeting in which there was no serious opposition to the BRM, and the only point worthy of comment is that the BRM lasted the distance. *(LAT Photographic)*

▶ Another view of Ken Wharton at Snetterton, leading Ron Flockhart's ERA. Despite it being an old car, the combination of R4D and Flockhart's driving had proved a potent force in Formule Libre racing. The fact that it had been Mays' car and that Mays was sexually attracted to the good-looking young Scot, led to Flockhart being invited to join the BRM team, but when Ron learned of how Mays felt about him he was horrified. *(LAT Photographic)*

A fine view of Ken Wharton, seen here with his V16 cantering to an easy win in the USAF Invitation Formule Libre race at Snetterton in the face of very weak opposition. *(LAT Photographic)*

▲ A handsome sight: Ken Wharton at speed on his way to victory in the Formule Libre race at Charterhall in August. *(Graham Gauld)*

Charterhall International Meeting

Charterhall, 15 August 1953

At this meeting at the Berwickshire circuit, jointly sponsored by the Scottish *Daily Record* and the *Newcastle Journal*, there were two 50-lap races – a Formula 2 race in which Ken Wharton entered his own Cooper-Bristol, recognisable by the broad yellow nose-band – and a Formule Libre race in which BRMs were entered for Reg Parnell and Wharton. During practice Parnell was travelling at around 100mph (161kph) and when he applied the brakes, those at the rear locked up and he spun, crashing backwards into a barrier.

Although Reg was unhurt, the rear bodywork of the car was badly damaged and there was no alternative but to scratch this entry. So, Wharton was the only BRM starter, and as his fastest practice lap was only 1min 24.4sec compared to the 1min 21.8sec, an unofficial circuit record, achieved by Farina with the Ferrari Thin Wall Special (now fitted with special Goodyear disc brakes), prospects did not look good.

The Formula 2 race was held first, and Wharton won this from the Connaughts of Roy Salvadori and Ron Flockhart, and he then switched to the BRM for the Formule Libre race. Farina led initially from Wharton and Moss (Cooper-Alta). Farina and the Thin Wall Special fell back because of ignition problems and retired. Moss also retired, and Wharton forged ahead to win the race and set a new outright circuit record. While Vandervell raced the Thin Wall to gain experience for his own Grand Prix cars and to test components, notably the Goodyear aircraft-type disc brakes, the BRMs were raced in an effort to salvage the team's reputation.

DAILY RECORD AND NEWCASTLE JOURNAL TROPHY, FORMULE LIBRE

15 August, Charterhall, 2-mile (3.2km) airfield perimeter circuit, 50 laps, 100 miles (161km)

1st	**Ken Wharton (BRM Type 15)**	**1hr 12m 32.2s, 82.70mph (133.1kph)**
2nd	Tony Rolt (Connaught A-series)	1hr 13m 30s
3rd	Jack Fairman/Roy Salvadori (Connaught A-series)	48 laps
4th	Ninian Sanderson (Cooper-Bristol)	48 laps
DNS	**Reg Parnell (BRM Type 15)**	**(accident damage in practice)**

Fastest lap: Ken Wharton, 1m 24s, 85.71mph (137.93kph), circuit record

▶ As can be seen from this photograph, Shelsley Walsh was and still is a power hill. On the day, the actual hill-climb was held in the wet and Ken Wharton, in giving a demonstration with the BRM, struggled with immense wheelspin. *(LAT Photographic)*

Shelsley Walsh

29 August 1953

On 29 August the Midlands Automobile Club staged their International Hill Climb at Shelsley Walsh and Ken Wharton made a demonstration appearance with a V16 BRM. It was a gesture of appreciation for the support received by BRM from the Club dating back to the early days of the project. The car was totally unsuitable, in theory at least, for a hill-climb, though Shelsley is recognised as a power hill and the BRM was much more at home than it would have been at, say, Prescott or Westbrook Hay. In addition, of course, Wharton was an RAC Hill Champion.

In practice on a dry hill Wharton was amazingly quick and, leaving black tyre marks at every bend, he ascended the Worcestershire hill in 37.97sec, which was only just over a second outside the record time. Torrential rain persisted on the day of the hill-climb itself, and with the BRM the intrepid Wharton could manage no better than 49.84sec, compared with his own BTD of 41.82sec at the wheel of a blown 2-litre ERA specially set up for hill-climbing.

BARC International Meeting

Goodwood, 26 September 1953

There was always a wonderful garden party atmosphere at Goodwood, even in the crisp, sharp air of the autumn meeting. All those who attended in those days, in whatever capacity, working or watching, remember it with great nostalgia. The level of blatant commercialism was much lower than at today's Goodwood Festival of Speed and Nostalgia meetings.

The September 1953 meeting witnessed a titanic clash between the stars, the V16 BRMs driven by heavyweights Fangio and Wharton and the Ferrari Thin Wall with Mike Hawthorn, the juvenile lead, at the wheel. There was a strong supporting cast of Connaughts and Coopers.

The Thin Wall, however, so nearly failed to make it and the Vandervell team members, unusually, were the ones in a panic. The Ferrari's engine had broken during Friday's practice and the mechanics had spent the night rebuilding it. Since the Albi race, BRM had only two V16s to field and at Goodwood these were driven by Fangio and Wharton.

The meeting opened with the five-lap Madgwick

211

Cup for Formula 2 cars. Roy Salvadori won this with a works Connaught, and in the process he lapped in 1min 35.0sec, thereby breaking the lap record set by González (Ferrari Thin Wall Special) at the Easter meeting at the circuit the previous year. Roy held the new record only briefly.

Woodcote Cup

This was a five-lap taster for the main race later in the day. The Vandervell mechanics were still working on Thin Wall up until the last moment, and Hawthorn joined the grid only 30sec before the start. Initially he lined up in the second row alongside Moss (Cooper-Alta), but Stirling and others waved him through to the front row; the Ferrari was projecting forward from the starting line some three feet when the starter dropped the flag and he seared off in a flurry of wheelspin. He was well ahead of the rest of the field by the first corner.

Salvadori held second place with his works Connaught until an oil pipe came adrift, and then Tony Rolt with Rob Walker's Connaught took up the chase of the BRM. As Wharton braked for the chicane on the third lap, a brake locked and he spun round facing Rolt's Connaught. Rolt swerved round the stricken BRM, but smacked into the concrete barrier on the inside of the circuit, wrecking the nose of the A-series.

Hawthorn won by a margin of 23.2sec from Fangio, with Wharton in third place a further 12.2sec behind. Hawthorn set a new outright circuit lap

record of 1min 32.0sec, 93.91mph (151.10kph). The BRM team was invited to protest Hawthorn's win because the Ferrari had its front wheels ahead of the line at the start. The team – especially Fangio – were adamant that they were soundly and fairly beaten and did not want to win the race on a technicality.

WOODCOTE CUP, FORMULE LIBRE

26 September, Goodwood, 2.4-mile (3.86km) airfield perimeter circuit, 5 laps, 12 miles (19.3km)

1st	Mike Hawthorn (Ferrari Thin Wall Special)	7m 42.2s, 92.11mph (148.23kph)
2nd	**Juan Manuel Fangio (BRM Type 15)**	**8m 5.4s**
3rd	**Ken Wharton (BRM Type 15)**	**8m 17.6s**
4th	Stirling Moss (Cooper-Alta)	8m 23.4s
5th	Bob Gerard (Cooper-Bristol)	8m 30.6s
6th	Geoff Richardson (RRA)	8m 42.6

Fastest lap: Mike Hawthorn, 1m 32s, 93.91mph (151.10kph)

GOODWOOD TROPHY, FORMULE LIBRE

26 September, 2.4-mile (3.86km) airfield perimeter circuit, 15 laps, 36 miles (58km)

1st	Mike Hawthorn (Ferrari Thin Wall Special)	23m 17.8s, 92.70mph (149.15kph)
2nd	**Ken Wharton (BRM Type 15)**	**23m 40.8s**
3rd	Bob Gerard (Cooper-Bristol)	14 laps
4th	Graham Whitehead (ERA B-type)	14 laps
5th	Roy Salvadori (Connaught A-series)	14 laps
6th	Horace Gould (Cooper-Bristol)	14 laps
Rtd	**Juan Manuel Fangio (BRM Type 15)**	**12 laps (gear selectors)**

Fastest lap: Mike Hawthorn, 1m 31.4s, 94.53mph (152.13kph)

◄ At the Goodwood meeting in September 1953 the combination of young Mike Hawthorn and the Ferrari Thin Wall Special proved too much for the BRMs, and the Vandervell-entered car won both Formule Libre races. *(Tom March Collection)*

► Before the Woodcote Cup, the first of the team's two races at Goodwood, Fangio listens to a locquacious Wharton. *(LAT Photographic)*

◀Fangio sits on the grid in pole position for the Woodcote Cup. Despite all the Argentinian's efforts, Mike Hawthorn won the race with the Thin Wall Special. *(Tom March Collection)*

▼At the September 1962 Goodwood meeting it can be seen that spillage during filling of the fuel tank has stripped the paint off the tail of the BRM. *(Grand Prix Library)*

▲ Ken Wharton was trying really hard to catch up with teammate Fangio, and he is seen here braking for the chicane. *(LAT Photographic)*

▶ Ken Wharton's brakes locked up at the chicane and he spun. This is Tony Rolt's view of Wharton as he tried desperately to avoid collision, and he hit the concrete barrier close to where the photographer was standing. *(LAT Photographic)*

Hastings Trophy Race

Castle Combe, 3 October 1953

The team sent a single car for Ken Wharton to drive in the 15-lap Hastings Trophy Formule Libre race at the meeting at Castle Combe on 3 October. This airfield perimeter road circuit had a length of only 1.84 miles (2.96km) because this had been a grass airfield with a quite short runway. The serious opposition in this race was limited to Bob Gerard (ERA) and Horace Gould ('The González of the West Country') at the wheel of his Cooper-Bristol.

Wharton was fastest in practice and he led throughout the race, despite suspension problems; the right strut of the suspension had failed and the right rear had lost pressure. In the ordinary way the Lockheed strut system was very reliable. Wharton set a new lap record and at the chequered flag he was 28.8sec ahead of Gerard, and Gould, hot on Gerard's exhaust, finished third.

HASTINGS TROPHY RACE, FORMULE LIBRE		
3 October, Castle Combe, 1.84-mile (2.96km) airfield perimeter circuit, 15 laps, 27.6 miles (44.4km)		
1st	**Ken Wharton (BRM Type 15)**	**18m 55.8s, 87.49mph (140.77kph)**
2nd	Bob Gerard (ERA B-type 2-litre)	19m 24.6s
3rd	Horace Gould (Cooper-Bristol)	29m 25.4s
4th	Tony Rolt (Connaught A-series)	
Fastest lap: Ken Wharton, 1m 13.8s, 89.77mph (144.40kph), circuit record		

▼ The start of the Hastings Trophy: from left, the front row comprises Horace Gould (Cooper-Bristol), Bob Gerard (ERA B-type) and Ken Wharton (BRM) in pole position. Gould was a motor trader from the Bristol area and he was a man of considerable 'corporation' – hence him being known as the González of the West Country. For a couple of years he was to race a 250F Maserati as a privateer, and he achieved a consistent level of success. *(LAT Photographic)*

▶ At the Castle Combe meeting the team sent a single V16 for Ken Wharton to drive. He is seen on his way to achieving a final win before the existing Grand Prix formula came to an end. Here, Wharton is maintaining a very tight line through the corners. *(LAT Photographic)*

Chapter 8
The 1954 season

A year of Formule Libre racing

It now seems illogical that, at the end of 1953, BRM dispatched one of the V16 cars to New Zealand to compete in the Tasman series with Ken Wharton at the wheel. The main reason (excuse would be a more accurate word) was that the Owen Organisation had growing business interests in New Zealand.

New Zealand Grand Prix

Auckland, 9 January 1954
The first race was the 204-mile (338km) Formule Libre New Zealand Grand Prix held on the Ardmore airfield circuit at Auckland. The V16 BRM was a class apart from a field that included Stan Jones' Maybach Special, Horace Gould's Cooper-Bristol, Tony Gaze's supercharged Alta-powered HWM, and Ron Roycroft's elderly ex-Salvadori Alfa Romeo Monoposto.

Mainly because of the shortcomings of the BRM, it was an exciting race, but it was reduced to a

◀ The flag has fallen at Goodwood for the start of the 21-lap Richmond Trophy race. Ron Flockhart (Mk II) on the left of the photograph and Reg Parnell (Ferrari Tipo 625) on the right have accelerated ahead. Between them and slightly further back are Ken Wharton with the Mk 1 and Kenneth McAlpine with his works Connaught (No. 45). Roy Salvadori (No. 9) has made a poor start, and this was to happen all season; the 250F, unknown to its driver and entrant, was fitted with a high, non-standard first gear. *(LAT Photographic)*

NEW ZEALAND GRAND PRIX, AUCKLAND, FORMULE LIBRE

9 January, Ardmore, 2.1-mile (3.38km) airfield perimeter circuit, 100 laps, 210 miles (338km)

1st	Stan Jones (Maybach Special 4.3-litre)	2hr 45m 20s, 74.90mph (120.51kph)
2nd	**Ken Wharton (BRM Type 15)**	**2hr 46m 13.3s**
3rd	Tony Gaze (HWM 2-litre s/c)	2hr 46m 22.3s
4th	Horace Gould (Cooper-Bristol)	2hr 47m 9.0s
5th	Ron Roycroft (Alfa Romeo Tipo B Monoposto)	2hr 48m 49.0s
6th	Jack Brabham (Cooper-Bristol)	2hr 54m 52.5s

Fastest lap: Ken Wharton, 1m 34.0s, 80.43mph (129.44kph)

◀ Seen here is the BRM carefully 'packed' in a crate for shipping to New Zealand by LEP Transport for Ken Wharton to take part in the Tasman series. *(LAT Photographic)*

▼ Before the New Zealand race Wharton is pushed onto the grid. Number 9 is the REDEX-sponsored Cooper-Bristol of Jack Brabham which fiinished sixth. *(Grand Prix Library)*

shambles by the timekeepers, who lost track of the number of laps that each competitor had covered, and the accuracy of the official results remains in doubt 60 years later, save for the fact that Jones was the undoubted winner.

With five laps completed, Wharton led the race and had lapped most of the field, but once again the BRM developed brake problems. Because of a grabbing brake he spun at the corner before the pits straight, scattering the oil drums and, after a push-start he rejoined the race without losing the lead. Rain started to fall and reduced tyre wear, which enabled a number of runners to go through the race without a pit stop. Wharton stopped at the pits after 44 laps of this 100-lap race, and refuelling and changing tyres cost him about 45sec.

Wharton had lost the lead to Stan Jones (Maybach Special), but he gradually closed the gap and took the lead again on lap 51. But then, on lap 60, he came past the pits streaming vaporised brake fluid from the front wheels, and many spectators thought that the BRM was on fire. He stopped at the pits, but it was impossible to repair the car under racing conditions; the front brakes were disconnected and Wharton rejoined the race, relying on the rear brakes and engine braking.

In its report of the race, *Autosport* quoted a local newspaper as saying of the BRM, '… the car could be heard at least 15 miles away. As soon as it was started … everyone … in the grandstand jerked to his feet, and all though the race people on the course were left gasping at the ear-shattering din the car produced.'

The winner was Stan Jones (father of World Champion Alan Jones) at the wheel of the Maybach. Wharton was classified second, but the results were protested by Horace Gould from Bristol ('The González of the West Country') who claimed that the organisers had credited him with a lap too few. During the interminable wranglings that followed, Wharton was classified, second, fifth, and ultimately third behind Horace Gould (Cooper-Bristol).

◄ Stan Jones, father of World Champion Alan Jones, is seen at the wheel of the Maybach Special with which he achieved an unexpected, sensational win at Auckland. The engine of this special originally powered a Maybach half-track scout car captured in the West African Desert and taken to Australia for examination by the Federal Government. It was sold to a Melbourne scrap merchant for £10, but Charles Dean, chief engineer of an Australian car component company bought it for £40.

Once he had realised the potential of the six-cylinder 4.6-litre single overhead camshaft Maybach engine, he installed it in a scratch-built, offset single-seater chassis. Jones bought the car in 1951, but Dean continued with responsibility for its development and preparation. It was reckoned that maximum speed was about 145mph (235kph) and it was said to have cost £1,000 to build.

After only three laps of practice for the Auckland race, it threw a con-rod, which went through the crankcase. It was bodged for the race with a con-rod from a General Motors truck, a new locally-made cylinder liner, and the crankcase was patch-welded. In the Auckland race, Jones won £1,800 of the available prize and starting money of a little over £3,000. (*LAT Photographic*)

▲ This photograph was taken just before half-distance in the Auckland race. Ken Wharton, having made his pit stop for fuel and tyres, had lost the lead and is now about to regain it from Stan Jones. *(LAT Photographic)*

▶ In the closing laps of the New Zealand Grand Prix, Ken Wharton, with only the rear brakes operative and slowing the car on the gearbox, struggles to reduce the speed of the V16 into a corner. When Wharton made his pit stop with the BRM, it was refuelled – rather sloppily – from churns, and the spilt alcohol-based fuel stripped the paint off the tail of the BRM. *(LAT Photographic)*

Lady Wigram Trophy, Formule Libre

Christchurch (NZ), 6 February 1954

This circuit was situated on what was originally Wigram Air Base. The base took its name from Sir Henry Wigram who owned the land on which it was situated. In 1949 Sir Henry's widow presented the Trophy for the winner of an International race of minimal importance.

In 1954 Wharton and the BRM headed the entry in that year's 100-mile Lady Wigram Trophy and the entry was generally similar to that at Auckland. The major difference in the entry list was the absence of Stan Jones and the Maybach Special, because the car had been shipped back to Australia to be properly repaired. Wharton took pole position on the starting grid and led the race for much of the distance.

In the words of Peter Greenslade who reported the race for *Autosport*:

Averaging 85.80mph with his 2-litre supercharged Ferrari, Peter Whitehead won the 102-mile Lady Wigram Trophy held at Christchurch on 6 February. Second was Tony Gaze's blown HWM, while Ken Wharton pushed a crippled BRM the last ¼-mile to the finishing line to take third place.

It was a race of much excitement, dominated by the three overseas competitors and particularly the

LADY WIGRAM TROPHY, FORMULE LIBRE		
6 February, Christchurch, 2.08-mile (3.35km) airfield perimeter circuit, 48 laps, 100miles (161km)		
1st	Peter Whitehead (Ferrari Tipo 166 2-litre s/c)	1hr 9m 51.3s, 85.80mph (138.05kph)
2nd	Tony Gaze (HWM 2-litre s/c)	1hr 10m 32.3s
3rd	**Ken Wharton (BRM Type 15)**	**1hr 16m 19.5s**
4th	John McMillan (Alfa Romeo Tipo B Monoposto)	1hr 16m 59.5s
5th	Arnold Stafford (Cooper-Norton)	1hr 17m 0.0s*
6th	Ray Archibald (Jaguar XK 120)	1hr 18m 19.5s

*This time may not be correct, precise time not issued by the organisers
Fastest lap: Ken Wharton, 1m 23.5s, 89.68mph (144.32)

BRM – at least for 42 of the 48 laps of the 2.1-mile circuit. Whitehead ran through non-stop and was never farther back than third.

With not much more than 12 miles left to go, the BRM in which Wharton had been lapping at terrific speed, appeared to lose all its power and came into the pits. Another two 90mph laps, and the car slowed down to a walking pace and finally stopped in the last lap a ¼-mile from home, leaving Wharton in the embarrassing position of having to push the car the rest of the way in blazing hot sunshine.

The official explanation for its failure was a 'broken oil pipe', but the BRM sounded very sick indeed, and its ailments must have been considerably more widespread. [According to Tony Rudd, he ran out of fuel.]

▼ After Ken Wharton ran out of fuel on the last lap of the Lady Wigram Trophy race, he pushed the car several hundred yards to the finish, and here he is seen taking the chequered flag. *(Author's collection)*

BRM Mk II

By the start of the European racing season in 1954 the BRM organisation was heavily engaged in the construction and development of the P25, the team's contender for the new 2,500cc Grand Prix formula. In contrast to the V16, the new car was a very straightforward design, and its 2,497cc engine, designed by Stuart Tresilian, was remarkably oversquare, with cylinder dimensions of 102.87 x 74.93mm. This car did not appear until late in the 1955 season.

To have a competitive car to race in Formula 1 and to gain experience in the category until the P25 was ready to race, the team ordered a new Maserati 250F Formula 1 car, and this was first raced with Ken Wharton at the wheel in the 1954 French Grand Prix on 4 July. The team substantially modified the Maserati 250F and, apart from the fitting of disc brakes – which was a genuine improvement – generally made it worse than it had been in its original form.

It was decided to continue racing the V16 cars in the diminishing number of Formule Libre races, and for 1954 Tony Rudd developed the Mk II version. At 7ft 7in (2.311m) the Mk II had a wheelbase 6in (152mm) shorter than its predecessor. One of the problems with the Mk I (as the earlier car now became known) was the flexibility of the cast aluminium-alloy pillars of the trailing arms of the Porsche-derived front suspension.

On the new version there was a steel front cross-member that had two strong and rigid tubes

bracing it back to the oval main frame chassis tubes. Additional rigidity was provided by an oval tubular cross-member to the rear of the engine and a round tubular cross-member at the rear of the gearbox. Whereas Mk I had a two-piece propshaft, it was replaced on the Mk II by a single-piece tubular shaft. The front bodywork was simply an aluminium-alloy shell, and it was the fitting of a small 42-gallon (170-litre) tank (with single central baffle) in the tail that enabled the wheelbase to be shortened.

As Rudd originally envisaged the Mk II, it was to have external surface radiator oil cooling and a much smaller radiator, as shown in the illustration overleaf. The ignition now incorporated four Lucas motorcycle magnetos, in place of the original coil ignition, and thereby dispensed with the battery needed by the coil system and at the same time saved some weight. The radiator was smaller than that of the original Mk I.

The dry weight of the car was reduced to 1,400lb (635kg) from the 1,624lb (736.5kg) of the original version. One of the Mk IIs was new and the other was a rebuild of an earlier car. They were ready before the start of the European season and the model was first raced at Goodwood on Easter Monday. In a limited number of respects these cars acted as test beds for the P25 car, although the number of occasions on which they could now be raced was very limited. They faced opposition from both the Thin Wall Special, in its last season, and the new 2,500cc cars.

▲ Tony Rudd developed the lighter, shorter Mk II version of the V16 for 1954 at very low cost. Here the new car is seen at Folkingham early that year. *(Grand Prix Library)*

◀ The original BRM organisation became the Owen Racing Motors Association after the BRM team was taken over by the Owen Organisation, and members were given this smart badge. *(Author's collection)*

▼ This sketch shows the original plan for the Mk II BRM. By the driver's right knee there was to be a Gallay honeycomb oil cooler from a Westland helicopter gearbox, with the oil tank on the other side. There was to be a new and much smaller water radiator, which provided a much lower nose line, and Rudd believed that only a small air intake was needed. This new layout was vetoed on cost grounds and the original 1951 radiators were used. *(LAT Photographic)*

BARC International Meeting

Goodwood, 19 April 1954

BRM entered an example each of the new Mk II and the old Mk I for Ken Wharton and Ron Flockhart, who each had a turn in the cars. And it turned out that both cars won a race, Wharton being the victorious driver on both occasions.

Chichester Cup, Formule Libre

In this short Formule Libre race, Ken Wharton drove the Mk II, while newcomer to the BRM team Ron Flockhart was at the wheel of the old Mk I. During practice the Mk II had engine trouble from part of a piston ring breaking off, but the car was repaired in time for the race. Despite an engine misfire, Wharton led throughout, but Roy Salvadori, with Gilby Engineering's new Maserati 250F, chased him hard and finished less than half a second behind.

Flockhart, with the Mk I, was badly crowded out by other competitors at Madgwick Corner, spun off, and rejoined the race in last place, but he managed to finish fourth.

CHICHESTER CUP, FORMULE LIBRE		
19 April, Goodwood, 2.4-mile (3.86km) airfield perimeter circuit, 5 laps, 12 miles (19km)		
1st	**Ken Wharton (BRM Mk II)**	**8m 7.2s, 88.70mph (142.72kph)**
2nd	Roy Salvadori (Maserati 250F)	8m 7.6s
3rd	Reg Parnell (Ferrari Tipo 625)	8m 8.4s
4th	**Ron Flockhart (BRM Type 15)**	**8m 28.4 s**
5th	Lance Macklin (HWM 2.5-litre)	
6th	Leslie Thorne (Connaught A-series)	

Fastest lap: Ken Wharton, Parnell, Roy Salvadori and Ron Flockhart, 1min 35.6sec, 90.38mph (145.42kph)

▼ Ken Wharton looks very pleased with himself as he puts on his goggles before the Mk II is pushed out for its racing debut in the Chichester Cup race. *(LAT Photographic)*

◀ The Mk II on the starting grid. Because of the smaller radiator the bottom of the air intake was blocked off – a quick way to recognise the Mk II. *(LAT Photographic)*

OVERLEAF At the wheel of the Mk II, Ken Wharton sits on the grid waiting for the rest of the field to line up. Peter Berthon supervises operations, and once the grid has formed up, the mechanics will push-start the BRM and then wheel it back into position. *(LAT Photographic)*

◀◣ These views of the Mk II's engine and cockpit were taken while the car was waiting on the grid for the start of the Chichester Cup race. As can be seen, the ribbon-type tachometer has been retained, but there are now further instruments, one each side of the tachometer. *(LAT Photographic)*

▶ Ken Wharton is seen at the wheel of the Mk II in the Chichester Cup race. Although the engine developed a misfire, he won from Roy Salvadori (Maserati 250F) by a narrow margin. *(LAT Photographic)*

▶ This view of Ken Wharton in the Chichester Cup race shows off well the truncated lines of the Mk II version of the V16. *(LAT Photographic)*

OVERLEAF As Ken Wharton hammers the Mk II BRM into the chicane in the Chichester Cup race, Roy Salvadori, with the Gilby Engineering 250F, is right on his tail. *(LAT Photographic)*

Richmond Trophy, Formule Libre

As the BRM drivers revved their engines on the starting grid, the shattering noise from the 32 cylinders overwhelmed everything and everybody. That very experienced driver Tony Rolt lost concentration and over-revved Rob Walker's A-series Connaught – as a result he retired on the fourth lap because of a bent valve. Parnell had already retired his Ferrari in this race because of gear-selector trouble. After a good start, Flockhart fell back because of magneto trouble.

Out in front was Ken Wharton, harassed every foot of the way by Roy Salvadori. Time and time again the Maserati driver closed up on the dark green supercharged V16, but Wharton kept a narrow lead, moving across to baulk Salvadori if there was any chance of him getting past. Of this race, Roy Salvadori wrote:

◀ Raymond Mays and Ken Wharton on the starting grid at Goodwood. As can be seen, Wharton's overall trousers are oil-soaked from the first race, the result of a leak from the Mk II's oil tank, which was positioned alongside the driver. *(LAT Photographic)*

▼ A few hundred yards after the start of the Richmond Trophy race, Ron Flockhart heads Ken Wharton, while well back are Reg Parnell and Roy Salvadori. Flockhart stayed in front for the whole of the first lap, but then Wharton went ahead and won the race by a margin of 40sec from Kenneth McAlpine (works Connaught A-series) and Leslie Marr, at the wheel of his private Connaught A-series. *(LAT Photographic)*

…I sat close behind the leading BRM of Wharton; the V16 was slowing through corners and throwing out oil and fuel, which soon spread over my windscreen, goggles and face. The BRM was a big car and I had difficulty in seeing my line through corners; I had no chance to get alongside and I was almost running into the back of it as it slowed for the corners. The race was getting progressively slower, but if I could have got ahead of the BRM, my lap times would have been very much faster…

As the Richmond Trophy progressed, so I became more and more bad tempered, waving my arms furiously. On lap 19 I tried to force my way through at Lavant Corner, hoping that Wharton would let me through. Ken was one of the very hardest drivers; I should have known better than to expect him to give way and the two cars collided [because Wharton moved across into the Maserati] and spun. Both cars restarted, but on the next lap my clutch blew up.

Sid Greene decided to enter a protest against the BRM, but this was rejected. However, even if Sid's protest had been upheld, it would not have benefited us as our car had retired. Nevertheless, the incident brought a lot of publicity, which was probably very good for the Goodwood circuit and Gilby Engineering.

Later I received from the Duke of Richmond and Gordon, the owner of Goodwood, a silver cigarette box inscribed, 'In acknowledgement of a splendid show at Goodwood on Easter Monday, 19 April 1954'. I was quite convinced that the Duke thought that I had been hard done by until I learned that Ken Wharton had also been presented with a similar cigarette box!

RICHMOND TROPHY RACE (for the Glover Trophy), FORMULE LIBRE

19 April, Goodwood, 2.4-mile (3.86km) airfield perimeter circuit, 21 laps, 50.4 miles (81km)

1st	**Ken Wharton (BRM Type 15)**	**35min 0sec, 86.40mph (139.04kph)**
2nd	Kenneth McAlpine (Connaught A-series)	35min 40sec
3rd	Leslie Marr (Connaught A-series)	36min 4sec
4th	**Ron Flockhart (BRM Mk II)**	**36m 8s**
5th	Peter Whitehead (Cooper-Alta 2.5-litre)	37m 29.4s
6th	Charles Boulton (Connaught A-series)	

Fastest lap: Ken Wharton and Roy Salvadori, 1m 37.8s, 88.34mph (142.17kph)

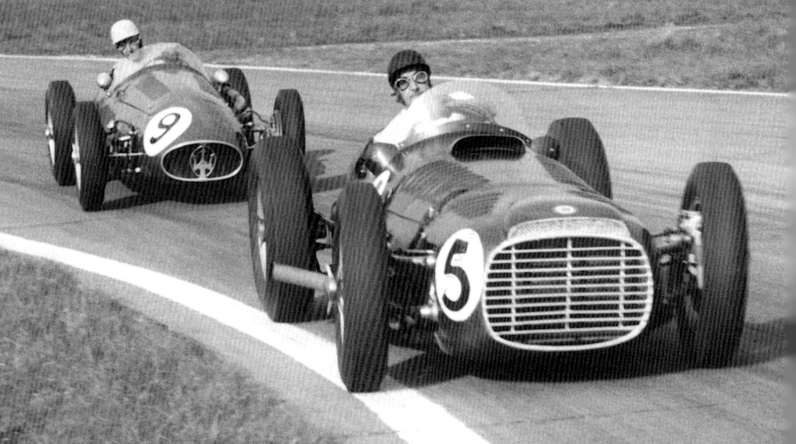

◀ Ken Wharton with the Mk I and Roy Salvadori with the Gilby Engineering Maserati 250F are locked in battle in the Richmond Trophy race. *(LAT Photographic)*

▶ The battle continues as Ken Wharton leads Roy Salvadori into the chicane. Behind them come Ron Flockhart (BRM MKII) and Parnell (Ferrari). Frustrated at being baulked by the BRM, on lap 19 Salvadori tried to force his way past; the BRM driver moved across to block the Maserati and the two cars collided and spun, but both rejoined the race. Almost incredibly, the damage to the Mk I incurred in the collision with the Gilby 250F was bad enough to make the BRM a write-off. *(LAT Photographic)*

▼ Roy Salvadori dropped out of the Richmond Trophy race when the clutch of his Maserati exploded on lap 20. Ken Wharton carried on serenely to win the race, and he is seen taking the chequered flag without another car in sight. What was unknown until the BRM was examined in the team's workshops back at Folkingham was that the chassis of the Mk I V16 had been so badly bent in the collision with Salvadori that the car was a write-off. *(LAT Photographic)*

AMOC Spring Meeting

Snetterton, 24 April 1954

The following weekend there was a national meeting at the Snetterton circuit in Norfolk, and the main event was a ten-lap Formule Libre race. The BRM team entered only a Mk II for Ron Flockhart and he won the race by nearly a minute from Horace Gould (Cooper-Bristol). *Autosport* commented:

It might be asked (and probably was) what purpose was served by the BRM taking part in such a race. But many were pleased to hear the car finish with an exhaust as crisp as it was at the start, and the happy smiles of that hard-worked and seldom elated contingent made the effort seem worthwhile.

In fact, the BRM finished the race with a split fuel tank.

▶ Ron Flockhart drove the sole BRM entry, a Mk II, in the Formule Libre race at Snetterton on 24 April. There was no serious opposition and he scored an easy, very hollow victory. *(LAT Photographic)*

▼ At the finish of the 10-lap Formule Libre race at the April Snetterton meeting Ron Flockhart takes the chequered flag to win the race without another car in sight. *(LAT Photographic)*

ASTON MARTIN OWNERS' CLUB TROPHY, FORMULE LIBRE		
24 April, Snetterton, 2.71-mile (4.36km) airfield perimeter circuit, 10 laps, 27.1 miles (43.6km)		
1st	**Ron Flockhart (BRM Mk II)**	**18m 12s, 89.01mph (143.22kph)**
2nd	Horace Gould (Cooper-Bristol)	19m 2.6s
3rd	Leslie Marr (Connaught A-series)	19m 20s

Fastest lap: Ron Flockhart, 1m 46.8s, 91.01mph (146.44kph), circuit record

▲ Ron Flockhart was again the only BRM driver at the Ibsley meeting. He is seen in the paddock before the race. *(Ferret Fotographics)*

◄ Seen here in the Formule Libre race at Ibsley in Hampshire is Ron Flockhart at the wheel of the BRM Mk II. There was no serious opposition and he won easily from two Écurie Ecosse-entered C-type Jaguars. *(LAT Photographic)*

WHDCC Trophy

Ibsley, 8 May 1954

The meeting at Ibsley close to the New Forest on 8 May was a closed Club meeting, so you had to be a member of one of the invited clubs if you wanted to take part. Ken Wharton should have driven in the Formule Libre race at this meeting, but he was unwell following a trip to Italy to test the Maserati 250F which had been ordered by the Owen Organisation.

So Ron Flockhart drove the Mk II again, but he spun off in practice damaging the car's wheels and tail. Roy Salvadori (Gilby Maserati) non-

WEST HANTS & DORSET CAR CLUB, FORMULE LIBRE	

8 May, Ibsley, 2.98-mile (4.80km) airfield perimeter circuit, 15 laps, 44.7miles (72.0km)

1st	**Ron Flockhart (BRM Mk II)**	**32m 9.3s, 83.48mph (134.34kph)**
2nd	Jimmy Stewart (Jaguar C-type)	
3rd	Ninian Sanderson (Jaguar C-type)	
4th	Graham Whitehead (ERA B-type)	
5th	Alistair Birrell (ERA)	
6th	Roy Salvadori (Maserati A6GCS)	

Fastest lap: Ron Flockhart, 87.39mph (140.61kph)

BARC *Daily Telegraph* 200

Aintree, 29 May 1954

On Saturday 29 May the BARC staged the inaugural meeting at the new Aintree circuit, the longest on the British mainland, that wended for three miles round the famous steeplechase circuit and used the grandstands and other features and facilities of the horse-racing course. It was a slow, flat, rather featureless course and for the first meeting only racing took place in an anti-clockwise direction, with the majority of corners left-handers. The reason for this was quite simply that it followed the direction of the horse-racing course. The direction of racing was reversed at all subsequent meetings.

The major race at this inaugural meeting was the *Daily Telegraph*-sponsored Aintree 200 race for 2,500cc Formula 1 and Formule Libre cars.

started at this meeting; repairs to the 250F had not been completed following its clutch problems at Goodwood. There were no serious single-seaters to challenge the BRM and Flockhart scored a very easy win from Jimmy Stewart and Ninian Sanderson with Écurie Ecosse C-type Jaguars.

▼ After winning the Formule Libre at Ibsley, Ron Flockhart, crash helmet removed, completed a lap of honour at the wheel of the BRM Mk II. *(LAT Photographic)*

The race consisted of two 17-lap 51-mile (82km) qualifying heats and a 35-lap 105-mile (169km) final. BRM had now completed a second Mk II car and the two were entered for Ken Wharton and Ron Flockhart. They faced the Ferrari Thin Wall Special, in its last season of racing, driven by Peter Collins. Formula 1 cars entered included the Maserati 250Fs of Stirling Moss and Roy Salvadori, the Ferrari Tipo 625 of Reg Parnell, and works Gordinis driven by Jean Behra and André Pilette.

Heat 1

Torrential rain fell during the first qualifying heat, and although Reg Parnell and Peter Collins accelerated away together, the Thin Wall soon rocketed ahead, opening up a gap of over seven seconds by the end of the first lap. Ken Wharton made a slow start with the Mk II BRM and was

back in fifth place, battling with Stirling Moss and Jean Behra. By the end of the fifth lap Collins led by almost 17sec, but then the Thin Wall engine started to misfire, and Parnell closed up on the big green Ferrari, swept into the lead and won the heat by over 20sec from Collins, with Moss, Wharton, and Behra in the next three places.

BARC *DAILY TELEGRAPH* 200 TROPHY, FORMULE LIBRE		
29 May, Aintree, 3-mile (4.8km) anti-clockwise circuit round horse-racing course		
Heat 1, 17 laps, 51 miles (82km)		
1st	Reg Parnell (Ferrari Tipo 625)	39m 45s 76.97mph (123.84kph)
2nd	Peter Collins (Ferrari Thin Wall Special)	40m 7s
3rd	Stirling Moss (Maserati 250F)	40m 12s
4th	**Ken Wharton (BRM Mk II)**	
5th	Jean Behra (Gordini Type 16)	
6th	Keith Hall (Cooper-Bristol)	
Fastest lap: Peter Collins, 2m 15.2s, 79.88mph (128.55kph)		

▼ The rain at Aintree was at its heaviest during the first heat of the BARC *Daily Telegraph* 200 race. This is Ken Wharton at the wheel of the Mk II BRM, which he drove into fourth place – a far from satisfactory result. *(LAT Photographic)*

BARC *DAILY TELEGRAPH* 200 TROPHY, FORMULE LIBRE		

29 May, Aintree, 3-mile (4.8km) anti-clockwise circuit round horse-racing course

Heat 2, *17 laps, 51 miles (82km)*

1st	**Ron Flockhart (BRM Mk II)**	**39m 47.2s, 76.92mph (123.76kph)**
2nd	Roy Salvadori (Maserati 250F)	39m 50.2s
3rd	Bob Gerard (Cooper-Bristol)	
4th	André Pilette (Gordini Type 16)	
5th	Philippe Étancelin (Talbot-Lago Type 26)	
6th	Rodney Nuckey (Cooper-Bristol)	

Fastest lap: Roy Salvadori, 2m 16.2s, 79.30mph (127.62kph)

Heat 2

Throughout the second heat Ron Flockhart, with the other BRM Mk II, and Salvadori (Maserati), battled for the lead, but the young Scot kept in front and won by a margin of 3sec. Bob Gerard (Cooper-Bristol) took third place.

Final

Although the rain had eased by the start of the final, the track was still very wet and the sky heavy and grey with more rain to come. The track, however, started to dry out as the race progressed. Again Peter Collins took the lead at the start, and the Thin Wall, having – apparently – been restored to good health, sounded superb. Collins gradually extended his lead, and after five laps he led Ron Flockhart by a margin of 21sec. Ken Wharton was third, Stirling Moss fourth, Roy Salvadori had dropped right down the field after a spin, and Jean Behra had brought his Gordini into the pits for a change of plugs. On the next lap Flockhart spun his Mk II BRM and rejoined the race in eighth place.

Now the Thin Wall started to misfire once more; Moss closed upon the Ferrari and took the lead when Collins pulled into the pits on lap 21. Parnell was now in second place, and Gerard clung on to the third spot with the Cooper-Bristol as Flockhart tried and tried again to get past the much slower Formula 2 car. Collins retired the Thin Wall after another slow lap and Wharton pulled out of the race because of brake problems. Moss led to the finish to win by 50sec from Parnell, slowed by handling problems. Flockhart snatched the third place from Gerard, and Salvadori recovered to finish fifth. It had been a good race, but the BRM team had little to be pleased about.

▶ On a streaming wet track Ron Flockhart, driving superbly at the wheel of his Mk II BRM, leads Roy Salvadori (Maserati 250F) in the second heat of the Aintree 200 race. They took the first two places in the heat, ahead of Bob Gerard (Cooper-Bristol). *(LAT Photographic)*

BARC *DAILY TELEGRAPH* 200 TROPHY, FORMULE LIBRE

29 May, Aintree, 3-mile (4.8km) anti-clockwise circuit round horse-racing course

Final, *35 laps, 105 miles (169kph)*

1st	Stirling Moss (Maserati 250F)	1hr 18m 48.4s, 77.70mph (125.02kph)
2nd	Reg Parnell (Ferrari Tipo 625)	1hr 19m 36.6s
3rd	**Ron Flockhart (BRM Mk II)**	**1hr 20m 32.6s**
4th	Bob Gerard (Cooper-Bristol)	1hr 20m 24s
5th	Roy Salvadori (Maserati 250F)	33 laps
6th	Kenneth McAlpine (Connaught A-series)	33 laps
Rtd	**Ken Wharton (BRM Mk II)**	**(overheated brakes)**

Fastest lap: Peter Collins, 2m 12s, 81.82mph (131.67kph)

▶ The front row of the starting grid of the final of the Aintree 200 race with, furthest from the camera, Peter Collins (Ferrari Thin Wall Special), and then Roy Salvadori (Maserati 250F), Ron Flockhart (BRM Mk II), and Reg Parnell (Ferrari Tipo 625). *(LAT Photographic)*

▼ By the closing laps of the final of the Aintree 200 race, the track was almost dry. Stirling Moss's head mechanic Alf Francis signals to Moss that he is leading the race from Reg Parnell and Ron Flockhart. *(LAT Photographic)*

Whitsun Trophy

Goodwood, 7 June 1954

BRM returned to Goodwood on Whit Monday, 7 June. It was a British National meeting, so there were no foreign entries; the two Mk II BRMs were driven by Ken Wharton and Ron Flockhart in the Whitsun Trophy Formule Libre race. Peter Collins was again at the wheel of the Ferrari Thin Wall Special; Reg Parnell entered his 2½-litre Ferrari, and Roy Salvadori drove Gilby Engineering's Maserati 250F.

At the fall of the flag the Thin Wall, in pole position, and the two BRMs surged off in a flurry of wheelspin, and Collins drew ahead into a comfortable lead that he held throughout the race. It was only his second race with the car and he performed magnificently.

Flockhart held station some way behind in second place and that was where he finished, 7.6sec ahead of Salvadori, and Wharton took fourth place. Flockhart had driven a good race and it was clearly recognised that the V16s were no match for the Thin Wall.

WHITSUN TROPHY, FORMULE LIBRE		
7 June, Goodwood, 2.4-mile (3.86km) airfield perimeter circuit, 15 laps, 36 miles (58km)		
1st	Peter Collins (Ferrari Thin Wall Special)	23m 35.4s, 91.35mph (147.01kph)
2nd	**Ron Flockhart (BRM Mk II)**	**23m 50.4s**
3rd	Roy Salvadori (Maserati 250F)	23m 58s
4th	**Ken Wharton (BRM Mk II)**	**24m 33s**
5th	Reg Parnell (Ferrari Tipo 625)	
6th	Keith Hall (Cooper-Bristol)	14 laps

Fastest lap: Peter Collins, 1m 32.6s, 93.30mph (150.12kph)

▼ Under the watchful eye of Peter Berthon the BRM mechanics push Ken Wharton out to the start of the Whitsun Trophy at Goodwood. The Smethwick driver was off-form in this race and he could do no better than finish fourth. After the race he claimed that a rear suspension strut had failed, badly affecting the handling. When the car was examined, nothing wrong with the rear suspension could be found. *(LAT Photographic)*

▶ The starting grid for the
Whitsun Trophy at Goodwood
with Peter Collins (Ferrari Thin
Wall Special) in pole position,
and alongside him Ken Wharton
and Ron Flockhart with their
Mk II BRMs. In the second row are
Gerry Dunham (Alvis) and Graham
Whitehead (ERA).
(LAT Photographic)

▲ The flag has fallen for the start of the Whitsun Trophy Formule Libre race, and although Peter Collins (Ferrari Thin Wall Special) and the two BRMs accelerate side-by-side, Collins pulled away into the distance and won from Ron Flockhart by a margin of 15sec. *(LAT Photographic)*

◀ Ron Flockhart (No. 2) made a super start in the Whitsun Trophy race at Goodwood and stayed in front for four laps. Early in the race he leads Collins, the eventual winner, through the chicane, watched by a large number of spectators. *(LAT Photographic)*

▶ Although his Gilby Engineering-entered Maserati 250F was not always reliable, Roy Salvadori remained a very serious threat all season. At the Whitsun meeting at Goodwood the English driver with an Italian name finished third in the Formule Libre race and beat Ken Wharton. *(LAT Photographic)*

◀A fine view of Ken Wharton at the wheel of his BRM Mk II in the Whitsun Trophy at Goodwood. Although he could be a very hard driver, and his style made few friends among his contemporaries, he was susceptible to anxieties about his cars. This was perfectly understandable in some ways as he had a bad crash at Albi in 1953, and this led him to look for problems. He was off the pace in the Goodwood race because he believed – wrongly – that one of the rear suspension struts had failed. This resulted in him finishing a poor fourth at the Sussex circuit. (LAT Photographic)

Shelsley Walsh Hill Climb

20 June 1954

Although the BRM was not demonstrated at this meeting, it was arranged for Ken Wharton to drive a Mk II in unofficial practice on 17 June. The actual car has not been identified. He made three runs, and on the second run he was badly slowed by a locking brake. His best time was 37.80sec, compared with the 37.97sec that he had achieved with a Mk I BRM at the previous year's meeting. In the hill-climb proper young Ron Flockhart drove R4D and set BTD and a new hill record.

The Owen Organisation Maserati 250F

The team took delivery of Maserati 250F in time for Ken Wharton to drive it in the French Grand Prix at Reims on 4 July. He retired because of propshaft failure. In the British Grand Prix on 17 July he finished eighth. He took sixth place, two laps in arrears, in the Swiss race; the team missed the Italian Grand Prix, and in the last Grand Prix of the season, the Spanish race on the Pedralbes circuit, he was in eighth place, six laps in arrears.

▼ Ken Wharton with the Owen Racing Organisation's Maserati 250F in the British Grand Prix at Silverstone where he finished a poor eighth. The writer recalls vividly Wharton's long, wild spin on a damp track at Abbey Curve. (Tom March Collection)

WECC Trophy

Snetterton, 14 August 1954

The only BRM in this 40-lap Formule Libre race was a Mk II driven by Ron Flockhart, and once again there was a fine display of power and speed by Peter Collins with the Ferrari Thin Wall Special in which he won with consummate ease. Other serious opposition was limited to Reg Parnell at the wheel of his Ferrari, with which he had won the 40-lap Formula 1 race held earlier, and Bob Gerard with his Cooper-Bristol. Parnell retired his Ferrari early in the race after his engine exploded, making very drastic and expensive noises.

Flockhart could offer no challenge at all to the Thin Wall, and the Bourne car was plagued by brake problems; he went off the road on the seventh lap and called into the pits for the car to be checked and the bonnet to be fastened back in place. On lap 18 of this 40-lap race Collins lapped the BRM, which almost immediately threw another fit of brake trouble; the V16 went straight on at Riches Corner, but Flockhart managed to gather it all up and retreated once more to the pits. His V16 was checked over and a cracked distributor cap replaced.

For the remainder of the race Flockhart lapped swiftly and serenely, but he was too far behind to challenge the winning Thin Wall. Second place, three laps in arrears, went to Cooper-Bristol driver Rodney Nuckey, whose check shirt gradually parted company with his body and he completed the race driving naked from the waist up. Flockhart finished third, four laps in arrears. Bob Gerard who had lost several laps during a long pit stop took fourth place.

WEST ESSEX CAR CLUB INTERNATIONAL RACE, FORMULE LIBRE		
14 August, Snetterton, 2.71-mile (4.36km) airfield perimeter circuit, 40 laps, 108.4 miles (174km)		
1st	Peter Collins (Ferrari Thin Wall Special)	1hr 10m 57.8s, 91.32mph (146.93kph)
2nd	Rodney Nuckey (Cooper-Bristol)	37 laps
3rd	**Ron Flockhart (BRM Mk II)**	**36 laps**
4th	Bob Gerard (Cooper-Bristol)	35 laps
5th	J. A. Williamson (ERA)	33 laps
6th	Alastair Birrell (ERA)	32 laps

Fastest lap: Peter Collins, 1m 43s, 94.37mph (151.84kph), circuit record

▼ After a very fraught drive, plagued by brake problems, Ron Flockhart finished third after two pit stops in the Formule Libre race at Snetterton on 14 August. He is followed by Rodney Nuckey (Cooper-Bristol) who took second place minus his shirt. *(LAT Photographic)*

BRISTOL MOTOR CYCLE AND LIGHT CAR CLUB HASTINGS TROPHY, FORMULE LIBRE

28 August, Castle Combe, 1.84-mile (2.96km) airfield perimeter circuit, 15 laps, 27.6 miles (44.4km)

1st	Bob Gerard (Cooper-Bristol)	19m 10.2s, 86.25mph (138.78kph)
2nd	**Ron Flockhart (BRM Mk II)**	**19m 10.6s**
3rd	Horace Gould (Cooper-Bristol)	19m 42.2s

Fastest lap: Gerard and Flockhart, 1min 15.0sec, 88.32mph (142.11kph)

Hastings Trophy

Castle Combe, 28 August 1954

BRM contested another British national race on 28 August and entered a single Mk II for Ron Flockhart in the 15-lap Formule Libre at the Castle Combe circuit in Wiltshire. Apart from the BRM, the entry was very weak: no Thin Wall Special, no Formula 1 cars, just Bob Gerard and Horace Gould with their Formula 2 Cooper-Bristols. Flockhart complained of grabbing brakes and an engine misfire, and his fastest lap in practice was 1min 16sec compared with the 1min 13.8sec achieved by Wharton the previous year.

Gould made the best start, but Flockhart was in front by the first corner and led easily until the seventh lap. It took three laps for Gerard to pass Gould and the Leicestershire driver then started to haul in the leading BRM. He was right up the V16's exhausts until the tenth lap when Gerard squeezed past, and in the absence of any serious straights on this little circuit there was no opportunity for Flockhart to retake the lead.

▼ Tony Rudd is at the wheel of Flockhart's V16 Mk II as it is towed out to the starting grid for the Formule Libre race at Castle Combe in September 1954. *(Author's Collection)*

◀ A fine view of Ron Flockhart at the wheel of his BRM Mk II at Castle Combe leading in the early laps of the Formule Libre Hastings Trophy race. Flockhart was a fine asset to the BRM team and always tried his hardest. *(LAT Photographic)*

▲ On the diminutive Castle Combe circuit just a short distance from 'Britain's prettiest village' of the same name, the power of the V16 was a handicap rather than an advantage. Here Ron Flockhart, plagued by a locking brake and an engine misfire, struggles to keep Bob Gerard's Cooper-Bristol at bay. *(LAT Photographic)*

▶ Another view of Ron Flockhart struggling to keep Bob Gerard (Cooper-Bristol) at bay. The BRM was beaten into second place by four-tenths of a second. It was a pointless waste of time and effort to continue racing the V16s when the team had its hands full entering the Maserati 250F as well as developing the new 2,500cc BRM. *(LAT Photographic)*

WJC Trophy

Charterhall, 4 September 1954

This was another British national meeting to which
BRM sent a single Mk II for Ron Flockhart. The
only other competitive cars were Roy Salvadori's
Maserati 250F and Bob Gerard's Cooper-Bristol. As
the cars accelerated away at the start of the Formule
Libre race, the BRM had covered only a couple of
hundred yards before the engine cut out; the cause
was a stone entering the carburettor and jamming it.
After four laps Salvadori dropped back with the 250F
and a lap later it was being wheeled away because of a
broken oil pipe. Gerard scored a very easy win.

▲ Flockhart's BRM in the paddock at Charterhall. Even in
their later days when the cars were regarded as failures,
they attracted great attention. *(Bill Henderson Collection)*

WJC (WINFIELD JOINT COMMITTEE) TROPHY, FORMULE LIBRE		
4 September, Charterhall, 2-mile (3.2km) airfield perimeter road circuit, 20 laps, 40 miles (64km)		
1st	Bob Gerard (Cooper-Bristol)	28m 59.2s, 82.70mph (133.06kph)
2nd	Geoff Richardson (RRA Special)	
3rd	Les Leston (Cooper Mk 8-Norton)	
Rtd	**Ron Flockhart (BRM Mk II)**	**first lap (jammed carburettor)**
Fastest lap: Bob Gerard, 83.72mph (134.71kph)		

BARC International Meeting

Goodwood, 25 September 1954

BRM sent both Mk IIs to the international meeting at Goodwood on 25 September. The main race of the day was the 21-lap Formula 1 Goodwood Trophy and Stirling Moss won this, totally unchallenged, with his own Maserati 250F painted red; he finished 20sec ahead of Peter Collins at the wheel of Vandervell's much-improved Vanwall Special, now running with a full 2.5-litre engine, and Roy Salvadori (Gilby Engineering Maserati 250F) took third place.

This was the new order, while the BRMs and the Thin Wall represented the old order and ran in a Formule Libre race. Peter Collins, with the Thin Wall, turned in another magnificent performance to win by a margin of 10sec from Ken Wharton's misfiring BRM, which was hounded to the finish by Stirling Moss (Maserati), Mike Hawthorn (Vanwall Special), and Roy Salvadori (Maserati). On the first lap Ron Flockhart, who made a typical slow BRM start, tried to overtake a gaggle of slower cars, but misjudged the situation and ended up in a turnip field and out of the race.

▲ Ron Flockhart is seen here in practice for the Formule Libre race at Goodwood; he went off the track on the first lap of the race. *(LAT Photographic)*

▶ Ken Wharton is on his way to second place; his engine has developed a misfire and he is being hounded by Moss with his own Maserati 250F now painted red in deference to his position as a works driver. *(LAT Photographic)*

BARC WOODCOTE CUP, FORMULE LIBRE	

25 September, Goodwood, 2.4-mile (3.86km) airfield perimeter circuit, 10 laps, 24 miles (38.6km)

1st	Peter Collins (Ferrari Thin Wall Special)	15m 38.4s, 92.07mph (148.14kph)
2nd	**Ken Wharton (BRM Mk II)**	**15m 44.4s**
3rd	Stirling Moss (Maserati 250F)	15m 48s
4th	Mike Hawthorn (Vanwall Special)	15m 48.2s
5th	Roy Salvadori (Maserati 250F)	16m 21.6s
6th	Bob Gerard (Cooper-Bristol)	16m 26.4s
Rtd	**Ron Flockhart (BRM Mk II)**	**first lap (accident damage)**

Fastest lap: Peter Collins, 1m 32.2s, 93.71mph (150.81kph)

BARC *DAILY TELEGRAPH* TROPHY, FORMULE LIBRE	

2 October, Aintree, 3-mile (4.8km) clockwise circuit round horse-racing course, 17 laps, 51 miles (82km)

1st	Stirling Moss (Maserati 250F)	35m 53.4s, 85.26mph (137.18kph)
2nd	Sergio Mantovani (Maserati 250F)	36m 4.4s
3rd	**Ron Flockhart (BRM Mk II)**	**36m 21.2s**
4th	André Pilette (Gordini)	
5th	Roy Salvadori (Maserati)	
6th	Don Beauman (Connaught)	
Rtd	**Ken Wharton (BRM Mk II)**	**(accident damage)**

Fastest lap: Stirling Moss, 2m 0.6s, 89.55mph (144.09kph), circuit record

BARC Trophy

Aintree, 2 October 1954

The British racing season ended on 2 October with an international meeting at Aintree. For a meeting so late in the year it attracted a very strong entry. There were six races and Stirling Moss won three of them: the Formula 1 and Formule Libre races with his own Maserati 250F, in which he ran as a works entry, and the race for 500cc single-seaters at the wheel of Francis Beart's modified Cooper.

BRM entered the Mk IIs for Ken Wharton and Ron Flockhart in the 17-lap Formule Libre race, and they faced Peter Collins with the Thin Wall Special, Mike Hawthorn at the wheel of the Vanwall Special, and works-entered Maserati 250Fs driven by Stirling Moss and Sergio Mantovani. Early in the race Wharton and Harry Schell (250F-engined A6GCM) collided at Cottage Corner and both were eliminated. Both Collins and Hawthorn retired. Moss and Mantovani took the first two places ahead of Flockhart.

Although the BRM V16s raced for another season, Vandervell retired the Thin Wall Special at the end of 1954. In 1955 he was able to field two of his new Vanwall Formula 1 cars. Although they failed at an international level that season and real success was two years away for the team, the Vanwalls performed well in British events of lesser importance.

◀ The first lap of the Formule Libre race at Goodwood: Ken Wharton (BRM Mk II) leads Peter Collins (Thin Wall Special) and Stirling Moss (Maserati 250F). Shortly after this photograph was taken, Collins streaked into the lead with the big Ferrari and stayed there to the finish. *(LAT Photographic)*

▶ Flockhart leads Wharton, Hawthorn (Vanwall Special) and André Pilette's Gordini. *(Grand Prix Library)*

▼ In the Formule Libre race at Aintree, Ron Flockhart, the paint stripped off the tail of the V16, drove a dogged race with an inadequate car to finish third behind the works Maserati. Although the grass has been turned to mud, earlier the race meeting was dry in both practice and the race. *(Grand Prix Library)*

Chapter 9
The 1955 season

The V16's final year of racing

Ken Wharton had left to drive for Vanwall in 1955, and Peter Collins left Vanwall for BRM, mainly of course to drive the new four-cylinder car when it was ready to race. Ron Flockhart remained as a regular test driver and as number two driver for the Bourne team.

Collins' behaviour had been rather peculiar; he signed up for BRM in December 1954, but he had misled Tony Vandervell into believing that he would be rejoining the Vanwall team to drive alongside Mike Hawthorn. He continued to string Vandervell along until March when it became clear that he would not be joining the team, and Vandervell then signed up Wharton. It seems that the Smethwick driver had defected from BRM rather than being pushed.

Although, on past form, the Owen Racing Organisation would have had more than enough on its hands with the Maserati Tipo 250F and the new Formula 1 car, the team ran the Mk II BRMs in minor events through to the Castle Combe meeting on 1 October 1955, but with very limited success.

The purpose was, in the words of Tony Rudd, 'to keep [Collins] interested.' Although the serious career of the Mk II was finished, Tony Rudd and his colleagues had carried out many minor improvements to the cars for their last season and they were considerably faster than in 1954 on both the straight and through corners.

◀ Peter Collins, with his Mk II BRM, ran away from the Formula 1 opposition in the Chichester Cup at Goodwood on Easter Monday 1955. In this short race he finished 5.4sec ahead of Roy Salvadori in the Gilby Engineering 250F. *(LAT Photographic)*

BARC International Meeting

Goodwood, 11 April 1955

The main race of the Goodwood Easter Monday meeting, the 21-lap Richmond Trophy, was for Formula 1 cars but the Owen Racing Organisation did not enter their Maserati 250F. Peter Collins drove the Mk II BRM in two short races.

Chichester Cup, Formule Libre

In the seven-lap Formule Libre Chichester Cup Collins ran away from the Maseratis of Roy Salvadori and Stirling Moss to win by a margin of 5.4sec from Salvadori. It was unusual for Roy to beat Stirling, but on this occasion he was very much on form, and the Moss 250F was not.

▶ On the first lap of the Chichester Cup race Peter Collins, with the V16, leads Stirling Moss through the chicane at Goodwood. Editor Gregor Grant reported the Goodwood meeting for *Autosport*, and of this race he wrote: 'Collins, holding the BRM at fairly high rpm, streaked ahead when "Ebby" dropped his flag, with Moss and Salvadori almost wheel to wheel into Madgwick. The Owen car came through in the lead, Collins' swerving technique at the chicane being something to admire. Behind the shrieking BRM came Moss and Salvadori locked in combat… Moss's Maserati was not all correct in the road-holding department, and on lap 2 he had to give way to Salvadori, who was bang on form.'
(LAT Photographic)

BARC CHICHESTER CUP, FORMULE LIBRE

11 April, Goodwood, 2.4-mile (3.86km) airfield perimeter circuit, 7 laps, 16.8 miles (27km)

1st	Peter Collins (BRM Mk II)	11m 9.8s, 90.29mph (145.28kph)
2nd	Roy Salvadori (Maserati 250F)	11m 15.2s
3rd	Stirling Moss (Maserati 250F)	11m 20.0s
4th	Tony Rolt (Connaught)	11m 28.2s
5th	Don Beauman (Connaught)	11m 35s
6th	Mike Keen (Cooper-Alta)	11m 38.8s

Fastest lap: Peter Collins, 1m 34.4s, 91.52mph (147.26kph)

Easter Handicap, Formule Libre

Collins' other race was the last of the day, the five-lap Easter Handicap for racing cars. The BRM was given an impossible handicap and he came through from scratch to finish fifth, but had the satisfaction of recording the fastest ever lap at Goodwood by a V16 BRM. In the results panel, the times stated in bold type are the number of seconds the runners started ahead of Peter Collins, who was the man on scratch. It is, of course, extremely doubtful whether running the BRMs in these very short races served any useful purpose.

BARC EASTER HANDICAP, FORMULE LIBRE		
11 April, Goodwood, 2.4-mile (3.86km) airfield perimeter circuit, 5 laps, 12 miles (19.3km)		
1st	Bob Gerard (Cooper-Bristol)	9m 9.8s, 88.25mph (132.74kph), **25s**
2nd	Roy Salvadori (Maserati 250F)	9m 11.0s, **10s**
3rd	John Young (Connaught A-Series)	9m 11.2s, **45s**
5th	**Peter Collins (BRM Mk II)**	**(scratch)**
Fastest lap: Peter Collins, 1m 33.0s, 92.90mph (149.48kph)		

▼ Alone in his 'scratch' position at the back of the starting line-up for the Easter Handicap at Goodwood, Peter Collins sits in his Mk II BRM with Tony Rudd (left) and Rivers-Fletcher (right) for company. *(Grand Prix Library)*

Daily Express Silverstone

On 7 May 1955 Peter Collins drove the Owen Organisation's Maserati 250F in the 176-mile (283km) International Trophy race at Silverstone, where the opposition consisted of works Vanwalls and Connaughts, plus several privately entered Maseratis. The race devolved into a battle between Collins and Roy Salvadori (with the Gilby Engineering 250F). Gradually Collins got the upper hand and he won the race by just under a minute from Salvadori, with 'B. Bira' (at the wheel of another 250F) third.

Although he was no longer a member of the BRM team, Ken Wharton drove a Ford Zephyr with Raymond Mays conversion in the Touring Car race at Silverstone. These conversions, developed and made by the Owen Racing Organisation, represented part of the effort to make BRM financially viable, and several hundred kits were sold. We do not know for certain the level of tune of Wharton's Zephyr, but the production model developed 68bhp at 4,200rpm, and the Raymond Mays version tested by John Bolster for *Autosport* magazine in December 1954 had a maximum power output of 106bhp at 5,000rpm and a maximum speed of 102mph (164kph). The version that Wharton drove into fourth place overall and a class win at Silverstone probably had a power output of 135–140bhp.

▲ Peter Collins on his way to a solid victory in the Maserati 250F run in 1955 by the Owen Racing Organisation, the owner of BRM. *(Tom March Collection)*

▼ In the Touring Car race at Silverstone Ken Wharton finished fourth overall and first in class with this potent Ford Zephyr, which was equipped with the Raymond Mays conversion marketed by the Owen Racing Organisation. *(Tom March Collection)*

▲ Collins made fastest lap in the Formule Libre race at Snetterton in May before he was eliminated in a collision. The long, heavy exhausts of the Mk IIs fouled the loading ramps of the team's now elderly Austin Lodestar transporters. They were detached, stowed separately, and fitted after the cars arrived at the circuit – a job that took only two or three minutes. *(Author's collection)*

▼ Here, Peter Collins is seen at Snetterton on 28 May 1955. In the ten-lap Formule Libre race the grid positions were decided by ballot. When Collins came up to lap Cunningham-Reid, the young and inexperienced driver of a Lister-Bristol endeavoured to move out of the way of the BRM, but went the wrong way and the two cars collided. A Lister spinner burst one of the BRM's tyres and Collins revolved out of the race. *(LAT Photographic)*

WECC Trophy

Snetterton, 28 May 1955

This was a British national meeting, so foreign licence-holders were not allowed to compete. The entry was dismally bad, with many well-known drivers and cars of the period missing. Roy Salvadori won the Curtis Trophy 10-lap Formula 1 race (from Scott-Brown's 2-litre Lister-Bristol sports car), and the last race of the day was the poorly supported Formule Libre race in which the two BRM Mk IIs were entered for Peter Collins and Ron Flockhart. As described in the caption, Collins was eliminated in a rather bizarre accident, and Flockhart finished second to Salvadori (Gilby Engineering Maserati 250F).

WEST ESSEX CAR CLUB TROPHY, FORMULE LIBRE		
28 May, Snetterton, 2.71-mile (4.36km) airfield perimeter circuit, 10 laps, 27.1 miles (43.6km)		
1st	Roy Salvadori (Maserati 250F)	17m 51.4s, 90.72mph (146kph)
2nd	**Ron Flockhart (BRM V16 Mk II)**	**18m 5.8s**
3rd	Archie Scott-Brown (Lister)	19m 14s
4th	Bill Smith (Jaguar)	19m 21.8s
5th	Nobby Spero (Maserati 8CM)	
Rtd	**Peter Collins (BRM V16 Mk II)**	**(accident damage)**
Fastest lap: Peter Collins, 1m 42.2s, 95.11mph (153.06kph)		

British Grand Prix, Aintree

Held at Aintree on 16 July 1955, the British Grand Prix was dominated by the Mercedes-Benz team, which took the first four places. Peter Collins had a poor race with the Owen Racing Organisation's Maserati 250F and he retired after 29 laps because of clutch failure.

▶ Peter Collins in the Owen Racing Organisation's Maserati 250F, which retired with clutch failure. The mechanics made a sloppy job of refuelling the car, and the alcohol in the spilt fuel has dissolved the paintwork on the tail. *(Tom March Collection)*

PREVIOUS SPREAD The BRM Mk II of Peter Collins in the Snetterton paddock in August 1955. Dzus fasteners have replaced the bonnet straps. *(LAT Photographic)*

◀ The V16 BRM was to be seen at only two more races in 1955, so Snetterton provided one of the last opportunities to examine the immensely complex V16 engine while the cars were still being raced. *(LAT Photographic)*

▲ Part of the starting grid for the Formule Libre race at Snetterton in August 1955. Car No. 142 is the Vanwall of Harry Schell, car No. 135 is the works streamlined B-series Connaught of Jack Fairman, and the C-type Jaguar is Bill Smith's ex-works, lightweight, disc-braked car. A few weeks later Smith, at the wheel of the works Connaught 1,500cc sports car, was killed in a multi-car accident on the Dundrod circuit. *(LAT Photographic)*

WECC International Trophy Meeting

Snetterton, 13 August 1955

The main event of the day at this unimportant international meeting was the 25-lap Formula 1 race in which Tony Vandervell's Vanwalls, driven by Harry Schell and Ken Wharton, took the first two places. For much of the race Stirling Moss, at the wheel of his very tired Maserati 250F, battled with Jack Brabham, driving his rear-engined 2-litre Cooper-Bristol, and they took third and fourth places. On the first lap Roy Salvadori had spun the Gilby Engineering-entered Maserati 250F, but recovered to finish fifth.

The survivors were joined in the Formule Libre race by Peter Collins (BRM Mk II), Geoff Richardson (supercharged ERA-powered RRA Special), and a couple of sports Jaguars. Because of a broken driveshaft Collins failed to complete the first lap, Schell retired the sole Vanwall starter three laps later, and Peter Walker, with Rob Walker's dark blue unstreamlined B-series Connaught, won by a margin of over 50sec from Salvadori (Gilbey 250F), Titterington (Écurie Ecosse Jaguar D-type), and Geoff Richardson (RRA).

WEST ESSEX CAR CLUB FORMULE LIBRE RACE		
13 August, Snetterton, 2.71-mile airfield perimeter circuit, 25 laps, 67.75 miles (109km)		
1st	Peter Walker (Connaught B-Series)	45m 3.8s, 89.86mph (144.61kph)
2nd	Roy Salvadori (Maserati 250F)	45m 54.4s
3rd	Desmond Titterington (Jaguar D-type)	46m 3.14s
4th	Geoff Richardson (RRA Special)	
Rtd	**Peter Collins (BRM V16 Mk II)**	**(broken drive-shaft)**
Fastest lap: Peter Walker, 1m 45.00s, 92.57mph (148.95kph)		

BARC Trophy

Aintree, 3 September 1955

Once again the main event of the day at the International Aintree was a Formula 1 race, the 51-mile (82km) *Daily Telegraph* Trophy. Stirling Moss (private Maserati 250F) battled for the lead with Reg Parnell (works streamlined Connaught), but Moss retired trailing blue smoke and then the Connaught slowed right off. Roy Salvadori (Gilby 250F) scored a totally unexpected win from Bob Gerard (Cooper-Bristol), Horace Gould (ex-works Maserati), Tony Brooks (Connaught A-series), and with Parnell fifth, a lap in arrears after pushing the Connaught to the finishing line.

So there was a significantly reduced field for the Formule Libre race with only ten starters. Gerard nosed ahead with his Cooper-Bristol at the start and then the rear wheels of the V16 bit the tarmac and Collins accelerated into a lead that he never lost. On that first lap Salvadori overcooked Mellow Crossing, slid off and stalled the Maserati's engine, rejoining the race after an illicit push start.

Cyril Posthumus reported the race for *Autosport* and commented: 'Gerard's valiant Cooper-Bristol broke a valve… Only six cars were now left running, and the BRM's progress on the far side of the circuit could clearly be heard.' Roy spent the next 17 laps making up lost ground and he finished second, 1min 18.2sec behind the V16. Third and fourth places went to Brooks (Connaught A-series) and Bruce Halford (Cooper-Bristol).

BARC *DAILY TELEGRAPH* FORMULE LIBRE RACE		
3 September, Aintree, 3-mile (4.8km) course round horse-racing track, 17 laps, 51 miles (82km)		
1st	Peter Collins (BRM V16 Mk II)	35m 54.8s, 85.20mph (137.09kph)
2nd	Roy Salvadori (Maserati 250F)	37m 13.0s
3rd	Tony Brooks (Connaught A-series)	37m 40.4s
4th	Bruce Halford (Cooper-Bristol)	16 laps
5th	Bill Holt (Connaught)	16 laps
6th	Horace Richards (HAR)	14 laps

Fastest lap: Peter Collins, 2m 4.0s, 87.10mph (141.11kph)

Castle Combe International Meeting

▲ The start of the *Empire News* Formule Libre race; Ron Flockhart sits in pole position, and immediately behind him is Les Leston with Moss's grey-painted 250F. Harry Schell's Vanwall is in the centre of the front row with Bob Gerard's Cooper-Bristol to his right. No. 10 in the second row is Roy Salvadori with the Gilby Engineering Maserati 250F. *(LAT Photographic)*

1 October 1955

The 1955 racing season ended in the UK with the international meeting on 1 October held on the short Castle Combe circuit and sponsored by the *Empire News* Sunday newspaper. Once again the main race of the day was a Formula 1 event, the 101-mile (162.51km) Avon Trophy race. The star in the Formula 1 race was a Vanwall driven by Harry Schell, with a supporting cast of four Maserati 250Fs driven by Peter Collins, Roy Salvadori, Horace Gould and Louis Rosier; Rob Walker's Connaught B-series with Peter Walker at the helm, and Bob Gerard with his Cooper-Bristol.

Schell led the Avon Trophy from start to finish, and behind him Horace Gould, the González of the West Country, was driving swiftly and smoothly to hold second place. Collins retired the Owen Racing Organisation Maserati because of a broken de Dion tube. Walker dropped out of contention when he pulled into the pits because of suspension problems. Salvadori was off-form because of a broken bone in his accelerator foot and he lost a race-long battle for third place to Gerard's Cooper-Bristol. Schell set a new circuit record of 1min 13.6sec, 90.00mph (144.84kph).

The field for the Formule Libre *Empire News* Trophy was headed by Ron Flockhart with the V16 BRM and included Schell, Salvadori, Les Leston (with Moss's Maserati 250F), Walker with the Rob Walker Connaught, and Gerard. Flockhart led initially, but then Schell steamed into the lead, and after a long battle with Leston, Gerard consolidated a safe third place. Peter Walker retired Rob Walker's car after only three laps. Salvadori took fourth place.

▶ In the Formule Libre race at Castle Combe, Ron Flockhart (V16) is about to lose the lead to Harry Schell (Vanwall). Following is Les Leston at the wheel of Stirling Moss's private Maserati 250F. *(Grand Prix Library)*

BRISTOL MOTOR CYCLE AND LIGHT CAR CLUB AND *EMPIRE NEWS* INTERNATIONAL, FORMULE LIBRE

1 October, Castle Combe, 1.84-mile (2.96km) airfield perimeter circuit, 20 laps, 36.8 miles (59km)

1st	Harry Schell (Vanwall)	25m 26.8s, 86.77mph (139.64kph)
2nd	**Ron Flockhart (BRM B26 Mk II)**	**25m 47.4s**
3rd	Bob Gerard (Cooper-Bristol)	26m 4.6s
4th	Roy Salvadori (Maserati)	

Fastest lap: Harry Schell, 1m 13.8s, 89.75mph (144.43)

278

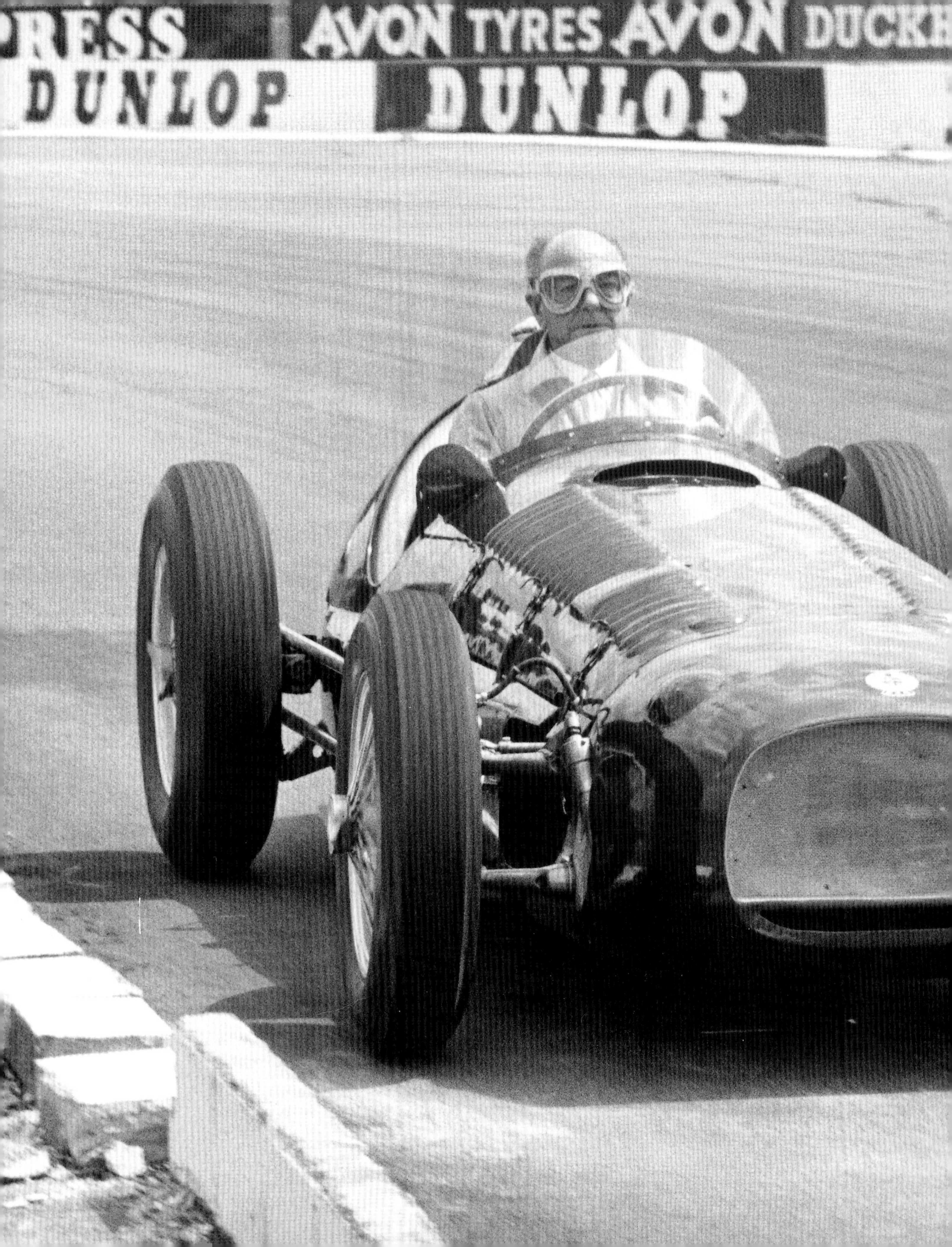

AVON TYRES AVON
DUNLOP
DUNLOP

Chapter 10
Postscript
After the V16

While the Owen Racing Organisation was still entering the V16s during the 1955 season, development of the new four-cylinder P25 progressed and the first car made two racing appearances during 1955. Compared with its V16 predecessor, the compact and well-proportioned P25, with its 2,491cc (102.87 x 74.93mm) engine designed by Stewart Tresilian, represented an exercise in simplicity, and it had a potential for speed. But beneath the apparent simplicity lay handling difficulties, and there were persistent valve problems, and equally persistent problems with the single rear transmission brake. The folly of the V16 seemed to have been replaced by the futility of the new design.

The first car was entered for Peter Collins at Aintree in September 1955, but it non-started after he crashed in practice. The car next ran three weeks later in the Gold Cup race at Oulton Park, but after a sensationally quick start brought Collins through to third place, the BRM lost its oil pressure and had to be withdrawn. Subsequent investigation revealed that the oil pressure gauge was faulty.

◄ What was both the first and last V16 BRM, the original chassis built in 1949 and rebuilt as a Mk II in 1954, ran at Folkingham in 1957 when it was driven by both Ron Flockhart and Rivers-Fletcher. Nearly ten years later this car was overhauled and driven by Raymond Mays in a demonstration at the British Grand Prix meeting at Silverstone. *(Tom March Collection)*

◀ This photograph of the BRM P25 Grand Prix car – the successor to the V16 – was taken at Folkingham in February 1956 when BRM held an open day for members of ORMA (Owen Racing Motors Association). *(Tom March Collection)*

▼ This is Tony Brooks's BRM P25 in the 1956 British Grand Prix. When he stopped at the pits because of a sticking throttle, the mechanics made a crude repair. The throttle jammed open and Brooks crashed. He was lucky to escape with minor injuries. *(LAT Photographic)*

For 1956 the team signed up Mike Hawthorn and Tony Brooks; the latter had achieved a sensational win with a works Connaught B-series car in the Syracuse Grand Prix in late October 1955. It was the first win in a Grand Prix by a British driver at the wheel of a British car since Sir Henry Segrave's victory with a Sunbeam in the 1924 San Sebastian Grand Prix.

The 1956 season proved disastrous and brought vivid memories of the disasters of the V16. Brake failures – and crashes – were combined with a tremendous turn of speed, and a season of promise was cut short when Tony Brooks walked away from an accident that could have proved fatal in the British Grand Prix at Silverstone. A bodged effort at repairing a broken throttle resulted in the throttle jamming open, the BRM turning end over end, and the team withdrew to concentrate on development work for the rest of the season.

For 1957 Colin Chapman of the fledgling Lotus company acted as consultant to BRM to sort out the handling problems. He redesigned the rear suspension and replaced the rear oleo struts used with the de Dion rear axle by a conventional coil spring and damper layout. The team sunk to near-despair with continuing failures in 1957, but Jean Behra stepped in and drove a P25 to a win in the non-Championship Caen Grand Prix.

Jean Behra and Harry Schell drove for the team in 1958 but, although the cars still showed great promise, no substantial success was achieved. The first World Championship race victory came in 1959 when Joakim Bonnier drove one of the cars to a win in the Dutch Grand Prix. By this time the rear-engined Cooper was the dominant Grand Prix car, and before the end of the season BRM had introduced their own rear-engined car, the P48, which was a conversion of the original front-engined P25 to rear-engined configuration.

Although the BRMs continued to show promise, nothing had been achieved. In the 1960 British race Graham Hill turned in a tremendous performance to come up through the field to take the lead and set fastest lap. But, in typical BRM fashion, it all came to naught when a locking brake caused Hill to spin out of the race.

A new 1,500cc unsupercharged Formula 1 came into force for 1961, and while BRM were developing their own V8 engine, the team was forced to race a modified version of the P48 with 1,464 four-cylinder Coventry Climax Mk II engines that developed about 150bhp. These cars were hopelessly underpowered compared with the Ferrari opposition, and 1961 proved yet another dismal and unsuccessful year.

For 1962 the long-suffering Sir Alfred Owen lost patience and made it clear that if the team did not enjoy a successful year it would be wound up. It proved an immensely successful year and, with wins in the Dutch, German, Italian, and South African races, together with second places in the British and United States races, Hill won the Driver's Championship for BRM, and the make won the Constructors' Cup. It had all come good at last, and it stayed good as Hill finished second in the Championship in 1963, 1964, and 1965. BRM survived in a series of ups and downs in the 3,000cc GP Formula of 1966 onwards, and ceased racing completely in 1978.

▲ During the years of the 2,500cc Grand Prix formula, BRM's only World Championship race victory was scored by Joakim Bonnier in the 1959 Dutch Grand Prix. *(LAT Photographic)*

Appendix 1

BRM Drivers

Peter Collins

Born 6 November 1931, died 3 August 1958

Collins's early experience was in Formula 3 (500cc) with Cooper-Norton and JBS-Norton cars. He was a strong contender and it was widely considered that there was no better learning curve than the tight, close, cut-and-thrust of racing in this category. Peter drove for HWM in Formula 2 in 1952–53, but the glory days of the team were over – the cars were underpowered, overweight and unreliable.

Aston Martin invited Collins to join their sports car team in 1952. He appreciated and enjoyed the tactics and long spells at the wheel that endurance racing entailed. In 1952 he co-drove the winning car in the Goodwood 9-Hours race with Pat Griffith. The pairing finished second in the following year's Goodwood event, and although generally the team had a poor year in 1954, Peter won the short Silverstone sports-car race outright.

In 1955 he and Paul Frère were second at Le Mans, and he stayed with the Aston Martin team through 1956, his first year with Ferrari in Formula 1. In 1954 Collins drove brilliantly at the wheel of the the Vanwall Special and the Ferrari Thin Wall Special. Then followed his year with BRM, where he found the behaviour and attitudes of both Mays and Berthon nauseating.

Peter joined Ferrari for 1956 and at different levels he had a close relationship with both Enzo Ferrari and Mike Hawthorn. He won the Belgian and French Grands Prix and finished third in the 1956 Drivers' Championship. He gained immortal fame for handing his car over to Fangio at Monza, when, if he had stayed at the wheel, he would have won the Championship by the narrowest of margins.

In 1957 the Ferraris were not competitive, but the team bounced back in 1958 and fought a season-long battle with Vanwall. Poor Peter was not there to see it through to the end of the season. He was very much a Championship contender, but he crashed heavily in the German Grand Prix and was flown to Bonn Hospital where he died from his injuries.

▼ A man of mixed repute. In his early racing days Peter Collins was considered something of a hooligan, but on the other hand he was highly regarded for his kindness and good humour. He is seen here at the wheel of an HWM Formula 2 car at the 1952 British Grand Prix. He stayed with HWM for 1953, joined Vandervell for 1954, and after a season with BRM in 1955 he was signed up by Ferrari and stayed with that team until his death at the German Grand Prix in August 1958. *(Guy Griffiths Collection)*

Juan Manuel Fangio

Born 24 June 1911, died 17 July 1995

Born in Balcarce, Argentina, Juan Manuel Fangio was the most talented and successful of the drivers promoted by the Argentine Automobile Club under the influence of President Juan Perón. Although Perón ensured that Fangio and others had superb cars to drive and all their expenses were paid, they did not get any income. In the early stages of his career he was very hard up, reliant on a small income from his modest garage business in Balcarce. Even Alfa Romeo paid him very little apart from a share of starting and prize money and the loan of a car.

The Maestro first raced in Europe in 1948 and the following year he competed for most of the season with a Maserati 'San Remo' entered by Scuderia Argentina, his successes including wins at Pau and Albi. For 1950 Alfa Romeo signed him as number two to Giuseppe Farina and he duly took second place behind his team leader in the newly inaugurated World Championship. The following year he won the World Championship and at the end of the season Alfa Romeo withdrew from racing.

While he was driving for Scuderia Argentina, Fangio became friendly with people in the racing department at Maserati and he was glad to sign up to drive the Maserati A6GCM Formula 2 car in 1952. Although by this time it was almost certain that World Championship and other important Grands Prix would be held to Formula 2 regulations, there would still be a considerable number of races held to the old Formula 1.

Raymond Mays adored 'stars' and 'stardom', and Fangio was undoubtedly a star. He needed the money offered by BRM and agreed to drive for the team. In early testing he made suggestions that improved the roadholding, comfort and driveability of the V16. He drove the V16 in only two races in 1952 before his dreadful accident at Monza, and after his return to the BRM team in 1953 he drove at three meetings in between commitments to Maserati in Grand Prix racing and Alfa Romeo in sports car racing.

Throughout 1953 Fangio battled for Maserati against Ferrari, won only one World Championship race and took second place in the title fight. In sports car racing Alfa Romeo was racing its *Tipo* 6C 34 3.4-litre coupés, the fastest cars in the Sports category, but with a reliability record too. With one of these cars Fangio took second place in the Mille Miglia, despite defective steering.

Mercedes-Benz returned to Grand Prix racing for the new 2,500cc Formula in 1954 and Fangio led the German team for two seasons. The new cars were not ready at the beginning of the season and he drove for Maserati in the first two World Championship races, at Buenos Aires and Spa-Francorchamps, and won both. The Mercedes-Benz made its debut in the French race at Reims and Fangio won this easily. He subsequently won three of the remaining five World Championship races to clinch the title.

In 1955 Mercedes-Benz raced in both Formula 1 and sports car racing. In a season cut short following the Le Mans disaster the Argentinian won four of the six Formula 1 World Championship races, and he was second in the British Grand Prix to team-mate Stirling Moss); in sports car events he finished second to Moss in the Mille Miglia and he and Moss together won the Tourist Trophy.

Fangio spent a miserable year with the Ferrari team in 1956 and he and Enzo Ferrari disliked and mistrusted each other. For his final full year of racing he rejoined Maserati and achieved his fifth World Championship title despite losing three of the season's last four races to Moss and the Vanwall. After driving in the Argentine and the French Grands Prix in 1958, Fangio retired from racing and returned to

▼ World Champion Juan Manuel Fangio looking rather grim before the 1953 Albi race: he was all too aware that on this very fast, very narrow road circuit – the sort of track on which drivers really earned their money – it was likely the BRMs would suffer tyre failure. *(LAT Photographic)*

his home town of Balcarce in the Argentine where he developed his car business and opened a motor museum.

It is recognised that it is impossible to compare drivers from different eras of racing but Fangio was undoubtedly one of the all-time greats. He had superlative judgement, he was a great tactician and he was certainly no car-breaker – and he won Five World Championships. He also came closer than anyone to mastering the V16 BRM.

Ron Flockhart

Born 16 June 1923, died 12 April 1962

▼ Ron Flockhart, seen here in the cockpit of a V16 BRM, scored his greatest successes in sports car racing, notably his victories at Le Mans in 1956 and 1957 co-driving the Jaguar D-types of Écurie Ecosse. *(LAT Photographic)*

During the years of WW2, Ron (William Ronald) Flockhart rose to the rank of Captain in the British Army. After the cessation of hostilities he entered the motor trade and started his motor sport career in 1948, racing motorcycles. He moved on to racing on four wheels with MG and 500cc JP-Vincent cars, but the most important step in his career came when he

bought Raymond Mays's R4D ERA in 1952. It was a very exceptional car and with Ron at the wheel it achieved some excellent performances.

Ron stayed with the BRM and Owen Organisations through 1959, but his finest performances were with other makes. In 1956 he achieved Connaught's best-ever performance in a World Championship race by finishing third in the Italian Grand Prix at Monza. He had joined Écurie Ecosse for 1956 and drove a Jaguar D-type in the 1957 Mille Miglia, also winning Le Mans for the team in at the wheel of D-type Jaguars, with Ninian Sanderson in 1956 and with Ivor Bueb in 1957. Although Ron continued to race after he left BRM, mainly with Lotus cars, he turned his attention more and more to flying which had become his greater enthusiasm.

He had gained his Private Pilot's Licence in 1954, and for some years he flew an Auster single-engined light aircraft. He became determined to break the record for flying from Sydney to London. He acquired a WW2 North American P51 Mustang for the attempt (powered by a Packard-built Rolls-Royce Merlin engine), but through no fault of his own, his efforts proved disastrous.

Flockhart started from Sydney and his first flight ended at Athens. It was as though he was sabotaged by the Athens airport authority. He was kept waiting to line up for take-off with his engine running and despite impassioned pleas to Air Traffic over the radio, he was holding so long that the Merlin engine caught fire and the aircraft was burnt out.

Back in 1962 Mustangs were cheap and he acquired another example. Before his second attempt on the record, he air-tested the aircraft over the Dandenong Mountains near Melbourne. He was killed when the Mustang broke up in exceptional turbulence. Those whose knowledge of Flockhart was slim have suggested that the incident happened because of his inexperience. It is simply untrue – he had vast experience, including blind flying (ie, flying on instruments alone), but what he lacked was an instrument rating or the equivalent.

José Froilán González

Born 5 October 1922

Born in Arrecifes, Argentina, Jose Froilán González was another driver nurtured by the Argentinian government through the national automobile club. He too raced Maseratis in Europe for Scuderia Argentina until Enzo Ferrari picked him to drive in the 1951 French Grand Prix at Reims as a substitute for Piero Taruffi, who was not fit to drive. Driving an obsolete single-plug car, González worked his way up to second place before handing over to team-leader Alberto Ascari.

The next race for Ferrari was the British Grand Prix at Silverstone and 'Pepe' again drove the single-plug car. Against all expectations he battled with Fangio and won, achieving the first defeat of the Alfa Romeo team since 1946. González joined Maserati for 1952, but the cars were not competitive until a twin-plug version of the A6GCM Formula 2 car appeared in the Italian Grand Prix at Monza where González finished second to Alberto Ascari (Ferrari).

During 1952 González accompanied Fangio during his early meetings with BRM and ended up driving the V16s all season. There was a very marked difference in González's driving of Ferraris and Maseratis on the one hand and the BRM on the other. His careful mental approach to racing, coupled with determination and tactics, helped him to his Grand Prix successes. In contrast, it was mindless driving that caused his crashes in the BRM at Silverstone and Boreham in 1952 – it has to be concluded that he was driving the V16 simply for the money.

González stayed with Maserati for 1953 and for 1954 he rejoined Ferrari. In his battles with Fangio and the Mercedes-Benz team he won the British Grand Prix. With Maurice Trintignant he won the Le Mans 24 Hours in a Ferrari after a long battle with the Jaguar D-type of Rolt/Hamilton. González crashed his sports Ferrari heavily in practice for the Tourist Trophy at Dundrod. Although he drove for Ferrari in Argentina at the beginning of 1955, his attitude towards racing changed and thereafter he raced only occasionally in local events.

Now the oldest living Formula 1 winner, González lives in Uruguay.

▼ At Silverstone in 1952 José Froilán González sits on the pit counter to watch the main race of the day, the British Grand Prix, which was followed by the Formule Libre race in which the BRMs took part. We know nothing of the people either side of the Argentinian driver, but the man on the left of the photograph is obviously English (and looks like a refugee from an Ealing Studios comedy) and the one on the right may be presumed to be a compatriot of González. *(Tom March Collection)*

◀ Stirling Moss regarded the BRM V16 as the worst car he ever drove and he appeared for the team only once, in the Ulster Trophy in June 1952. Here he is seen with Fangio at Goodwood on Easter Monday 1953. *(Guy Griffiths Collection)*

Stirling Moss

Born 17 September 1929

So much has been written by and about Stirling Moss that little remains to be said other than to summarise his attitude to the BRM V16. He tested it extensively at Monza and drove it in one race, the 1952 Ulster Trophy at Dundrod in Northern Ireland.

He disliked the handling and the engine characteristics; he had contempt for the persistently poor preparation of the cars and the inability of the team to make them raceworthy; he did not trust either Mays or Berthon; he considered the cars to be dangerous and that it was not worth risking life or limb to drive them.

Despite walking away from the BRM team after that one outing, Stirling Moss became an icon of his generation; the V16 remained a failure.

Reg Parnell

Born 2 July 1911, died 7 January 1964

A very successful pig farmer by occupation, Derby-born Reg Parnell started racing in pre-war days. He was practising with his MG at Brooklands in 1937 and lost control and spun when he went higher on the banking than the speed of his car allowed, colliding with Kay Petre who was lapping her Austin at a lower level. Petre was badly hurt and had facial injuries, but she made a full recovery, although she remained scarred and used make-up to hide the blemishes. Parnell's licence was suspended, but it was reinstated a year later; there were many who thought Parnell had been victimised for what was a pure racing accident because he was working-class.

During the war Parnell collected a large number of racing cars at a time when they could be bought for 'peanuts' and he had the space to store them at his pig farm. When racing resumed after the end of the war there was immediate demand for racing cars and from the sale of his 'stock' Reg was able to finance his post-war racing career.

He entered into a deal with Count 'Johnny' Lurani's Scuderia Ambrosiana whereby he was supplied with Maserati racing cars, at first a 1939-type 4CL and subsequently a 4CT San Remo. These cars remained in Italian ownership and came into the UK on a carnet

and Parnell, in breach of the currency regulations, paid in cash, either by giving the money to Lurani when he was in the UK or sometimes an Italian ice cream salesman living in the UK would visit his family in Italy and when he did so, he acted as courier for Lurani and carried large quantities of cash.

From 1950 onwards Reg was a member of the Aston Martin works team and he was invited by Alfa Romeo to drive a *Tipo* 158 in the 1950 European Grand Prix at Silverstone. The Milan cars took the first four places and despite a collision with an unfortunate hare Reg duly finished fourth.

Parnell was Britain's most successful racing driver at the time and the ideal man to drive the BRM. A member of the team from 1950 to early 1953, he was one of very few drivers who understood the V16 and fully exploited it – but he did not like it and that is why he and BRM went their separate ways.

Subsequently, in 1954, Parnell raced the ex-Bobby Baird Ferrari *Tipo* 500 in another deal with Scuderia Ambrosiana. This 2-litre car had been completely rebuilt at the factory in the latest 2.5-litre form

and with it Reg enjoyed a very successful year. He had also continued driving for Aston Martin and occasionally he drove other cars. He crashed Rob Walker's Grand Prix Connaught at Crystal Palace in 1956 and this made him to decide to retire.

From 1956 he became Aston Martin's Racing Manager, and after Aston Martin retired from racing he managed the Bowmaker Racing Team. It was an important team and in 1962 it raced the new Lola Formula 1 cars with Coventry Climax V8 engines and John Surtees as number one driver. The team showed immense promise but it failed to win a Grand Prix in 1962, although Surtees finished second in two World Championship races.

Bowmaker withdrew from racing and so Parnell took over the team, which he ran as Reg Parnell Racing. It was underfunded and never achieved much – apart from giving Chris Amon his first chance in Formula 1. Parnell died in 1964 of peritonitis when an operation for appendicitis went wrong. Son Tim took over the team and later forged strong links with BRM. What comes round, goes round!

▲ Reg Parnell looks weary here, at Goodwood in 1950, and the mechanics' overalls are dirty and wet. *(LAT Photographic)*

Raymond Sommer

Born 31 August 1906, died 10 September 1950

Of Raymond Sommer it has been written that he epitomised all that is good about motor racing: courage, tenacity, enthusiasm, persistence and sportsmanship (Steve Small, *Grand Prix Who's Who*). He first became recognised at international level in 1932 when he and Luigi Chinetti won the Le Mans race and what was notable about the victory was that Sommer was at the wheel for 21 of the 24 hours; he won again at Le Mans in 1933 when he partnered Tazio Nuvolari.

Throughout the latter part of the 1930s Sommer was always seen at the wheel of private Alfa Romeos because he was not interested in driving works cars and being subject to the discipline and constraints of works teams and the whims of team managers. Although he never won a 'proper' Grand Prix, he revelled in harassing and often beating Scuderia Ferrari-entered Alfa Romeos and works Maseratis.

His only Grand Prix win was in the 1936 French race (held as an event for sports cars) in which he partnered Jean-Pierre Wimille at the wheel of the winning Bugatti 'Tank'.

In 1946 Sommer won the first post-war Grand Prix, the St Cloud race near Paris, with a Maserati after the failure of the works Alfa Romeo 158s. The following year he was entered to drive France's grand prix hopeful, the CTA-Arsenal, in the French Grand Prix on a makeshift circuit at Lyon. The car was very slow in practice and, at the start of the race, the clutch jammed and as Sommer struggled to free it, it went in suddenly, the car jerked forward and the back axle broke. History was destined to repeat itself.

During 1948 Sommer drove a semi-works Ferrari and among his successes was a win in the Formula 2 race at Reims. He raced a Talbot-Lago in 1949–50 Grands Prix and he was invited to drive the V16

▼ Raymond Sommer (right), seen here with Harry Schell at the Silverstone International Trophy meeting in 1950. *(Guy Griffiths Collection)*

BRM in the International Trophy race at Silverstone in August 1950. It proved a disastrous repetition of the Lyon race. At the start of his heat, Sommer fed in the clutch of the V16 and a driveshaft failed. Not only was BRM vilified, but so was Sommer, who was blamed for another start-line failure. Neither this incident nor the failure at Lyon was in any way his fault and in the case of the BRM the driveshafts proved to have been made to a specification of inadequate strength.

A fortnight later Sommer was dead. His Cooper 500 crashed with fatal results on 10 September on the Cadours circuit, near Toulouse in the Haute Garonne *département* of France. The cause of the accident was believed to be a seized wheel bearing.

Peter Walker

Born 7 December 1912, died 1 March 1984

Peter Walker came from a prosperous farming background and went to Oxford University where he and Peter Whitehead met. The two became firm friends and shared an interest in motor racing that they indulged in the years up to the war. When Whitehead bought one of the early 1,100cc Alta twin-cam sports cars, he let Walker compete with it; when Whitehead bought ERA R10B, he let Walker drive that as well.

Post-war, when Jaguar entered sports car racing in 1951, Walker was invited to join the team and he partnered Peter Whitehead in the C-type to a win at Le Mans that year and to second place in the Tourist Trophy race on the Dundrod circuit in Northern Ireland. In the period 1952–54 he regularly and satisfactorily partnered Stirling Moss, closely matching his lap times until they both left the team at the end of the 1954 season. Their best performance was second place in the 1953 Le Mans race in which Jaguars finished first, second and fourth.

As a leading British driver, Walker was a natural choice to drive for BRM alongside Parnell. Walker believed in the future prospects of the V16 and after the 1950 Penya Rhin Grand Prix he wrote a long and constructive appraisal of the race and the car. One of the many problems with BRM was that it had a board of Trustees who meddled, interfered and adversely criticised; most of them had experience of the motor industry and not of racing and most of them were abysmally ignorant of the sport.

After the Spanish race, Walker was criticised for not trying hard enough, whereas he drove a cautious race with a car that was almost completely unproven under racing conditions. He was nominated to drive for BRM for the second and last time in the 1951 British Grand Prix. He had the guts to keep going when he was in agony from the burns caused by the badly insulated exhaust system. Even so, some Trustees criticised him again for not trying hard enough.

In 1952 Walker competed with a special Cooper with lengthened Cooper chassis and 2-litre ERA engine, but it was not a success. At the end of 1954 he felt that it was time for a change and left Jaguar to drive for Aston Martin. He also drove Rob Walker's new B-series Connaughts in some events and achieved a stirring win in a Formule Libre race at Snetterton in August 1955.

Walker crashed his DB3S heavily at Le Mans in 1956 and suffered serious injuries. His confidence was shattered and he retired from racing after driving Rob Walker's B-series Connaught at Siracusa. Thereafter he began to drink heavily and as a result of financial difficulties he lost his farm and became a derelict roaming the streets of London and 'dossing' where he could. He caught pneumonia and was taken into hospital where he met and fell in love with a nurse who responded to his feelings in the same way. There are not many stories of this kind with a happy ending, but they married and stayed contentedly together until Peter died in 1984.

▼ In early post-war years Peter Walker proved himself to be one of the fastest and gutsiest of British drivers. In 1951 he co-drove the winning C-type Jaguar at Le Mans with Peter Whitehead, and during the period 1952–54 he regularly partnered Stirling Moss in the Jaguar team. He was a nominated BRM driver in 1950–51, but he was much criticised for lack of enthusiasm by BRM Trustees. Here he is in the cockpit of the ERA that he drove in the International Trophy race at Silverstone in August 1949. *(Guy Griffiths Collection)*

▶ After Ken Wharton's winning drive in the Richmond Trophy at Goodwood in 1953, the great all-rounder stayed in the cockpit to allow the press to take photographs. Here, Wharton consoles Reg Parnell, who retired because of engine problems and looks suitably doleful, while between them stands a gleeful Alfred Owen, and Raymond Mays is on the right. *(Guy Griffiths Collection)*

Ken Wharton

Born 21 March 1916, died 12 January 1957

Ken Wharton was an extremely talented driver, but at the same time one of the most difficult and irritating that it was possible to meet. He ran a garage business in Smethwick, a suburb of Birmingham, and he was an outstanding motorsport enthusiast. It is doubtful whether anyone in the history of motor racing has been so successful in so many different areas of the sport.

He was a great trials driver (he won the British Trial Drivers' Championship in 1951), he was a superb rally driver (he won the Dutch Tulip Rally outright in 1953), he was a fine hill-climber (he won the RAC Hill Climb Championship in 1954) and as a racing driver he was well above average.

During 1952 he drove a Formula 2 Frazer Nash for Peter Bell. From 1952 onwards he was the works Frazer Nash driver and very much involved in the development of the prototype owned by the manufacturer, AFN Limited. In 1953 he raced very successfully a Cooper-Bristol painted British Racing Green with a yellow nose-band. He was a works Jaguar driver in 1954 and he was Daimler Competitions Manager in 1955.

The real problem with Ken that he was as hard as they come; he never gave an inch and he would push you off as soon as look at you. Almost needless to say, few of his contemporaries would give him

the time of day. He was the sort of driver that some entrants liked, but it came at a price; he whinged and complained and he was superstitious.

Wharton joined BRM in 1952 and he stayed with the team until the end of 1954. He tried very hard and it is difficult to forget his heroics in the New Zealand Grand Prix in 1954 when the V16 'conked out' and he pushed this hulking brute of a car hundreds of yards to the finish. Over three seasons he gained vast experience of the V16 and he came to love its foibles and failures.

When the Owen Organisation bought a 250F Maserati in 1954, he simply could not get on with it. It has never been clear why he left the BRM team, but it may have been because he felt unable to master the 250F. He joined Vanwall for 1955, but he crashed badly in the International Trophy at Silverstone in May; the car punctured its fuel tank, caught fire and Ken suffered bad burns to the arms.

He left Vanwall at the end of simply because Tony Vandervell did not want him and he was reduced to driving for private owners. He was killed in January 1957 in the sports car race at Ardmore, New Zealand, when he overturned a Ferrari Monza and he was crushed in the cockpit. He deserved better and recently his talents have been recognised by the opening in Smethwick of a museum dedicated to him.

Appendix 2

BRM V16 Specification in Detail

Where the figures for the Mk II are significantly different, they are given in square parentheses.

Engine

Configuration	16 cylinders in 'V' formation at an included angle of 135°
Valves	Two per cylinder at an included angle of 80°, dimensions of 1.25in (31.75m) inlet, 1.09in (2.7.69mm) exhaust
Valve actuation	Twin overhead ten-bearing camshafts per bank of cylinders, spur gear-train driven from centre of crankshaft
Cylinder block	Aluminium-alloy, Brico cast-iron wet cylinder liners
Cylinder heads	Light alloy
Crankcase	Light alloy
Connecting rods and pistons	Nickel-chrome steel connecting rods and Hepolite pistons
Crankshaft	Two-piece ESC Nitralloy crankshaft running in ten Vandervell Thin Wall three-layer main bearings
Piston area	47.8sq ft
Piston speed	3,800ft/min at 12,000rpm
Carburation	Rolls-Royce twin-stage centrifugal supercharger with maximum pressure of 5.7 atmospheres and two SU carburettors
Ignition	Four Lucas magnetos (or distributors), single Lodge plug per cylinder
Compression ratio	7.5:1
Lubrication	Dry sump with a capacity of 5 gallons (22.7 litres)
Cooling	Water-cooled, radiator capacity of 4 gallons (18.18 litres)
Firing order	1-10-6-13-2-16-5-11-8-15-3-12-7-9-4-14
Capacity (bore x stroke)	1,496cc (49.53 x 47.8mm) 91.256cu in (1.95 x 1.90in)
Maximum power	430bhp at 12,000rpm [485bhp at 12,000rpm]

Transmission

Clutch	Dry multi-plate (three driven plates) mounted in unit with the engine
Gearbox	Jointed propshaft to final drive unit; five-speed gearbox of the countershaft type with the drive taken through a pair of dog-engaged constant-mesh gears; shafts transversely across the car which drive a pair of input bevel gears on the left side
Final drive	Incorporating ZF limited-slip differential, sliding block universal joints either side of gearbox, short shafts, Hooke-type universal joints inboard of rear hub carriers

Chassis

Chassis frame	Ladder-type chrome-molybdenum steel with double-tube side members and four cross-members
Front suspension	Trailing arms and Lockheed air struts
Rear suspension	De Dion axle, single radius rods, sliding block, Lockheed air struts
Steering	Worm and nut, 2¼ turns lock-to-lock
Brakes	Girling hydraulic three-shoe drum, 14in (356mm) drums front and rear; from 1952 the team adopted Girling hydraulically operated disc brakes with 13.5in (343mm) diameter front and 13in (330mm) diameter rear discs
Wheels	Dunlop wire-spoke centre-lock on Rudge splined hubs, 18in (457mm) front, 17in (432mm) rear
Tyres	Dunlop racing, 5.25 x 18 front, 7.00 x 17 rear

Dimensions & weights

Wheelbase	8ft 2in (2,490mm); [Mk II. 7ft 7in (2,310mm)]
Front track	4ft 4in (1,321mm)
Rear track	4ft 3in (1,295mm)
Overall length	13ft 2in (4,013mm); [Mk II, 12ft 7in (3,835mm)]
Overall height	2ft 11in (889mm); [Mk II, 2ft 10in (864mm)]
Frontal area	9.5sq ft
Dry weight	1,624lb (736.5kg); [Mk II, 1,400lb (635kg)]
Starting line weight	2,140lb (970.5kg); [Mk II, 1,904lb (863.9kg)]

Appendix 3

BRM V16 Race Record Summary

1950		
International Trophy (F1) Silverstone, 26 August Two qualifying heats, each of 34 miles, and 101-mile final	Rtd	R. Sommer, No. 8 (drive-shaft failure at start of heat)
BARC International Goodwood, 30 September		
Woodcote Cup (F Libre) 12 miles	1st	R. Parnell, No. 1, 78.50mph
Goodwood Trophy (F Libre) 29 miles	1st	R. Parnell, No. 1, 82.48mph
Penya Rhin Grand Prix (F1) Barcelona Cup,	Rtd	R. Parnell, No. 8, supercharger drive failure
Pedralbes, 29 October, 194 miles	Rtd	P.D.C. Walker, No 10, gearbox failure

1951		
British Grand Prix (F1) Silverstone, 14 July, 260 miles	5th	R. Parnell, No. 6
	7th	P.D.C. Walker, No. 7

▶ Froilán González at the wheel of his BRM V16 in the Woodcote Cup Formule Libre race at Goodwood in September 1952. González won ahead of Farina's Ferrari Thin Wall Special and Parnell's BRM. *(Guy Griffiths Collection)*

1952		
Albi Grand Prix (F1) Circuit des Planques, 1 June, 189 miles	Rtd	J.M. Fangio, No. 2, engine
	Rtd	J.F. González, No. 4, engine
Ulster Trophy (F1) Dundrod, 7 June, 252 miles	Rtd	J.M. Fangio, No. 7, fuel starvation
	Rtd	S. Moss, No. 8, engine overheating
British GP meeting, Silverstone F Libre race, 17 July, 102 miles	Rtd	J.F. González, No. 7, accident damage
	Rtd	K. Wharton/J.F. González, No. 8, gearbox
Daily Mail Trophy (F1 & F2 races run together), Boreham, 2 August, 201 miles,	Rtd	J.F. González, No. 25, accident
	Rtd	K. Wharton, No. 26, gearbox
Scottish Daily Express National Trophy (F Libre) Turnberry, 23 August, 35 miles	1st	R. Parnell, No. 53, 79.50mph
	Rtd	K. Wharton, No. 52, steering
BARC International, Goodwood, 27 September Woodcote Cup (F Libre) 12 miles	1st	J.F. González, No. 5, 87.64mph
	3rd	R. Parnell, No. 6
	DNS	K. Wharton, No. 7, fuel-feed problems on starting grid
Daily Graphic Goodwood Trophy (F Libre), 36 miles	1st	J.F. González, No. 5, 88.13mph
	2nd	R. Parnell, No. 6
	3rd	K. Wharton, No. 7
Glasgow Daily Herald International Trophy (F Libre), Charterhall, 11 October, 80 miles	2nd	K. Wharton, No. 2
	Rtd	R. Parnell, No. 1, transmission

1953		
BARC International, Goodwood, 6 April		
Chichester Cup (F Libre) 12 miles	2nd	K. Wharton, No. 2
	4th	R. Parnell, No. 1
Glover Trophy (F Libre) 36 miles	1st	K. Wharton, No. 2, 90.47mph
	Rtd	R. Parnell, No. 1, supercharger drive failure
Charterhall (F Libre), 23 May, 40 miles	3rd	K. Wharton, No. 2
Albi Grand Prix (F1 and F2), Circuit des Planques, 31 May, heats of 55.5 miles for F1 and F2 cars, final for both 99.4-miles	F1 HEAT	
	1st	J.M. Fangio, No. 7, 110.48mph
	2nd	K. Wharton, No. 9
	5th	J.F. González, No. 11
	FINAL	
	2nd	J.F. González, No. 11
	Rtd	J.M. Fangio, No. 7, tyre failure causing damaged hub
	Rtd	K. Wharton, No. 9, accident caused by tyre failure
British GP support race (F Libre), Silverstone, 18 July, 50 miles	2nd	J.M. Fangio, No. 3
	3rd	K. Wharton, No. 2
USAF Trophy meeting, Snetterton, 25 July		
AMOC Trophy (F Libre), 40.6 miles	1st	K. Wharton, No. 1, 88.79mph
USA Invitation (F Libre), 27 miles	1st	K. Wharton, No. 1, 87.79mph
Daily Record International Trophy (F Libre) Charterhall, 15 August, 100miles	1st	K. Wharton, No. 35, 82.70mph
	DNS	R. Parnell, No. 34, accident in practice
BARC International, Goodwood, 26 September		
Woodcote Cup (F Libre), 12 miles	2nd	J.M. Fangio, No. 1
	3rd	K. Wharton, No. 2
Goodwood Trophy (F Libre), 36 miles	2nd	K. Wharton, No. 2
	Rtd	J.F. Fangio, No. 1, gearbox
Hastings Trophy (F Libre), Castle Combe, 3 October, 28 miles	1st	K. Wharton, No. 62, 87.49mph

1954		
New Zealand Grand Prix (F Libre), Ardmore, Auckland, 9 January, 210 miles	2nd	K. Wharton, No. 1
Lady Wigram Trophy (F Libre), Christchurch, 6 February, 100 miles	3rd	K. Wharton, No. 1, fuel-feed problems, pushed car across the line
BARC International, Goodwood, 19 April		
Chichester Cup (F Libre), 12 miles	1st	K. Wharton (Mk II), No. 4, 88.70mph,
	4th	R. Flockhart, No. 5
Glover Trophy (F Libre), 50 miles	1st	K. Wharton, No. 5, 86.40mph
	4th	R. Flockhart (Mk II), No. 4
AMOC spring meeting (F Libre), Snetterton, 24 April, 27 miles	1st	R. Flockhart (Mk II), No. 1, 89.01mph)
WHDCC Trophy (F Libre), Ibsley, 8 May, 31 miles	1st	R. Flockhart (Mk II), No. 102, 83.48mph
BARC *Daily Telegraph* 200 (F Libre), Aintree, 29 May, two 51-mile qualifying heats and 105-mile final	HEAT 1	
	4th	K. Wharton (Mk II), No. 9
	HEAT 2	
	1st	R. Flockhart (Mk II), No. 9, 76.92mph
	FINAL	
	3rd	R. Flockhart (Mk II), No. 10
	Rtd	K. Wharton (Mk II), No. 9, brakes
Whitsun Trophy (F Libre), Goodwood, 7 June, 36 miles	2nd	R. Flockhart (Mk II), No. 2
	4th	K. Wharton (Mk II), No. 1
WECC Trophy (F Libre), Snetterton, 14 August, 108 miles	3rd	R. Flockhart (Mk II), No. 2
Hastings Trophy (F Libre), Castle Combe, 28 August, 27.6 miles	2nd	R. Flockhart (Mk II), No. 54
WJC Trophy (F Libre), Charterhall, 4 September, 40 miles	Rtd	R. Flockhart (Mk II), No. 61, fuel-feed blockage at start
BARC International, Goodwood, 25 September Woodcote Cup (F Libre), 24 miles	2nd	K. Wharton (Mk II), No. 4
	Rtd	R. Flockhart (Mk II), No. 5, accident damage
BARC Trophy (F Libre), Aintree, 2 October, 51 miles	3rd,	R. Flockhart (Mk II), No. 10
	Rtd	K. Wharton (Mk II), No. 9, accident damage, collision with Schell's Maserati

1955		
BARC International, Goodwood, 11 April Chichester Cup (F Libre), 17 miles Easter Handicap, 12 miles	1st	P.J. Collins (Mk II), No. 25, 90.29mph
	5th	P.J. Collins (Mk II), No. 25
WECC Trophy (F Libre), Snetterton, 28 May, 27 miles,	2nd	R. Flockhart (Mk II), No. 98
	Rtd	P.J. Collins (Mk II), No. 97, tyre burst and spin, after collision with Cunningham-Reid's Lister
WECC International Trophy (F Libre), Snetterton, 13 August, 68 miles	Rtd	P.J. Collins (Mk II), No. 146, driveshaft universal joint failure
BARC Trophy (F Libre), Aintree, 3 September, 51 miles	1st	P.J. Collins (Mk II), No. 22, 85.20mph
Empire News Trophy (F Libre), Castle Combe, 1 October, 37 miles	2nd	R. Flockhart (Mk II), No. 48

Appendix 4

BRM Suppliers

(List published in 1951)

Accles and Pollock Ltd
Aeroplane and Motor Castings Ltd
Alexandra Machinery Ltd
André Rubber Company Ltd
James Archdale and Co. Ltd
Austin Motor Co. Ltd
Automotive Products Ltd
R. M. Birkett and Sons Ltd
Birmingham Aluminium Castings Ltd
James Booth and Co. Ltd
Britcovmo Ltd
British Wire Products Ltd
The Brooke Tool Manufacturing Co. Ltd
Brown Bros (Aircraft) Ltd
David Brown and Sons Ltd
Burgess Products Ltd
Burman and Sons Ltd
The Chloride Electrical Storage Co. Ltd
Charles Churchill and Co. Ltd
Clyde Alloy Co. Ltd
Cooper's Mechanical Joints Ltd
Coventry Gauge and Tool Company Ltd
Coventry Precision Ltd
Delaney Gallay Ltd
Doncaster & Sons Ltd
Ductile Steel Ltd
Dunlop Rubber Company Ltd
Electro Hydraulics Ltd
English Steel Corporation Ltd

ENV Engineering Co. Ltd
Equipment and Engineering Co. Ltd
Fairman Precision Tools Ltd
Ferodo Ltd
Firth Derihon Ltd
Thos Firth and John Brown Ltd
Firth Vickers Stainless Steel Ltd
W. T. Flather and Co. Ltd
Garrington and Sons Ltd
N. Greening and Sons Ltd
Guest, Keen and Nettlefold Ltd
Hall and Pickles Ltd
Hardy Spicer and Co. Ltd
T. S. Harrison and Sons Ltd
Heenan and Froude Ltd
Hepworth and Grandage Ltd
Alfred Herbert Ltd
High Duty Alloys Ltd
Hoffmann Manufacturing Co. Ltd
Richard Klinger Ltd
Langley Alloys Ltd
Laycock Engineering Co. Ltd
Arthur Lee and Sons Ltd
F. H. Lloyd and Co. Ltd,
Lodge Plugs Ltd
Joseph Lucas Ltd
John Lund Ltd
Marston Excelsior Ltd
Midland Motor Cylinders Ltd

Motor Panels (Coventry) Ltd
Napier and Sons Ltd
National Standard Co. Ltd
Northern Aluminium Co. Ltd
F. Perkins Ltd
Plessey Co. Ltd
Power Flexible Tubing Co. Ltd
Pyrene Ltd
Rolls-Royce Ltd
Rubery Owen and Co. Ltd
Rylands and Brothers Ltd
Geo Salter and Co. Ltd
Skefco Ball Bearing Co. Ltd
Slack and Carr Ltd
Specialloid Ltd
Standard Motor Co. Ltd
Standard Valves Ltd
Super Oil Seals and Gaskets Ltd
Tecalemit Ltd
Richard Thomas, Baldwin and Co. Ltd
Tube Investments Ltd
Universal Steel Co. Ltd
Universal Grinding Wheel Co.
Vandervell Products Ltd
Vickers Armstrong Ltd
Vigzol Oil Co. Ltd
H. Wiggin and Co. Ltd
James Woodhead and Sons Ltd
Yorkshire Copper Works Ltd

Appendix 5

An Engineering Exercise

Some Notes on the BRM Formula 1 Grand Prix
Engine, an Original Project which has Exceeded All
Previous Standards of Brake Horsepower per Litre of
Swept Volume
By Laurence Pomeroy, FRSA, MSAE
(Reproduced from *The Motor* of 25 November 1953)

November 25, 1953   669   *THE MOTOR*

An ENGINEERING EXERCISE

Some Notes on the B.R.M. Formula I Grand Prix Engine, an Original Project which has Exceeded All Previous Standards of Brake Horsepower per Litre of Swept Volume

By LAURENCE POMEROY, F.R.S.A., M.S.A.E.

SINCE it was first described in The Motor of December 21, 1949, the B.R.M project has had a chequered, controversial and, be it admitted, a disappointing history. Designed to equal the performances achieved with pre-war 3-litre cars this 1½-litre Formula I model has failed to secure any success in the Grandes Epreuves organized under this formula which has now expired. Nevertheless, the car as a whole remains a most interesting technical project and the engine in particular stands out as a landmark in design for it develops more h.p. per litre than any orthodox engine yet built, and may well maintain this record into the future, for it is probable that Grand Prix engines to come will be either unsupercharged or built with some system of compounding or turbine final drive if supercharged.

We are therefore particularly grateful to Mr. Alfred Owen for providing permission to reproduce working general arrangement drawings of the B.R.M. power unit, coupled with a perspective broken-open drawing. We are also indebted to Messrs. Mays and Berthon for their co-operation in securing these drawings and for the provision of relevant technical information.

CONCEIVED in 1947, the general layout of the B.R.M. engine was based upon the following premises:

1. It would be impossible to construct, with modern tyre dimensions, a single-seater racing car with a frontal area of less than 9½ sq. ft.

2. To secure such a frontal area it was desirable to have an engine low in height, driving a propeller shaft below the wheel centres.

3. To secure the required maximum speed an output of at least 45 h.p./sq. ft. of frontal area would be needed, calling for an engine output in excess of 400 b.h.p.

4. On the basis of information existing in 1947 such an output would need at least 40 sq. in. of piston area and a boost pressure of not less than 30 lb./sq. in. or 3 ata.

Reference to the drawings will now show how these conditions were met. By the choice of 16 cylinders of approximately equal bore and stroke, a piston area of 47.8 sq. in. was achieved, coupled with an inlet valve area (based on overall diameter) of 20 sq. in., sufficient on previous practice to pass enough air at 3 ata. to give approximately 360 h.p.

By disposing of these cylinders in two banks of eight at an included angle of 135 deg. a very low engine was obtained, the maximum height above the base of the crankcase being only 11.8 in. By the adoption of central gearing upwards to the camshafts (as used since 1932 by Alfa Romeo) and also downwards to a sub main driving shaft connected to the clutch (as first used on the Ricardo-designed Alfa Romeo V.16 3-litre engine of 1939-40) the required low drive for the propeller shaft was provided, together with a normal clutch speed.

Finally, by employing a second subshaft to give a torsionally resilient drive to a two-stage centrifugal blower it was possible to guarantee supercharger pressures of 3 ata. upwards with a high level of adiabatic efficiency—a highly important factor where large mass air flows are concerned, as a 1% variation in blower efficiency can quite easily make a change of over 5% in engine output.

It can be seen from the perspective drawing that the two subshafts are carried in a single light alloy casting which also forms the (dry) sump of the engine. Seventeen bearings are housed in this section which number includes those supporting two transverse drives to the oil pressure and scavenge pumps and, on the same shafts, two water pumps which discharge through an external manifold to the lower (exhaust) side of two separate castings, each of which contain the water jackets for four opposed sets of cylinders and the apertures for the wet liners which form the cylinder bores.

Each pair of cylinder block castings also carries five main bearings to support one half of the two-piece crankshaft. Two roller bearings are provided on each side of the double spur wheels which drive down to the subshafts and up through a train of four intermediate gears to a central spur wheel driving the camshafts. The intermediate wheels are mounted upon a separate carrier which is located between the two cylinder blocks.

Steel connecting rods with a length of only 4.125 in. (stroke × 2.36) have split big ends carrying Vandervell thin-wall bearings, the crankshaft being fed through two full-flow filters at not less than 50 lb./sq. in. The light alloy pistons give a compression ratio of 6:1 and run in detachable cast iron liners which are quite deeply spigoted into the base of the block. At their top end they are recessed into the combustion chamber and sealed by pulling down the detachable head on to a flange. After the water has been delivered to the cored space in the lower side of the block it passes around the liner and through channels on both sides of the head, the off-take pipe being immediately above the inlet valves. There is thus no direct flow of high velocity water on to the exhaust valve seat, but the exhaust valve guide is finned and in direct contact with the coolant. The exhaust valve stem is hollow and uses sodium cooling to extract heat from the head.

THE B.R.M. ENGINE

Dimensions and Construction

Cylinders: V.16 at 135 deg. between banks.
Bore: 49.53 mm.   **Stroke:** 48.26 mm.
Cubic capacity: 1,488 c.c.   **Piston area:** 47.8 sq. in.
Valves: Two per cylinder, four overhead camshafts.
Compression ratio: 6:1.
Diameter of inlet valve: 1.25 in.
Diameter of exhaust valve: 1.1 in.
Total inlet valve area: 19.63 sq. in.
Total exhaust valve area: 15.2 sq. in.
Cylinder heads: Four light alloy detachable castings.
Included angle of valves: 90 deg.
Crankcase: Two light alloy castings vertically divided.
Sump: Single light alloy casting carrying auxiliary and final drives.
Crankshaft: Two-piece eight-throw running in 8 Vandervell thin-wall bearings and two roller bearings.
Connecting rods: Steel with split big ends carrying Vandervell thin-wall plain bearings.
Lubrication: Dry sump with oil fed at 50 lb./sq.in. through two full-flow filters.
Camshaft drive: Through centrally-mounted gears.
Main drive: Through subshaft driven from double gears in centre of crankshaft.
Supercharger drive: Through quill shaft driven by double gears from main drive.
Supercharger type: Two stage centrifugal.   **Supercharger pressure:** 5.7 ata.
Carburetters: Dual horizontal S.U.

Performance Factors

Maximum b.h.p.: 525.
Max r.p.m.: 10,500.
B.h.p./sq.in. piston area: 10.98 at 3,300 ft./min. piston speed.
B.m.e.p.: 434 lb./sq.in.
H.p./sq. in. of inlet valve area: 26.75.

(Text continued on page 672)

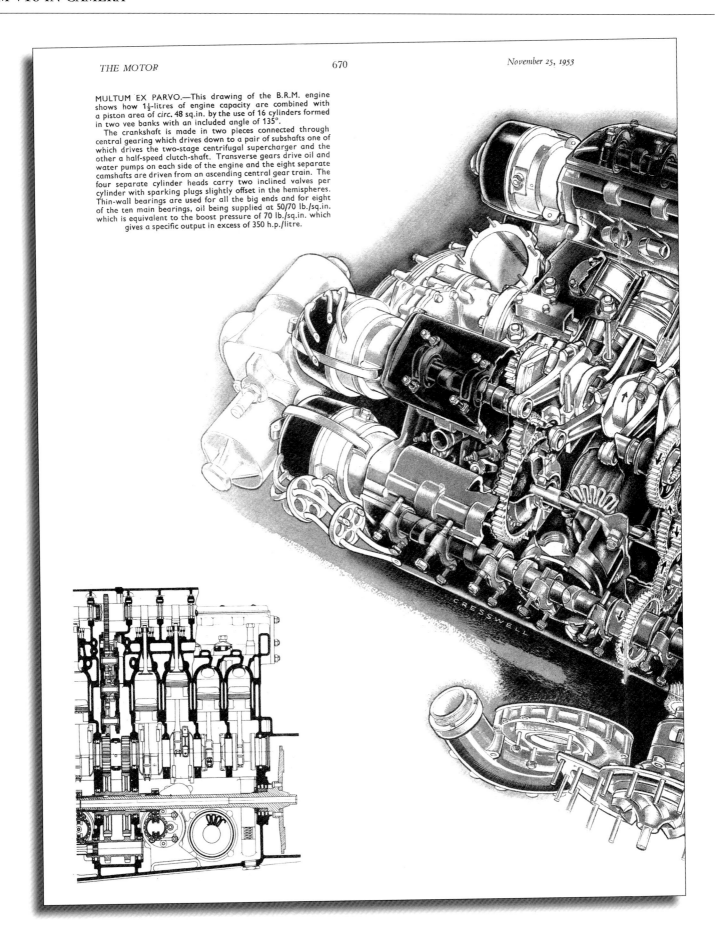

MULTUM EX PARVO.—This drawing of the B.R.M. engine shows how 1½-litres of engine capacity are combined with a piston area of *circ.* 48 sq.in. by the use of 16 cylinders formed in two vee banks with an included angle of 135°.

The crankshaft is made in two pieces connected through central gearing which drives down to a pair of subshafts one of which drives the two-stage centrifugal supercharger and the other a half-speed clutch-shaft. Transverse gears drive oil and water pumps on each side of the engine and the eight separate camshafts are driven from an ascending central gear train. The four separate cylinder heads carry two inclined valves per cylinder with sparking plugs slightly offset in the hemispheres. Thin-wall bearings are used for all the big ends and for eight of the ten main bearings, oil being supplied at 50/70 lb./sq.in. which is equivalent to the boost pressure of 70 lb./sq.in. which gives a specific output in excess of 350 h.p./litre.

An Engineering Exercise - - - - - - - **Contd.**

→ → MASS FLOW
⊶ ⊶ RESTRICTED FLOW
.° °° °° OIL MIST

THE MOTOR   672   *November 25, 1953*

An Engineering Exercise - - Contd.

The eight separate camshafts attack the valves through followers which have inset hardened faces and each valve is closed by a pair of hairpin valve springs.

In order to obtain maximum valve area the Lodge 14 mm. sparking plugs are offset in the hemispheres and are masked, communicating with the combustion chamber through passages of small diameter.

High-tension current is provided through Lucas coils and four Lucas distributors driven from the front end of each camshaft.

Fuel is supplied by mechanical pumps to a pair of specially developed S.U. carburetters, early experiments with fuel injection into the eye of the supercharger impeller having proved abortive.

A Record Boost

The speed of the supercharger rotors has been increased on a number of occasions since the first trials on the engine, and the blowers now provide mixture at a boost of 70 lb./sq./in., which corresponds with the maximum air flow which the carburetters are capable of passing. As is well known, centrifugal supercharger boost is inherently sensitive to speed variations, and the stated figure is attained at 10,500 r.p.m., at which speed some 525 b.h.p. can be relied upon, although on one engine a maximum of 585 b.h.p. has been realized. A normal "passing off" figure from the test-bed is 412 b.h.p. at 9,000 r.p.m. The performance factors are not as high as one might perhaps expect in relation to the absolute manifold pressure, and this underlines the difficulties of developing a multi-cylinder engine with very small individual components from the viewpoint of port shapes, combustion chamber lay-out, and so on. Moreover, although the design sprang logically from the original premises it resulted in an engine of considerable size, weight and complexity. The overall length of the power unit from the air entry to the blowers to the end of the clutch housing amounts to 36 in. or no less than 35% of the wheelbase. An equivalent length of frame cannot be cross-braced. It can also be seen that the building up of the unit from six sections divided in two planes leads to the need for highly accurate machining (always difficult to achieve when small numbers are being made) and exceedingly careful assembly.

This notwithstanding, the engine has proved generally reliable, although in the early stages of development some crankshaft balance weights became detached with disastrous results. The use of plain bearings has been fully justified despite the high rotational speeds and the somewhat extreme L/D ratio of 0.27 : 1. It is essential to keep the S.A.E. 30 oil exceptionally clean, and owing to the low crankcase area in relation to the power developed operating oil temperatures as high as 140° C. have to be faced.

Development Difficulties

For a long time the progress of the engine was delayed by cracked cylinder liners and after such theories as hydraulic lock due to incorrect fuel distribution, mechanical excitation, and wrongly timed sparking due to pick up between the electrical leads, had been investigated, and rejected, the cause was found to be a leak through the sealing joint between the liner and the head. This permitted water to enter the combustion chamber when the throttle was shut.

Another and more persistent trouble arising from part-throttle conditions has been seepage of oil into the blower past the driving shaft seals, this oil being then discharged into the engine when it carbonizes on the exhaust valve guides with resultant valve flutter and misfiring. It remains true, however, that the biggest disadvantage of the chosen lay-out has been the sharply rising torque curve arising from the blower characteristics. This has called for a high degree of driving skill, for not only does it impose an abnormally large number of gear changes, but the tendency to wheelspin increases as the r.p.m. rise, and this presents the driver with a particularly difficult problem if the road surface be loose, or worse still, wet.

Despite this, the car holds the record for race lap speeds on four circuits—Albi at 115.57 m.p.h.; Charterhall at 85.71 m.p.h.; Castle Combe at 89.77 m.p.h.; and Snetterton at 90.5 m.p.h. Only one car has bettered its speed on the present Goodwood and Silverstone circuits.

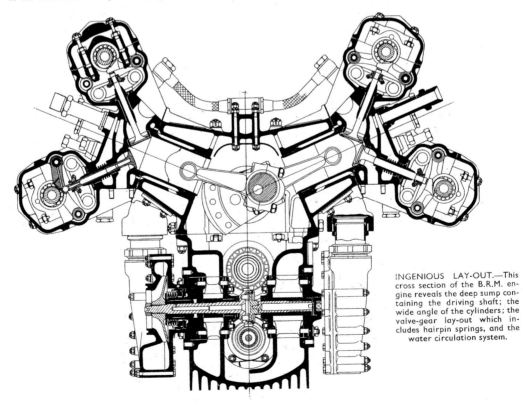

INGENIOUS LAY-OUT.—This cross section of the B.R.M. engine reveals the deep sump containing the driving shaft; the wide angle of the cylinders; the valve-gear lay-out which includes hairpin springs, and the water circulation system.

Appendix 6

Supercharging the 1½-Litre V16 BRM Racing Engine

By G. L. Wilde (Associate Member), Chief Designer (Projects), Aero Division, Rolls-Royce Limited) and F. J. Allen, Senior Research Engineer, Aero Division, Rolls-Royce Limited published in Volume 179 of the Proceedings

SUPERCHARGING THE 1½-LITRE V.16 BRM RACING ENGINE

By G. L. Wilde (*Associate Member*)* and F. J. Allen†

The BRM racing car project was initiated in 1945 by Messrs Automobile Developments Limited and supported by the British motor industry. The engine was a 1½ litre V.16 cylinder supercharged unit required to give 400 b.h.p. This paper gives an account of the work carried out by Rolls-Royce Limited in the design, building and development of the supercharger, and also deals with the problems of estimating the power output of the engine based on a method for calculating the charge consumption. The problems encountered in the development of the power unit are discussed, and the experience gained may be of some interest to others who may be considering a supercharged engine for the new racing Formula in 1966.

INTRODUCTION

THE RECENT BOOK *BRM* by Raymond Mays (**1**)‡ covering the history of his racing car project has revived a certain amount of technical interest in the original 1½ litre V.16 supercharged engine. It will be recalled that the first BRM cars suffered from a number of difficult development problems. Some of these were associated with the power unit which in its day was of very advanced design and performance standard. The authors have been approached to give an account of certain aspects of the work.

The original BRM racing car and engine were designed by the firm of Automobile Developments Limited, Bourne, Lincs. during 1945–46, and the motor industry gave substantial support to the project. The contribution by Rolls-Royce Limited was to undertake the design, building and development of the supercharger. Mr E. W. Hives, C.H., M.B.E., Managing Director (later Lord Hives), and Mr A. G. Elliot, C.B.E., Chief Engineer, gave their full support to the project, and the work was assigned to the Compressor Section, Experimental Department, which was responsible for the aerodynamic design and performance development of the aero superchargers and gas turbine compressors. The authors and others in the firm were soon caught up in the enthusiasm of the racing car world, so much so that it was necessary from time to time to remind ourselves that the development of the aero compressors was still our main job! In due course, and

particularly when engine testing began, the BRM project and its supercharger became for the authors an exciting week-end sport from which we derived much enjoyment after spending the week on the more sober and exact problems involved in aero engines.

This paper describes the basis of the design and some of the problems encountered during the development of the V.16 BRM engine with particular reference to the supercharger.

Notation

b.h.p.   Engine brake horsepower.
s/c hp   Supercharger horsepower.
d Cylinder bore, in.
f.h.p.   Engine friction horsepower.
G Gas constant.
H Heat liberated per unit mass charge, chu/lb.
i.h.p.   Indicated horsepower.
J Joule's equivalent of heat, ft lbf/chu.
N Engine crank speed, rev/min.
P_c Boost pressure total, lbf/in² abs.
P_e Exhaust back pressure, lbf/in² abs.
r Cylinder volume ratio.
s Cylinder clearance volume, in³ or absolute units.
S Engine swept volume, litres.
s.h.p.   Crankshaft horsepower.
T_c Cylinder charge temperature, °K or °C abs.
T_{ct} Induction pipe temperature, °K or °C abs.
T_e Exhaust temperature, °K or °C abs.
T_z Cylinder temperature at end of suction stroke, °K or °C abs.
T_1 Air intake temperature to supercharger, °K or °C abs.

The M.S. of this paper was received at the Institution on 31st January 1964. A report of the meeting at which this paper was presented is on p. 72.
* Chief Designer (Projects), Aero Division, Rolls-Royce Limited.
† Senior Research Engineer, Aero Division, Rolls-Royce Limited.
‡ References are given in the Appendix.

Proc Instn Mech Engrs 1964–65

Vol 179 Pt 2A No 1

U_1 First stage+impellor tip speed, ft/sec.
U_2 Second stage impellor tip speed, ft/sec.
U_e Equivalent single stage impellor tip speed, ft/sec.
V Mean piston speed, ft/sec.
W_c Charge flow, lb/min.
η_t Indicated thermal efficiency.
η_m Engine mechanical efficiency.
η_g Supercharger gearing efficiency.
$\varDelta T$ Supercharger temperature rise, °C.

ORIGIN OF THE PROJECT

During the years before the war British racing cars in the Grand Prix category had been completely outclassed by foreign competition, notably by the German Mercedes and Auto Union racing cars which achieved remarkable standards of performance. This situation was recognized in this country and regretted by racing enthusiasts, many engineers and a large proportion of the motoring public, who believed that this was an adverse reflection on our technical competence in the design of automobiles. Racing has been a source of technical development in the progress of the automobile, although the authors appreciate that this is a controversial subject and that there are examples of racing car design having progressed from developments in the passenger car.

After the war when Grand Prix racing was resumed it appeared that this situation would repeat itself, but with the Italian Maserati and Ferrari racing teams gaining supremacy. As far back as 1945 Mr Raymond Mays foresaw this probability, and realizing that Government support would not be forthcoming, decided to launch an enterprise calling for the support of the British motor industry as a whole to share in the project of designing, building and developing a racing car of Grand Prix class. The firm of Automobile Developments Limited was formed to promote the project, and the design of a racing car was started under the engineering direction of Mr Peter Berthon. The general direction of the enterprise, which included seeking support for the project by the many firms in the industry, was carried out by Mr Mays with great enthusiasm, drive and persuasion. In 1950 the late Mr Tresilian joined A.D. Limited, as engineering consultant.

Rolls-Royce were approached in the autumn of 1945, when a meeting took place between Mr Mays and Mr Elliot. The Grand Prix Formula I at that time called for engines of either 4½ litre unsupercharged or 1½ litre supercharged. A.D. Limited had decided to base their car on the latter, and asked Rolls-Royce to design and build a supercharger which would enable a 1½ litre engine to develop 400 hp. No doubt this approach to Rolls-Royce was influenced by the known advances that had been made in Merlin aero engine power output by single and two stage centrifugal supercharging during the war years, and implied the choice of a centrifugal supercharger for the proposed racing engine which was a V.16 cylinder 1½ litre unit with a bore of 1·95 in and stroke of 1·90 in designed to run at a maximum speed of 14 000 rev/min.

The authors had worked for a number of years on the supercharging of aero engines. They were well aware that the problem of supercharging a racing car engine requiring high power over a range of engine speeds is a different problem from supercharging an aero engine which requires ground level boost pressures to be maintained to high altitudes, but over a restricted engine speed range.

There were three main problems. Firstly there was the problem of predicting the power output of a small highly supercharged engine. Secondly, an investigation was required to compare the power developed with different types of supercharger. Finally, if the centrifugal supercharger was estimated to develop the required engine power, there was the problem of designing a small high performance centrifugal unit of considerably smaller dimensions and running at much higher speeds and duties than had been attempted before.

THE V.16 BRM ENGINE AND THE ESTIMATION OF POWER OUTPUT

BRM Engine details

The Grand Prix Formula was based on engine capacity or cylinder swept volume. Since for geometrically similar cylinders operating at the same mean gas pressure and stresses the power varies as the square of the linear dimensions, for a specified total swept volume the power output is proportional to the cube root of the number of cylinders. Thus by using a large number of small cylinders, A.D. Limited were exploiting this principle and were also aiming to achieve the high volumetric efficiency said to be associated with short stroke engines. However, these considerations lead to very high rotational speeds, high acceleration and inertial forces, and high valve frequencies. The last proved a difficult mechanical problem in the development of the engine. Design details of the engine were as follows:

Number of cylinders in 135°V	.	16
Bore (hemispherical head with 1 sparking plug)	. .	1·95 in
Total piston area	. .	47·8 in²
Stroke	. . .	1·90 in
Capacity	. . .	1490 cm³
Crank speed (maximum)	. .	14 000 rev/min
Mean piston speed (design)	.	4432 ft/min
Cylinder compression ratio	.	7·8:1

Valves 1 inlet, 1 exhaust (sodium cooled). Twin overhead camshaft, hairpin springs.
Valve timing. Inlet opens 21° BTDC
                    Inlet closes 76° ABDC
                    Exhaust opens 55° BBDC
                    Exhaust closes 24° ATDC

Port areas. Inlet	. .	0·88 in²
Exhaust .	.	0·6125 in²
Power required	. .	400 b.h.p. at 10 000 rev/min
b.h.p./piston area (in²)	.	8·36

Fuel:
   Initially 80% Methanol, 10% Benzol, 10% Alcolate Iso-pentane.
   Later: 70% Methanol, 20% Benzol, 10% Alcolate Iso-pentane.

The eight throw crankshaft was in two parts coupled at the centre from where a spur gear step down drive (27/52) was taken to the clutch and five speed gearbox at the rear of the engine. A torsionally flexible driving shaft running at 27/21 times crankshaft speed extended forward to drive the supercharger at the front of the engine through a step up spur gear train giving an overall ratio of 3·25:1. This was later increased to 4:1 relative to the crankshaft.

In this paper the authors are not intending to give a complete description of the engine, as this can be found in Mr May's book and elsewhere (I) (2), but a general arrangement cutaway drawing of the engine and supercharger is shown in Fig. 1, and photographs of the engine and super-charger are shown in Figs 2 and 3.

Estimation of power output

The methods of estimating piston engine power output were not too well developed at the beginning of the last war, and this applied especially to supercharged engines. It became an urgent matter to devise a method for estimating the power output of aero engines which were required to operate at very high altitudes, and in the course of development of the Merlin engine and its centrifugal supercharger during the period 1939 to 1941 an improved method of estimation was worked out. Under the direction of Dr S. G. Hooker, C.B.E., who was then Assistant Chief Experimental Engineer, Aero Division, a small team, which the authors were privileged to join, conducted a comprehensive series of tests on the Merlin engine in which engine power and air flow were measured when tested over a wide range of speed, boost pressure and temperature, and exhaust back pressure. The friction and pumping losses were also deduced from these and other tests. However, a detailed description of this work is beyond the scope of this paper.

In parallel with these engine tests, a series of super-charger tests were conducted over a substantial range of inlet pressure, temperature and rotational speed to enable a system of dimensional analysis to be established. This included an empirical correction for the effect of fuel evaporation at entry to the supercharger. The BRM engine was originally intended to have a petrol injection pump spraying fuel into the intake of the supercharger, but this unit was never developed and choke type carburettors were substituted. These caused a loss of pressure at the intake and a significant loss of power at high engine speed.

The first objective was to devise a formula for calculating the air consumption of the engine, or rather the 'charge' of fuel/air mixture consumption. This is discussed in the next section.

Estimation of the charge consumption of a 4 stroke engine

The most important factor in governing the power output is the charge consumption, for with a constant air/fuel

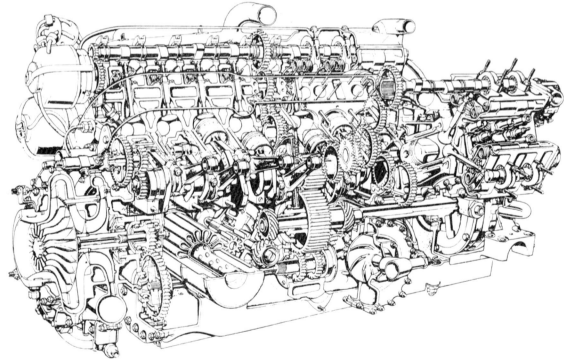

Fig. 1. Cutaway perspective drawing of BRM engine

G. L. WILDE AND F. J. ALLEN

Fig. 2. The BRM engine

ratio this is a direct measure of the heat energy supplied to the engine. If the charge consumption can be calculated, and if the thermal efficiency of similar engines has been deduced from bench tests, we shall be able to calculate the crankshaft horsepower (s.h.p.) from which the mechanical losses and supercharger power are subtracted to give the useful brake horsepower (b.h.p.).

The charge consumption depends upon the following variables:

(1) The engine rotational speed N,
(2) the induction pipe temperature T_{ci} °K abs.,
(3) the boost pressure P_c abs., and
(4) the back pressure P_e abs.

The first step is to consider the effect of these various factors on charge consumption, and we will now consider a single cylinder unit and confine our attention to the exhaust and suction strokes. Reference should be made to Fig. 4; the following assumptions are made:

(*a*) The pressure of the residual exhaust gases in the clearance space above the piston at the end of the exhaust stroke is equal to the back pressure P_e in the exhaust ports.

(*b*) The pressure of the charge mixed with the residual exhaust gases at the bottom of the suction stroke is equal to the boost pressure P_c in the inlet manifold.

These assumptions are tantamount to assuming that no throttling takes place at the valves, and the tests carried out on the supercharged Merlin aero engine, which included light spring indicator diagrams, supported this assumption up to the normal maximum mean piston speeds of 3000 ft/min.

Starting with the conditions at the beginning of the suction stroke, the weight of the residual exhaust gas remaining in the cylinder is:

$$\frac{P_e s}{G T_e}$$

where s is the clearance volume, G is the gas constant, and T_e the exhaust temperature (absolute units).

Similarly, the weight of gas in the cylinder at the end of the suction stroke is:

$$\frac{s}{G} \frac{(r P_c)}{T_z}$$

where r is the cylinder volume ratio (usually called the compression ratio) and T_z is the final temperature of the mixture of exhaust gas and fresh charge (°C abs.). It follows that the weight of fresh charge inhaled on the suction stroke is the difference of the above quantities, viz.:

$$\frac{s}{G} \left(\frac{r P_c}{T_z} - \frac{P_e}{T_e} \right) \quad . \quad . \quad . \quad . \quad (1)$$

Fig. 3. The BRM engine—side view

Assuming the specific heats of the charge and exhaust gases to be equal we have:

Heat lost by gas = heat gained by charge

$$\frac{P_e s}{G T_e}(T_e - T_z) = \frac{s}{G}\left(\frac{rP_c}{T_z} - \frac{P_e}{T_e}\right)\times(T_z - T_c) \quad (2)$$

We can now eliminate T_z from equations (1) and (2) leaving the following equation for the weight of charge inhaled per cycle:

$$W_c = \frac{rs}{GT_c}\left(P_c - \frac{1}{r}P_e\right) \quad . \quad . \quad . \quad (3)$$

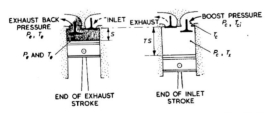

Fig. 4. Estimation of charge flow with assumed cylinder conditions

Proc Instn Mech Engrs 1964–65

In this expression T_c is the temperature of the charge as it enters the cylinder, and this is not necessarily the same as the temperature of the charge leaving the supercharger since heat is picked up from the hot metal surfaces of the inlet ports and valves.

For a four-stroke engine of capacity S litres, operating at N rev/min, the charge consumption per minute is:

$$W_c = \frac{1}{37\cdot 8}\frac{r}{r-1}\frac{NS}{T_c}\left(P_c - \frac{1}{r}P_e\right)\text{ lb/min} \quad . \quad (4)$$

where the pressures are measured in lbf/in² abs.

In this equation all the quantities can readily be measured on an engine test with the exception of the cylinder charge temperature T_c.

Analysis of the Merlin engine tests already referred to in which all the above quantities were measured, including the induction pipe temperature T_{ci}, enabled an empirical formula to be derived for the value of cylinder charge temperature T_c as follows:

$$T_c = T_{ci} + \tfrac{1}{4}(440 - T_{ci}) \quad . \quad . \quad . \quad (5)$$

This was based on a correlation of charge temperature rise $(T_c - T_{ci})$ against induction pipe temperature T_{ci}

Vol 179 Pt 2A No 1

50   G. L. WILDE AND F. J. ALLEN

covering a wide range of values of T_{ci} from 260° to 400°C abs.

The value of T_{ci} can be calculated from the known supercharger tip speed, the ambient temperature and the temperature drop caused by the latent heat of evaporation of fuel. The last is about 28 degC for high grade aero fuel, but for alcohol fuels used in racing car engines the temperature drop may be as high as 120 degC, and this was one of the unknown factors when estimating the charge consumption and power output of the BRM engine and the performance of the supercharger.

Evaluation of engine power output from the charge consumption

It is convenient to consider the conversion of the heat energy of the fuel into useful work at the gearbox input shaft in three separate stages.

Let the heat evolved by the combustion of one pound of charge be H c.h.u. Then the total heat supplied to the engine per minute is $H \times W_c$ c.h.u's, and the three separate stages can be considered as follows:

(1) Of this total heat supplied only a fraction appears as work done on the piston, or indicated horsepower (i.h.p.), viz.:

$$\text{i.h.p.} = \frac{HW_cJ}{33\,000} \times \eta_t \quad . \quad . \quad . \quad (6)$$

where η_t = the thermal efficiency

(2) Of the total i.h.p. only a fraction appears as useful horsepower at the crankshaft (s.h.p.)

$$\text{s.h.p.} = \text{i.h.p.} \times \eta_m \quad . \quad . \quad (7)$$

where η_m = the mechanical efficiency.

(3) From the total shaft horsepower, the power absorbed in driving the supercharger must be subtracted in order to obtain the b.h.p. available at the gearbox input. Thus we have:

$$\text{b.h.p.} = \text{s.h.p.} - \text{s/c hp} \quad . \quad . \quad (8)$$

Now the power required to drive the supercharger can easily be shown to be

$$\text{s/c hp} = \frac{W_c \Delta T}{100\eta_g}$$

$$= \frac{W_c \Delta T}{95} \quad . \quad . \quad . \quad (9)$$

where ΔT is the supercharger temperature rise in degC, and η_g the gearing efficiency assumed to be 95 per cent for the three tooth conversions in the BRM supercharger drive.

Hence we have

$$\text{b.h.p.} = W_c \frac{HJ}{33\,000} \eta_m \eta_t - W_c \frac{\Delta T}{95} \quad . \quad (10)$$

In this expression both the thermal efficiency η_t and the mechanical efficiency η_m are unknown quantities the absolute values of which it is difficult to determine. However, the product of these two quantities can be determined from experimental results on a given engine.

For example, equation (8) can be written in the form

$$\frac{\text{s.h.p.}}{W_c} = \frac{\text{b.h.p.}}{W_c} + \frac{\Delta T}{95} \quad . \quad . \quad (11)$$

The charge consumption for a given b.h.p. can be measured on the test bed, and with any given supercharger and driving gear ratio the value of ΔT is known, so that the s.h.p. developed per pound of charge can be obtained from the above equation. In fact it was found on the Merlin engine tests that the s.h.p./W_c was independent of the supercharger gear ratio, and hence independent of the supercharger temperature rise. This implies that both the thermal efficiency and mechanical efficiency are sensibly independent of charge temperature.

Following on from this it was possible to plot curves of s.h.p./W_c against charge flow W_c per unit piston area for different engine speeds or piston speeds. The results are shown in Fig. 5.

Later, tests in which the engine friction horsepower (f.h.p.) was measured by motoring a Merlin engine with piston crowns and supercharger impellor vanes removed gave the result that f.h.p. $\propto N^2$. From this and the data of Fig. 5 an empirical formula was deduced, viz.:

$$\text{s.h.p.} = 10W_c - \text{f.h.p.} \quad . \quad . \quad (12)$$

where f.h.p. $= 110(N/3000)^2$ for Merlin engines (bore 5·4 in, stroke 6 in, capacity 27 litres), and

$$\text{s.h.p.} = \text{b.h.p.} + \text{s/c hp} \quad . \quad . \quad (13)$$

This was reduced to a generalized form for the b.h.p., viz.:

$$\text{b.h.p.} = 10W_c - \frac{0·84}{10^6} d^2 V^2 - \frac{W_c \Delta T}{95} \quad (14)$$

Calculation of V.16 BRM engine power

These methods of calculating charge flow, boost pressure and b.h.p. were used in order to define the required supercharger capacity and pressure ratio needed to produce the 400 b.h.p. required at 10 000 crank rev/min. The authors would not like it to be thought that the analysis presented on pages 47–50 represented the whole of the analysis

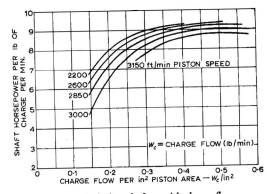

Fig. 5. Variation of s.h.p. with charge flow

work carried out at Rolls-Royce on aero engine performance. In fact, Merlin engine performance analysis was extended considerably during 1942–43 to determine the cylinder breathing capacity at higher than normal piston speeds, and to deduce the inlet and exhaust stroke pumping losses caused by the cylinder charge pressure being lower than boost pressure, and the cylinder exhaust pressure being higher than exhaust port pressure. At piston speeds above 3000 ft/min the assumptions (a) and (b) made on page 48 are no longer valid, and aero engine tests indicated a marked falling off in the rate of increase in charge flow with engine speed.

It will be appreciated that the methods established for estimating the charge flow and power output of a large 27 litre V.12 engine like the Merlin might be found in error when applied to a very much smaller engine like the 1½ litre V.16 BRM, and the following factors were considered by the authors to be possible sources of discrepancy:

(1) Thermal efficiency lower due to the larger surface/volume ratio of the BRM cylinder. This is a scale effect.

(2) Friction hp greater than proportional to N^2 at the higher piston speeds owing to relatively larger crankshaft main bearings and crank pin diameters of the BRM.

(3) Higher volumetric efficiency expected for the BRM cylinder due to the hemispherical head and large valve areas (two valves) compared with the flat head and four valves of the Merlin. The high valve and piston frequencies corresponding to the extremely high crank speeds of the BRM might invalidate the estimation of charge flow by the methods described.

(4) The use of alcohol fuel of low calorific values (about 5000 c.h.u's/lb) and very high latent heat of evaporation (278 c.h.u's/lb) should produce a temperature drop of the air passing through the supercharger of approximately 120 degC, which is roughly four times that with high octane aviation fuel.

(5) The efficiency of a small centrifugal supercharger could be expected to be lower than the much larger aero superchargers owing to the relatively higher boundary layer thicknesses and owing to the limitations of vane thickness and clearances determined by practical manufacturing considerations. The performance with such large fuel evaporation characteristics was also unknown.

After a good deal of thought the following assumptions were made:

The heat losses from the cylinder due to the higher surface volume ratio would be compensated for by the higher compression ratio of 7·8 of the BRM compared with 6 of the aero engines investigated.

The friction hp was assumed to be the same as that of the large aero engines after correcting for piston area at the same mean piston speed.

The higher volumetric efficiency expected from in-

creased valve areas relative to piston area was disregarded in view of the high piston frequencies.

The large temperature drop owing to the evaporation of alcohol fuel was assumed to take place as follows: ⅓ before the first stage of the supercharger, ⅓ between the two stages, and ⅓ in the induction pipe and cylinder port. At this point it is worth mentioning that we had originally assumed that high octane leaded fuel would be used which would give a much lower temperature drop (about 28 degC), and at the high boost pressures required to produce 400 b.h.p. at 10 000 rev/min an after cooler would have been necessary to reduce the charge temperature to prevent catastrophic detonation. The high evaporation of alcohol fuel achieves the same effect as an after cooler in this respect.

In order to check the accuracy of the charge flow formula on smaller engines Mr R. Kauffmann, Head of the Experimental Department of the F.N. Company, Liège, Belgium, generously undertook to conduct a series of tests on a 4·275 litre petrol engine, and on a 5·4 litre diesel engine. These tests were useful in giving us additional confidence in applying the methods to smaller engines.

A loss of power was allowed to cover inlet and exhaust pumping, the details of which are beyond the scope of this paper. However, the magnitude of the loss was roughly equal to the friction hp referred to on page 50 at the higher speeds.

Variation of power with boost pressure

Making these assumptions, and using the methods outlined, the first step was to calculate the variation of b.h.p. with boost pressure and to examine the effect of supercharger efficiency on power output. To obtain 400 b.h.p. at 10 000 rev/min requires the engine to operate at about 420 i.m.e.p. and a boost pressure of 34·5 lbf/in² (abs.) assuming that the supercharger would have an isentropic efficiency of 75 per cent. A Rootes type supercharger operating at this pressure ratio of 2·45 would be expected to have an efficiency of the order of 50 per cent, although a two stage Rootes would be higher. These estimations are summarized in Fig. 6 and assume no loss of pressure in the supercharger intake which is justified in the case of fuel injection. Also with alcohol fuel there is an overall reduction in charge temperature of 120 degC of which 40 degC is assumed to occur before the charge enters the supercharger.

Variation of power with engine speed

Assuming that the pressure rise ratio $(R-1)$ is proportional to $N^{2\cdot8}$ the full throttle engine power was calculated for a range of speeds up to 10 000 rev/min. This data is given in Table 1 and Fig. 7.

If the supercharger is geared to give a boost pressure of 34·5 lbf/in² abs. at 10 000 rev/min, 400 b.h.p. is developed. At 7000 rev/min the boost pressure is 22 lbf/in² abs. at which the power has fallen to 220 b.h.p. Above 10 000 rev/min the boost pressure would rise rapidly to 65·5 lbf/in²

G. L. WILDE AND F. J. ALLEN

abs. at 14 000 rev/min, and this would lead to an impossibly high cylinder i.m.e.p.

We therefore proposed that the boost pressure should be automatically regulated above 10 000 rev/min by introducing a special method of throttling the supercharger, which may be called vortex throttling. With this system an array of vanes is designed into the supercharger intake which can be moved to vary the swirl into the impellor. Below 10 000 rev/min these vanes are set in the axial position causing negligible pressure loss. Above 10 000

rev/min the vanes are progressively moved to swirl the incoming air/fuel mixture in the same direction of rotation as the impellors. This reduces the change of angular momentum through the impellors, and hence the temperature rise and pressure ratio, while still maintaining a good compression efficiency. The effect achieved is that of a variable gear over a limited range of ratio. Ahead of these variable swirl vanes there is a normal butterfly throttle under the control of the driver, which he uses in the normal manner, and which is overriding. The swirl vanes may be controlled by a servo piston regulated automatically by boost pressure or engine speed. This system was designed into the BRM supercharger from the start, but was never actually used in a race owing to the priorities of

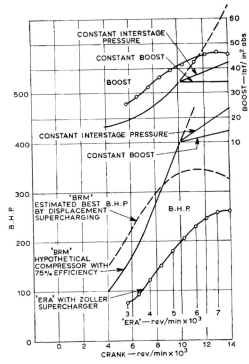

Fig. 6. *Engine estimates—variations of power with boost pressure and supercharger efficiency*

Fig. 7. *Engine estimates—variation of power with engine speed*

Table 1. Derivation of Fig. 7

Crank rev/min	Piston speed, ft/min	Press ratio	Boost, P_e	T_{ci}	T_c	W_c	i.h.p.	i.m.e.p.	$f+p$* hp	s/c hp	b.h.p.
7 000	2215	1·497	22·0	208·3	266·5	23·92	239·2	298·0	7·8	10·4	221·0
8 000	2532	1·721	25·3	223·4	277·7	30·58	305·8	333·0	10·8	17·3	277·7
9 000	2850	2·002	29·42	240·4	290·3	38·70	387·0	374·3	19·5	28·6	338·9
10 000	3167	2·350	34·5	259·0	304·2	48·70	487·0	424·0	37·0	45·3	404·7

* $f+p$ = friction+pumping.

other development problems. The same applied to the fuel injection system which was designed to deliver fuel into the supercharger intake. The injection carburettor was replaced by S.U. variable choke type carburettors which introduced a pressure drop in the intake of approximately 1 lbf/in² and consequent loss of boost pressure amounting to 2½–3 lbf/in² at 10 000 rev/min.

With a two stage centrifugal supercharger we can decide either to regulate the boost pressure to be constant, or some intermediate supercharger pressure such as interstage pressure to be constant. Fig. 7 gives the estimated power above 10 000 rev/min on the basis of constant interstage pressure, and hence the boost pressure is shown to rise steadily from 34·5 lbf/in² abs. at 10 000 rev/min to 43 lbf/in² abs. at 14 000 rev/min. The power curve therefore rises steeply up to 10 000 rev/min, and then has a much flatter slope from 10 000 to 14 000 rev/min. This slope, and the speed at which it cuts in, may be regulated to match the mechanical capabilities of the engine by selecting any other intermediate supercharger pressure tapping to be kept constant through variable swirl control.

We considered that the useful speed range of the engine in the car would be from approximately 7000 rev/min to 14 000 rev/min over which the b.h.p. varies from 220 to 470 (Fig. 7), and the driver would make full use of his five speed gearbox, which is accepted racing practice. It did not seem possible to achieve this high engine power/speed relationship by any other method, and these recommendations were accepted for the project.

For comparison the authors show an estimated power curve for the BRM engine supercharged with a displacement type supercharger, and also a power curve taken from an early test of a 1½ litre ERA racing engine. These show that higher relative powers and torques can be obtained at the lower engine speeds, but that boost pressures are not maintained constant at the low speeds. We understand this is partly due to internal leakage losses between the casing and vane system (which deteriorates with wear) of these types of supercharger. Engine valve overlap may also be a contributing factor.

Choice of supercharger gear ratio

In order to give a margin of power over the 400 b.h.p required at 10 000 rev/min, the authors proposed designing for a higher boost pressure than the 34·5 lbf/in² abs. referred to on page 51. Instead, a boost pressure of

41 lbf/in² abs. was chosen corresponding to a full throttle supercharger pressure ratio of 2·8. It was estimated that this could be obtained from the two-stage supercharger with alcohol fuel running at 32 500 rev/min requiring a driving gear ratio of 3·25 relative to the crankshaft. The estimated power curve is shown in Table 2 and Fig. 8 for standard barometric pressure and temperature.

At 10 000 rev/min the boost pressure is 41 lbf/in² abs. and the b.h.p. is 450. This power curve was based on estimated supercharger characteristics, and the resulting boost pressures were very nearly achieved on the engine, as will be seen later. It should be noted that the estimated i.m.e.p. is nearly 500 lbf/in² abs. at 10 000 rev/min.

During early engine testing it became apparent that the maximum engine speed of 14 000 rev/min would have to be reduced to below 11 000 rev/min, although this was raised later to 12 000 rev/min. The main reason for this

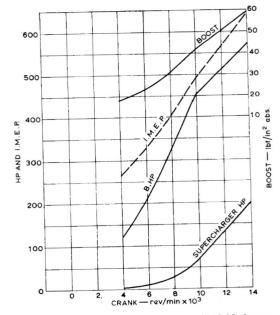

Fig. 8. Original estimated performance with 3·25 : 1 supercharger gear

Table 2. Derivation of Fig. 8, 3·25 : 1 supercharger drive ratio

Crank rev/min	Piston speed, ft/min	Press ratio	Boost, P_c	T_{ct}	T_c	W_c	i.h.p.	i.m.e.p.	$f+p$ hp	s/c hp	b.h.p.
5 000	1583	1·410	20·7	189·5	252·0	16·95	169·5	295·5	1·5	5·0	163·0
7 500	2373	1·945	28·6	221·0	276·0	32·85	328·5	382·5	8·25	22·0	298·0
10 000	3167	2·823	41·5	279·0	319·0	56·3	563·0	490·0	43·5	69·0	450·0
12 000*	3800	3·490	50·0	302·0	336·0	77·85	778·5	565·5	125·0	140·0	513·5

* Vortex controlled.

54   G. L. WILDE AND F. J. ALLEN

was the inability of the valve gear to operate satisfactorily in the range 11 000–14 000 rev/min, and because valve bounce and rapid wear of cams and rocker mechanism occurred. The engine suffered from irregular and violent backfires at high speeds, and it is a remarkable fact that these did not wreck the supercharger. The induction pipe blow off valve may have saved this.

The restriction of maximum engine speed to 12 000 rev/min, at which the mean piston speed is only 3800 ft/min, was a serious limitation to power output. As there seemed little prospect of developing the valve gear to operate at the original speed within the time available it became necessary to consider raising the boost pressure by increasing the supercharger gear ratio to 4·0:1. This is discussed in the next section.

Engine bench tests

The first bench tests of the engine were made in June 1949 at the headquarters of A.D. Limited in Bourne. A new test bed had been built specially for the new engine. This was well equipped. The authors participated in some of these tests using air flow measuring equipment from Derby. There was great excitement, as can be expected, and the authors in particular were concerned about the estimates of power output, and the breathing capacity of the engine. We were also anxious about the ability of the dynamometer to absorb the power, and in particular its stability because of the steepness of the slope of the power curve.

Initial testing proved difficult because of the unsteady running of the engine. In addition to the backfires at high speeds the engine was at first uncontrollable on the brake, with engine speed at full throttle either soaring or fading from a given setting. The maldistribution of fuel to the cylinders was partly responsible, aggravated by the high alcohol content and incomplete evaporation of all fractions of the fuel before reaching the cylinders. The problem had been met many years before at Rolls-Royce with methanol fuel on the 37 litre V.12 R engine developed for the Schneider Trophy. At the higher speeds it was suspected that ignition of the plugs was occurring on the wrong cylinder due to static induction and leakage paths in the high tension distributor, and a proposal to earth HT points on either side of the 'live' plug was considered. Gas leakage at the joint between the cylinder liner and cylinder head was suspected as being a cause of engine roughness and power fade at full throttle on the bench.

Progress was made in tracing and overcoming these troubles, and in parallel with this work an engine was prepared for installing in the car. A.D. Limited were in the unenviable position of having to develop a very ambitious project under pressure from the public, press and motor industry to get a car into a race, and this situation was to hamper the methodical development of the car and power unit throughout its life.

In February 1950 a power curve reaching 395 b.h.p. at 10 000 rev/min was obtained, with the 3·25 supercharger

gear, but subsequent testing with a larger capacity dynamometer, twin S.U. variable choke carburettors replacing the fuel injection pump, and some degree of induction pipe heating to improve distribution gave much lower powers. These are shown in Fig. 9, and were much lower than expected.

Meanwhile, the authors reconsidered the assumptions on which these estimates were based, and recalculated the powers with the following modified assumptions:

(1) Increasing the engine friction and pumping hp by 50 per cent supported by one engine test in which heat to oil was assessed.

(2) A reduction in the i.h.p. per pound of charge flow from 10 to 9·4 which was a correction for the high proportion of low calorific value alcohol fuel in the mixture.

(3) Actual supercharger characteristics measured on the rig at Derby.

The effect of these new assumptions reduced the estimated power at 10 000 rev/min from 450 b.h.p. (Fig. 8) to 375 b.h.p. (Fig. 9), but the measured power was only 295 b.h.p. This was obtained with twin S.U. carburettors producing a pressure drop in the supercharger intake of

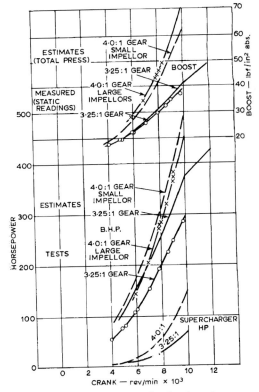

Fig. 9. BRM engine—actual and estimated powers

about 0·85 lbf/in². Without this loss the boost pressure would have increased from 39·0 to 40·5 lbf/in² abs., compared with the estimated figure of 41 lbf/in² abs., and the power would have increased to 305 b.h.p. This is still 70 b.h.p. lower than the revised estimate which the authors had considered pessimistic. This discrepancy was never satisfactorily explained, but we believed from the analysis of the measured air and fuel flows that these were at least 12 per cent lower than expected suggesting a deficiency in breathing capacity.

Effect of increasing the supercharger gear ratio

The effect of increasing the gear ratio to 4·0:1 on the estimated power with revised assumptions is shown in Fig. 9. At 10 000 rev/min the power increases to 495 b.h.p. and the boost to 61 lb/in² abs. Although it will be seen that the increase in power is 120 b.h.p., the supercharger power itself has increased by as much as 75 hp, and it is clearly becoming uneconomic to increase the supercharger speed much further.

For the reasons explained on page 54 the supercharger gear ratio on the actual engine was increased from 3·25 to 4·0:1. When this was done the supercharger was also modified in two respects. Firstly, the discharge flow capacity was reduced to match the engine better at lower speeds, and secondly, the first stage impellor was increased in diameter from 6·0 to 6·50 in. This was done to improve the flow matching between the two stages at the higher rotational speeds and pressure ratio with the 4·0:1 gears.

The measured engine power and boost (corrected to standard atmosphere conditions) with the 4·0:1 gear and the other supercharger modifications mentioned are shown in Fig. 9. The power at 9 000 rev/min has increased by 115 b.h.p. to 360 b.h.p., which is greater than the increase in power estimated to be due to the higher gear ratio alone. Extrapolating to 10 000 rev/min suggests that approximately 450 b.h.p. would have been obtained with a boost pressure of 69 lbf/in² abs.

If twin S.U. carburettors had been replaced by fuel injection into the supercharger intake, thus eliminating the intake pressure loss of about 1 lbf/in² on these tests, the boost pressure would have been 74 lb/in² abs. at 10 000 rev/min. A figure of over 70 lb/in² abs. was observed in the car under racing conditions. At these high boost pressures and speeds, maximum engine powers in the region of 500 b.h.p. should have been recorded on the bench.

Rolls-Royce participation in this project terminated in August 1952, and although higher powers are believed to have been measured later by A.D. Limited (by now BRM Limited), the authors are not in possession of the test data. However, the supercharger was not developed any further after this date.

SUPERCHARGER PERFORMANCE CHARACTERISTICS

The BRM supercharger and final gear train were installed on the 400 hp Compressor Test Plant at Derby as shown

in Fig. 10. The Laurence Scott dynamometer had a swinging field and ran at a maximum speed of 4000 rev/min. A Merlin engine supercharger gear train of 7·06:1 step-up ratio was interposed between the motor shaft and BRM 3·25:1 final train. It was therefore possible to test up to speeds of the order of 70 000 rev/min, if required.

The overall performance characteristics were based on inlet and outlet total pressures and temperatures. The outlet temperature was measured by a special calibrated glass thermometer immersed in a non-conducting stagnation pocket, and the outlet pipe was lagged. The hp input to the rig gear drive was recorded on the tests, but the gear losses were high in relation to the powers being transmitted, and in consequence the mechanical efficiency of the drive appeared low. We did not therefore have a reliable check on the measured supercharger temperature rise (with uncarburetted air) from the hp per unit air flow, but the power measurements were definitely useful in the analysis of the supercharger performance with a fuel/air mixture flow when the outlet temperature measurements are rendered inaccurate by the effect of fuel evaporation on the bulb.

The air flow was measured by the calibrated orifice shown in Fig. 10. The pressure/mass flow characteristics on the rig were obtained by running at a given speed and progressively closing the throttle on the outlet side of the supercharger while adjusting the rig throttle on the inlet side between the air meter and supercharger to keep the inlet total pressure constant. The outlet throttle was progressively closed until the supercharger began to surge, which is a condition of violent pressure fluctuations set up as soon as the diffuser vanes of either the first or second stage stall. The last stable point before surge sets in is the minimum flow value at any given speed, and the locus of these points over the speed range considered is referred to as the surge line.

Estimated characteristics and initial tests with dry air

The first tests of the supercharger were carried out in March 1949 with air only (uncarburetted) in order to establish the basic performance compared with the estimate with air alone under which conditions the temperature rise and efficiency can be assessed with reasonable accuracy. These results are shown in Fig. 11, going up to a speed corresponding to a maximum pressure ratio of 4·1:1.

At this point it should be mentioned that it was our practice to define the non-dimensional speed as $U_e/\sqrt{T_1}$, where U_e is the equivalent single stage impellor tip speed, and $U_e = \sqrt{(U_1{}^2 + U_2{}^2)}$. The usefulness of this index is in comparing the performance characteristics of single and two stage superchargers at the same input hp per unit airflow, and gives an immediate indication of whether the stage performance is satisfactory. Interstage pressures were also taken for stage performance analysis.

56   G. L. WILDE AND F. J. ALLEN

The performance design speed is $U_e/\sqrt{T_1} = 67.9$ corresponding to 32 500 impellor rev/min (10 000 crank rev/min). It will be seen that the estimated pressure ratio of 2·43 with air only was slightly exceeded, and the design isentropic efficiency of 72 per cent was very nearly reached. The design mass flow was achieved, but the surge flow was 37 per cent higher than estimated. It had often been observed that two stage superchargers seldom had the mass flow range estimated from their separate stages, and so this result was not entirely unexpected. It is a consequence of two stages very rarely being perfectly matched, and surging of one stage occurring before the other and propagating the surge of the complete unit. The small size of this supercharger may have introduced a scale or Reynolds number effect which could cause the diffuser vanes to stall at a lower incidence.

The choking flow, which is the maximum flow at any given speed, was 6 per cent higher than estimated. This together with the higher surge flows suggested that we would have to reduce the capacity of the supercharger to match the engine by fitting new diffuser vanes of smaller throat area. However, we decided to carry out tests with

air/fuel mixture before making any modifications of this kind.

Effect of vortex throttling

The object of vortex throttling is discussed on page 52, and initial tests were carried out with air only at a speed of $U_e/\sqrt{T_1} = 82.5$ corresponding to 12 160 crank rev/min. The results are shown in Fig. 12 covering vortex vane settings of 0° (axial), 40° and 60° to the axial direction.

As the vanes are moved from the axial position there is a reduction in temperature rise. The efficiency falls slowly at first, and then more rapidly as the vane angle exceeds 40°. Considering peak efficiency points, the temperature rise is reduced from $\Delta T/T_1 = 0.62$ at 0° to $\Delta T/T_1 = 0.585$ at 60°, or just over 5 per cent. This is not a large effect, but the authors believed that this feature was well worth developing and applying to the second stage as well as the first thereby more than doubling the reduction in impellor work capacity. It is evident from these tests that the vortex vanes are becoming inefficient swirl generators at the higher angle settings because the peak efficiency is falling rapidly.

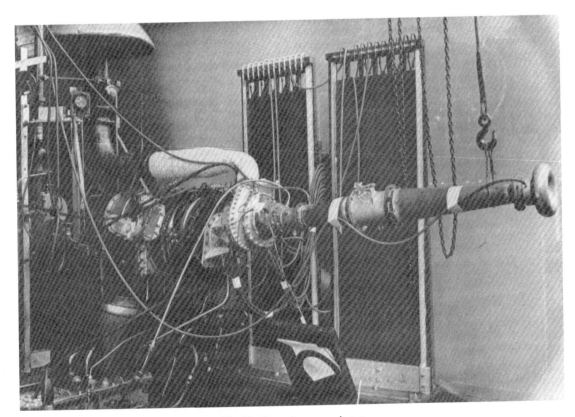

Fig. 10. Supercharger on rig test

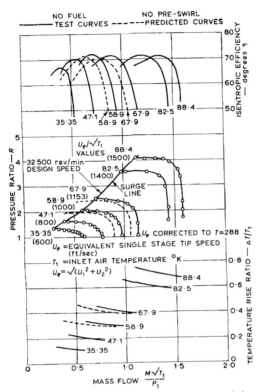

Fig. 11. Results of tests of supercharger characteristics

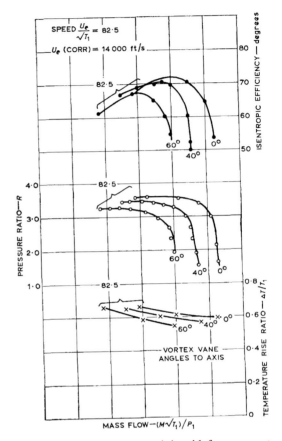

Fig. 12. Supercharger characteristics with first stage vortex throttling

Tests and overall characteristics of the two stages with fuel

The second series of tests was a full calibration of the supercharger with fuel consisting of a mixture of 70 per cent methanol; 20 per cent benzol; 10 per cent alcolate iso-pentane. These tests were done over a range of air/fuel ratios of 5:1, 7:1 and 9:1. As the pressure ratio did not vary significantly with air/fuel ratio, the results for 9:1 only are shown in Fig. 13. Fuel was introduced into the eye of the supercharger and distributed from a centrifugal spinner. Fuel flows were regulated manually to give the correct air/fuel mixture ratio.

These results with fuel correspond to the test results shown in Fig. 11 with air alone for the four speeds $U_e/\sqrt{T_1}$ of 35·35, 47·1, 58·9 and 67·9. Referring to $U_e/\sqrt{T_1} = 67·9$, it will be seen that the pressure ratio has increased from 2·5 (Fig. 11) to 2·84 owing to the effect of fuel evaporation. The estimated design pressure ratio of 2·8 for the engine working point was therefore achieved on these tests.

We also show the estimated characteristic of $U_e/\sqrt{T_1} = 67·9$ for fuel with a latent heat of evaporation of 278 c.h.u's/lb and air/fuel ratio of 9:1 which peaks at a pressure ratio of 2·92. This is higher than the test, but is at least partly

explained by the test fuel having a lower latent heat of evaporation (240 c.h.u's/lb) compared with the quoted fuel.

On the face of these results it appeared that the assumptions we had made on page 50 regarding the way in which the fuel evaporated to reduce the temperature of the air and charge passing through the supercharger were reasonably correct. On the other hand the treatment of fuel evaporation entirely as the lowering of intake temperature at entry to each stage is clearly an approximation to what must actually happen. The impellors act as both a fuel separator and atomizer, and it would be surprising if the impellor compression efficiency were unaffected by these processes, which are too obscure for analysis.

Above the speed $U_e/\sqrt{T_1} = 67·9$ in Fig. 13 all the characteristics shown are with vortex throttling set to maintain a given first stage pressure ratio of 1·7 (based on a static tapping). These and other tests show a greater degree of fuel evaporation with vortex throttling, the only useful consequence of which on the engine is a small reduction in charge temperature. It will be seen that even

SUPERCHARGING THE 1½-LITRE V16 BRM RACING ENGINE

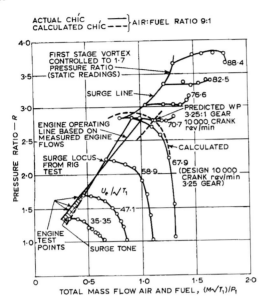

Fig. 13. Supercharger characteristics with fuel and vortex throttling

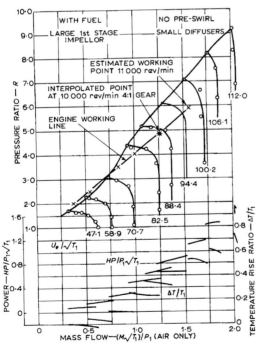

Fig. 14. Performance characteristics of developed super-charger

with vortex throttling a maximum pressure ratio of 3·82 was obtained at $U_e/\sqrt{T_1} = 88·4$, which on the engine would give a boost pressure of 56 lbf/in² abs. at 13 000 crank rev/min with the 3·25 gear.

Matching of the supercharger and engine

The supercharger characteristics described on page 57 were those which related to the first engine tests. We had estimated the charge flow consumption of the engine by the methods described, and had calculated a working line on these characteristics. This is shown on Fig. 13, and it intersects the supercharger surge line at a pressure ratio of about 2:1 corresponding to 7800 crank rev/min. Below this speed supercharger surge was expected at full throttle as indicated in the shaded area. At part throttle settings this is frequently damped and the engine runs quite stably.

The supercharger pressure ratios and flows measured at low speeds on the first engine tests are indicated on Fig. 13, and are shown to be in this region. As engine speed increases the working line moves away from the surge line, which is a normal matching characteristic of a dynamical supercharger and a piston displacement engine. These test results indicated that the flow capacity of the supercharger would have to be reduced, or the flow through the engine increased. Either change would result in a fall in boost pressure at the high full throttle speeds on the engine. This is because the matching pressure ratio points move to higher flows away from peak pressure as speed increases.

High speed tests with developed supercharger

During 1949–50 the engine was under development at Bourne, and the supercharger was modified to incorporate the new performance and mechanical features, based on test experience, described on page 60. The higher supercharger gear ratio of 4·0:1 referred to on page 55 was also introduced, and when this was done new smaller capacity diffuser vanes were fitted to both stages, and the larger 6·50 in diameter first stage impellor was incorporated.

It is not necessary to give an account of all the modifications introduced, many of which were detail design changes. By August 1951 a new supercharger specification had been evolved, the performance characteristics of which are presented in Fig. 14. There were not any further changes specially introduced to alter the performance after this date.

These test results were obtained with an air/fuel mixture ratio of 8:1, and covered much higher speeds than any previous tests. All the characteristics shown on Fig. 14 are at full throttle without any vortex throttling, and the highest speed tested $U_e/\sqrt{T_1} = 112·0$ corresponds to 51 200 impellor rev/min or 12 800 crank rev/min with the 4·0:1 gear. At this speed a peak pressure ratio of 9·2 was achieved. This gives a good idea of the performance capability of this small supercharger, which exceeded our expectations. But of course, the boost corresponding to this would be far beyond the useful maximum on the

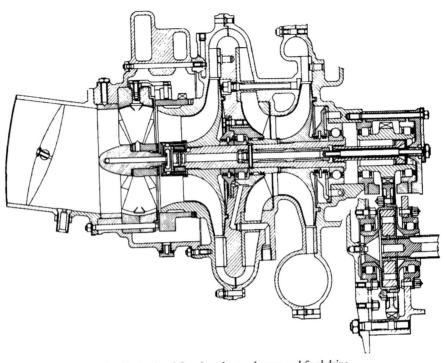

Fig. 15. Sectional drawing of supercharger and final drive

engine and the supercharger would be automatically vortex throttled to the safe maximum boost that the engine could withstand.

It would not have been possible to carry out these very high speed tests with air alone because bearings and casings would have been overheated, and the second stage impellor would almost certainly have burst. The reduction of outlet temperature due to fuel evaporation was of the order of 110 degC at the highest speeds in these tests.

The full throttle range on the engine up to 10 000 crank rev/min corresponds to a $U_e/\sqrt{T_1} = 87\cdot3$ at which the pressure ratio by interpolation is 4·9 giving 72 lbf/in² abs. boost as mentioned on page 55. This would have been the boost measured on the engine if fuel injection had been used. From this it will be seen that there was good agreement of boost pressures between supercharger rig tests with fuel, and engine bench tests.

The mass flow scale of Fig. 14 is now shown based on air flow only, not charge flow. We reverted to this because the value of intake temperature T_1 applies to the air before the fuel is introduced, and we found it more straightforward in performance comparisons to treat the introduction of the fuel and its effect in supercharger performance as equivalent to aerodynamic changes affecting stage matching.

Although the diffuser capacity had been reduced, the engine working line still intersected the surge line at about

3:1 pressure ratio, but in spite of this the engine seemed to run in a stable manner, and we thought that the rig assessment of surge flow was probably higher than registered on the engine. Since surge is an oscillating condition, we have found before in aero work that the surge flow is affected by the volume of ducting at inlet and outlet, and there have often been discrepancies between rig assessment and engine experience. Nevertheless, we would recommend a further reduction in diffuser capacity unless the engine volumetric flow could be increased by improved breathing. It was the intention to carry out engine air flow tests without the supercharger and running under normally aspirated conditions to investigate this properly.

GENERAL DESIGN CONSIDERATION OF TWO STAGE CENTRIFUGAL SUPERCHARGER AND DRIVE

We have discussed the boost pressures, mass flow and efficiency necessary to give the required high powers. The original full throttle conditions fixed for the design of the supercharger were as follows:

Rotational speed . . .	32 500 rev/min
Air mass flow . . .	0·84 lb/s
Fuel flow (alcohol mix at 7:1 air/fuel ratio)	0·12 lb/s
Boost pressure . . .	41 lbf/in² abs.
Supercharger pressure ratio (Full throttle with fuel) . .	2·8
Efficiency (isentropic) . .	72 per cent

Proc Instn Mech Engrs 1964–65

Vol 179 Pt 2A No 1

G. L. WILDE AND F. J. ALLEN

and these corresponded to the engine speed of 10 000 rev/min chosen as the performance design speed at which 400 b.h.p. was required as outlined on page 50.

High performance centrifugal superchargers had been developed for the Merlin aero engine, and from this work it was apparent that these design conditions could be met with a single stage supercharger running at 70 000 rev/min. However, the impellor diameter would have been only 4½ in, and we were concerned that the efficiency would deteriorate in such a small size, and that such a high rotational speed would lead to mechanical difficulties in the design of bearings, shaft, seals and drive. Furthermore, there would be little scope for future development.

We therefore chose to design a two stage supercharger running at a maximum speed of 45 500 rev/min (14 000 crank rev/min), which speed we felt was a reasonable extrapolation beyond known practice at that time requiring a 3·25:1 driving gear ratio. The two stage supercharger was appreciably larger and heavier than the single stage, but was nevertheless appreciably smaller than displacement types of supercharger to meet the same design conditions. The overall dimensions were approximately 10 in diameter by 10 in long, and other leading particulars are given below:

Intake diameter . . .	3·30 in
(First stage impellor, dia. 6·0 in) tip speed .	1190 ft/s (14 000 crank rev/min)
Number of vanes (radial) .	18
(Second stage impellor, dia. 5·5 in) tip speed .	1091 ft/s (14 000 crank rev/min)
Number of vanes (radial) tip speed . .	18
	780 ft/s (10 000 crank rev/min)
First stage diffuser inside dia.	6·16 in
First stage diffuser outside dia.	8·4 in
First stage diffuser width .	0·325 in
First stage diffuser vanes .	10
Second stage intake dia. .	3·05 in
Second stage diffuser inside dia.	5·625 in
Second stage diffuser outside dia.	7·625 in
Second stage diffuser width	0·315 in
Second stage diffuser vanes	10
Volute outlet dia. . .	2·08 in
Weight (including the final step-up gear train and slipper clutch) . .	54 lb

A general arrangement cross-sectional drawing of the supercharger is shown in Fig. 15, and Fig. 16 shows a perspective cutaway drawing of the first stage intake and vortex throttles. External views of the unit are shown in Figs 17 and 18, and Fig. 19 shows the component parts.

A racing car engine is subject to sudden and rapid changes of speed when changing gear, and the authors were concerned that this would impose excessive stresses on the supercharger drive shafts and gears unless some degree of flexibility were introduced. Accordingly, two features were designed into the supercharger transmission. The first was a long torsionally flexible shaft between the first gear train from the crankshaft and the final step-up gear train to the supercharger rotors. This can be seen in Fig. 1. The second feature was the incorporation of a slipper drive or centrifugal clutch in the centre of the large

step-up gear to the rotor pinion. This can be seen in Figs 1 and 15. Any sudden changes of engine speed because of gear changes, backfires, or mechanical failure cause the clutch to slip and so protect the supercharger gear and impellors from excessive shock load and torque.

The vortex throttles are seen in Figs 15 and 16. There are 9 radial vanes in the intake which can swivel on their axes and which are operated by a servo piston working on boost pressure (or oil pressure if desired). The piston rod is coupled to an arm which has a quadrant with teeth engaging an actuator ring to which each vane is coupled by a lever working in a sliding pin.

It was the intention to incorporate later an array of annular vanes in the intake of the second stage to swirl the flow in the same direction of rotation as the impellor in the same manner as the first stage, thereby doubling the benefit from variable swirl and extending their approximation to a variable gear ratio. This was never done, but it would be a good feature to incorporate in any future two stage supercharger.

Ahead of the vortex throttles in the intake there is a normal butterfly throttle under the direct control of the driver.

With a fuel injection carburettor, fuel could be introduced as an atomized spray into the intake just ahead of the vortex throttles, or into a rotating cup on the rotor shaft at the hub of the first impellor and introduced as a centrifugal spray as shown in Fig. 15. Neither of these features was introduced owing to the priority of other development problems.

SUPERCHARGER MECHANICAL FEATURES

As far as possible the mechanical design followed the practice established on the aero superchargers, but because of the very small size of the BRM supercharger it was necessary to make a number of design changes. The original design schemes were made at Rolls-Royce and the detail drawings were done at A.D. Limited. The finally revised scheme based on development experience was completed at Rolls-Royce.

In this section we give some account of the design and development problems which had to be faced. Mechanical and aerodynamic aspects are often interconnected. When this is so, they are discussed together.

Impellors

Had the engine been able to run up to 14 000 crank rev/min giving an impellor speed of 56 000 rev/min with the 4:1 gear, the 6·5 in diameter first stage impellor would have had a tip speed of 1587 ft/sec. Such speeds were not outside our experience, although stresses then reach very high values and special care was required in the design of the impellor discs and blades to avoid stress concentration and unnecessary bending stresses in the blades. The small scale of the machine did not warrant making separate steel rotating inlet guides or inducers requiring expensive machine tools and fixtures as they are on the aero engines. Consequently they had to be milled integral with the main

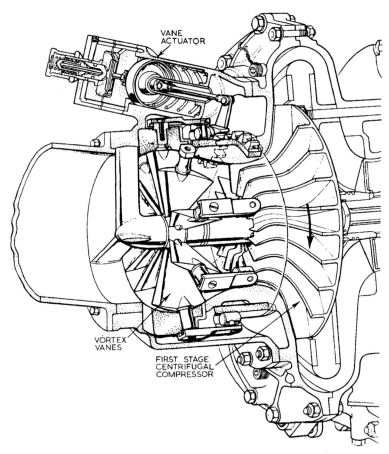

Fig. 16. Vortex throttles of the supercharger

blades which meant that they were shaped wholly by hot bending from the axial direction instead of only partially by bending from an oblique milled form as was the case with separate inlet guide vanes. Since we had no aluminium alloy of adequate strength for the impellors which we could be confident of bending without risk of cracking, the impellors were made of steel. The grade used was En 22, a $3\frac{1}{2}$ per cent nickel type whose strength was more or less proportional to its density compared with the aluminium alloys generally used for impellors. The weight addition was not serious, but a greater consideration was their moment of inertia which is of consequence in the acceleration of the car. A rotating body geared to a linearly moving one imparts to it an extra linear inertia or equivalent mass. In this case, with the 4:1 gear ratio, while the impellors possessed only about $\frac{1}{10}$ lb/ft² moment of inertia on their own shaft they added some 2 per cent to the equivalent mass of the car even when travelling in top gear. In lower gears the effect was greater.

Proc Instn Mech Engrs 1964–65

Later we found we were able to make reliable impellors of aluminium alloy without any change in design, and this naturally reduced the inertia effect to about a third of that of the steel impellors. The 18 blades adopted on each impellor had been proved satisfactory on an experimental supercharger and had the advantage of giving a better inlet guide vane space/chord ratio. We experienced some trouble in both materials with cracking at blade roots, but this was overcome by careful attention to the radii and good polishing.

Diffuser vanes

These followed well proved practice. The first designs, which can be seen in Fig. 18, had ten thin parallel section vanes. They were made as separate parts in aluminium as in the aero engines so that they could be easily exchanged for alternative diffuser vane rings of different throat area. The throat area of these vanes largely determines the mass flow of the supercharger. Later, these thin parallel section

Vol 179 Pt 2A No 1

62   G. L. WILDE AND F. J. ALLEN

vanes were replaced by vanes of narrow wedge form with leading edges of very small radius. The wedge form allowed additional casing bolts to pass through to strengthen the casings against the gas pressures resulting from the higher boost ratings.

Casings and interguide

The casings were of cast aluminium and were in five major parts. These can be seen in Fig. 19. The interguide, which has ten cast vanes, is designed to remove the swirl from the first stage before entering the second, and this component can be seen on the right of Fig. 19. The axial width of the vanes increases as the radius from the centre decreases, and the cast integral ring which forms the intake lip into the second stage supports the inner ends of the interguide vanes against the likelihood of vibration and cracking.

Figs 17 and 18. Two views of the BRM supercharger

Fig. 19. The components of the BRM supercharger

Impellor, shaft, and bearing arrangement

The mechanical aspects of the construction naturally claimed a good deal of attention and in fact involved a fair amount of development though there was no occasion to depart from the original general scheme in which, like the two stage aero superchargers, there was a ball bearing at the impellor high pressure end taking the considerable end thrust (which under most conditions is towards the intake) resulting from aerodynamic loads on the impellor discs. There was a roller bearing between the stages and the first stage was overhung. We did not meet any whirling problems.

The drive input was at the high pressure end, but one departure from the normal aero practice was that having only a single gear wheel engaging with the impellor shaft pinion, the journal loads at the highest speeds would be very great. Therefore the pinion was mounted entirely separately on its own pair of roller bearings and connected to the impellor shaft by a short quill. This proved completely satisfactory as it could be lavishly lubricated without risk of adding to the oil contamination of the charge.

It was found that the ordinary bronze ball or roller cage with riveted cover ring was liable to disintegrate under the severe conditions of running and either solid or symmetrically split cages had to be adopted.

The greatest revision arising from experience on the project concerned the assembly of the impellors on the shaft. Originally they, with all spacers, bearing races, etc., were threaded on from the intake end to a shoulder at the driving end, the whole being tightened by a nut at the intake end. The impellors were individually balanced statically and the complete rotating assembly was then checked dynamically and adjusted to within a limit of 0·01 oz in which results in an out of balance force of 40 lbf at 48 000 rev/min.

It was often found that after running, the balance had deteriorated and this was thought to be possibly due to the fact that the impellors were engaged on the shaft by 48 Vee shaped serrations. Any expansion of the impellors caused by temperature or centrifugal effects combined with driving torque would relax the centralizing rigidity of the assembly, and this might be further aggravated by the fact that both impellors with all their associated bearing races, seals, spacers, etc. were threaded on from the inlet end in a single stack abutting an integral collar at the driving end. Accordingly the collar was transferred to the centre of the shaft, and the respective impellors with their attendant parts (carefully pruned to a minimum number) were assembled from opposite ends. Moreover, rectangular section splines were used instead of serrations and the impellors located on the sides of the splines with clearances at tips and roots so that they would remain centralized in spite of any expansion. The result was greatly improved preservation of balance and no further trouble from this source.

Lubrication and seals

Much detail work had to be done to control oil flows both

to and from the bearings so as neither to starve them nor to allow excessive ingress of oil to the engine. A small oil leakage into the engine was beneficial, but the widely varying conditions produced by the range of speeds and between open and closed throttle were not easy to meet. The impellor had the usual holes drilled through the discs to relieve end thrusts, and there were some intricate passageways in the assembly for oil draining and pressure relief of bearing chambers. These were not entirely satisfactory as it was found that under throttled conditions an excessive quantity of oil entered the supercharger and found its way into the engine.

The eventual system of shaft seals comprised piston-ring types adjacent to bearings, and so-called labyrinth types elsewhere. Whilst the rings afforded a better seal, they had a tendency to seize up unless they received a small amount of oil. They were made of bronze running in steel grooves, while the labyrinths (which were simple sharp-edged grooves) were of steel running in an aluminium bore with a clearance no greater than the bearing slack (about 0·002 in diameter).

Control of the lubrication was always a delicate matter. Some boost leakage inevitably reaches the bearings in spite of all seals and vent chambers, and this is very sensitive to speed variations. Moreover, on the engine, when the throttle closes, the boost is suddenly transformed into a strong depression. This does not occur in normal rig testing so that whilst on the rig we could afford to supply oil at 10 or 15 lbf/in² on the engine this would have resulted in oiling up of the plugs. It was found that for the conditions prevailing in races a workable balance was struck at 2 lbf/in² pressure. Towards the end of the car's career as a Formula 1 model a scheme of settling tank was devised which promised to be a great improvement. However, as it was by then less urgently needed, it was never adopted.

Flexible drive and clutch

The protection against torsional oscillations afforded by the flexible quill and clutch on the BRM was probably greater than it was on the aero engines since the drive was taken from the same part of the crankshaft (the centre) as the main transmission, instead of from the opposite end as on the aero engines. In fact it gave very little trouble though when the gear ratio was raised to 4:1 the clutch was redesigned and the quill diameter increased from 0·350 in to 0·450 in diameter. Angular twist was limited to 15° by stops and the surface stress at this condition was 35 ton/in². The quill was embodied in the shaft going forward from the 21 toothed wheel to the final wheel engaging with the impellor shaft pinion.

The clutch, of segmental bronze block type, was housed in the 56 toothed wheel. These blocks can be seen just above the foot rule in Fig. 19 showing the component parts of the supercharger. This actually shows the original design in which the frictional surface was cylindrical. In the redesign it was made a double cone. From the beginning the blocks carried pins engaging in slots cut in plates at each side to provide a drive, the slots being at an angle from the radial such as to give a wrapping action in the forward direction thus adding to the clutch rating and more easily permitting overrun on a sudden shut-down of the engine. On the engine test-bed the supercharger could be heard running down after a quick engine stop. Most of the engine running was done with only 8 of the 10 blocks assembled.

There was, in fact, a suggestion put forward at one time that the supercharger should be driven through a free-wheel so that it would overrun the engine when slowing down for corners and provide a better boost for picking up than the more rigid drive could do. An analysis showed, however, that to obtain any appreciable extra boost in this way, the moment of inertia of the blower would have to be so much increased (presumably by adding a flywheel) as to swamp any benefit in acceleration on account of the added equivalent mass of the car.

CONCLUSIONS

The design and development of a small highly supercharged engine like the V.16 BRM is a complicated and difficult project which requires technical backing and experimental manufacturing facilities on a generous scale. As the specialist groups contributing to this project were widely dispersed, it was an extremely difficult task for A.D. Limited to coordinate the effort and in the authors' opinion this was the main factor which retarded the systematic development of the car and power unit, and which robbed the V.16 BRM of the success it might have had.

The conclusions which the authors are able to draw are confined to the specialized problems entailed in the design and development of the supercharger and how this performed on the engine. These are set out below:

(1) A small compact two stage centrifugal supercharger can be designed to meet the highest supercharging demands ever likely to be required on a high performance piston engine. Boost pressures of well over 50 lbf/in² g can be obtained with an isentropic efficiency of the order of 70 per cent.

(2) The estimated engine power of 400 b.h.p. at 10 000 rev/min was almost certainly exceeded, but it was necessary to run at appreciably higher boost pressure than originally predicted to obtain this power. This was done by increasing the supercharger gear ratio from 3·25:1 to 4·0:1. Such engine tests as were carried out and analysed by the authors suggest that the breathing capacity of the cylinders was at least 12 per cent lower than expected. There would appear to be scope for developing the engine to give higher powers at a given boost pressure by improving volumetric efficiency and also raising the piston speed. The supercharger could quite easily be made to pass 30–40 per cent more flow at a given rotational speed, if required.

(3) The wide variation of boost pressure with speed, which is the well known characteristic of a centrifugal supercharger, can be largely overcome by incorporating a system of vortex throttling linked to a boost control. With this device high engine powers can be obtained over a sufficiently wide range of engine speeds to give good performance in the car with a multi-speed transmission gear box. The vortex throttling system which was designed into the BRM supercharger from the beginning was never installed in the car.

(4) The vortex throttles were designed into the first stage only and had tests proved successful in the car it was intended as a development to apply them to the second stage. This would have further increased the engine speed range at high powers. The authors suggest the further exploitation of this principle in a three stage supercharger designed with impellors having a larger ratio of intake to tip diameter in each stage to increase the effect of variable swirl. Such a supercharger would approximate to a variable gear drive arrangement, which is probably not feasible.

(5) In general, when not baulked by mechanical troubles the BRM cars seemed to run well, and did not appear to be seriously handicapped by the peculiar characteristics of the centrifugal supercharger. More power at the very low speeds was certainly called for, but if the limitation of maximum engine speed had been removed, and vortex throttling had been developed, it would seem to the authors that the cars would have had considerably more power available than the competitors over most of the useful speed range. The supercharger transmission with torsion shaft, centrifugal clutch and gearing worked reliably. Supercharger bearing lubrication and oil leakage was never completely satisfactory, and further development of sealing was required.

(6) If supercharged engines using standard fuels are required to be developed, thereby losing the advantage of the high latent heat of evaporation of alcohol fuels, it will almost certainly be necessary to reduce the supercharger delivery temperature by some form of radiator cooling. This will add appreciably to the volume and weight of the supercharging system.

ACKNOWLEDGEMENTS

The authors wish to thank the Directors of Rolls-Royce for permission to publish this paper. They also acknowledge with thanks the loan of the diagrams of Figs 1, 2, 3, 15 and 16 by the *Autocar* and Iliffe Press Limited.

APPENDIX
REFERENCES

(1) MAYS, R. and ROBERTS, P. *BRM*. 1962 (Cassell, London).
(2) COOPER, J. A. 'Design for a purpose', *Autocar* 1951 XCVI (No. 2910), 1062.

Discussion

Mr H. Mundy (*Associate Member*)—The authors have done a magnificent job in presenting their work on a complex subject which is of great topical interest as the new formula 1 for Grand Prix cars reverts to the use of 1·5 litre supercharged engines in 1966; I refer to this matter later. The method which the authors used for estimating the power output of a supercharged engine was new to me and it is something which many engineers will find useful.

As I was concerned with this project from its inception, it is of particular interest to me and I think that some project history should be known as it bears an important relationship to the point made by the authors, that the engine never developed its full potential when related to their supercharger work. Incidentally, to the best of my knowledge and contrary to most published figures, the maximum power ever developed by the engine was 485 b.h.p. at 12 000 rev/min.

The design was started almost 20 years ago and therefore in terms of progress it is now like comparing the 1939 all conquering Mercedes with their 1914 Grand Prix car —which swept to victory in the last race before the First World War.

The 16-cylinder BRM unfortunately became something of a laughing stock in the racing world, but many people are not aware of the enormity of the programme in relation to our resources. In addition to the very complex engine, with the exception of the supercharger, the transmissions, including the clutch, suspension, chassis, body and the obviously complicated fuel, oil and water systems were designed from scratch in their entirety by Automobile Developments Ltd. Apart from previous experience with the ERA racing cars and the knowledge gleaned from Mercedes, Auto-Union, Alfa Romeo, etc., we had no established organization on which to build. There were no workshop facilities in existence, and these, together with development facilities, had to be established on a very meagre budget; furthermore, the whole of the design was undertaken by only four senior draughtsmen and three or four juniors.

Many people considered that the combination of 16 cylinders and a centrifugal supercharger was completely wrong for balanced power. This is not wholly true. In the current 1½ formula there are already two 12-cylinder engines in use, and next year Coventry Climax will have a flat 16 engine. What has been learned since 1945–46 is the ability to maintain cylinder filling over a relatively wide engine range, even in unsupercharged form. The end re-

sult means that the drivers have a usable combination of torque and power and do not need to change gear continuously with its waste of time, the effect it has on the need for more concentration when entering and leaving a tricky corner, and the obvious reduction of fatigue. Usually five or six speeds are sufficient, which contrasts with eight and twelve on modern two-stroke racing motor cycles.

The main difficulty experienced by drivers of the BRM was the continuously rising torque curve, which meant that when accelerating through a fast corner, the limit of tyre adhesion could be reached with the car under the influence of considerable cornering forces; sideways adhesion was then lost and the car became frighteningly unstable. With modern wide rims and low tyre profiles, this problem would not be so severe. A part throttle power curve was never taken on the engine and I suspect that the constantly rising torque curve was more severe in this condition, such that the drivers could not 'feather' the throttle.

The authors have said that the engine never produced the power expected and this undoubtedly resulted from the basically poor breathing. As originally laid out it was intended to run on fuel injection, but apart from a very short initial period, this was never pursued. Throughout its racing life the engine operated on 2½ in diameter S.U. carburettors connected to a $3\frac{9}{16}$ in diameter throttle with a cross-sectioned area of 9·96 in². The original air throttle body was 4·0 in diameter with an area of 12·6 in².

However, the greatest restriction on breathing was undoubtedly the valve gear; although the inlet valve head of 1·25 in diameter was adequate for the cylinder capacity, its lift was only 0·25 in or $d/5$. This feature in conjunction with a valve opening period of 300 crankshaft degrees, enabled the maximum valve acceleration to be kept to 52 000 ft/sec² at 12 000 engine rev/min and the valve gear was reliable at these speeds, but it was achieved at the cost of obvious air throttling. This undoubtedly also explains the small gains of power when the supercharger speeds were increased.

The BRM engine really failed from lack of intensive development. When the first three engines were built, they did not complete thirty test-bed hours between them in the first eighteen months, during which time at least six new body shells were made merely to make the car more attractive. As the authors pointed out, vortex throttles would have counteracted the undesirable characteristics of the centrifugal supercharger. In spite of the throttling of the inlet valves, the supercharger could have been speeded up still further to improve bottom-end power and the boost cut off at a predetermined point to limit its pressure and so modify the torque curve. Three sets of vortex throttles were made but never fitted to the engine.

In retrospect there were mistakes made in the conception of the BRM. Primarily, it was very heavy. The dry engine weight (including the supercharger of 54 lb) totalled 525 lb compared with the current 1·5 litre V.8 Grand Prix engine scaling 285 lb. With present knowledge, a 16-cylinder unit could be built to approximately 320 lb dry weight. The dry chassis weight in Mk.1 form was 1624 lb and for the Mk.2, 1400 lb. This compares with 1000 lb (including oil and water) for a modern 1·5 litre unsupercharged Grand Prix car. Starting line weight was 2128 and 1904 lb respectively with 75 gallons of fuel aboard and the consumption was under 3 mile/gal. However, with continued development, the car could have been made reliable and had sufficient power to have been successful on several of the European circuits such as Rheims, Spa and Monza where handling is not all-important.

With the possibility of using a 1·5 litre supercharged engine in 1966—bearing in mind that fuel is restricted to 100 octane Super Premium grade as distinct from alcohol with its high latent heat values as used in the BRM—would the authors care to comment on the following:

(a) Given a 16-cylinder engine with similar cylinder proportions to the BRM would they again recommend a centrifugal supercharger, or perhaps choose a multi-stage Rootes type with its more suitable delivery characteristics and its superior adiabatic efficiency, despite its greater bulk and weight for a given capacity. If choosing a centrifugal supercharger, what changes would they make compared with the BRM?

(b) Would it be necessary to have interstage and/or aftercooling to obtain satisfactory charge temperatures and would water injection be necessary as this appeared to be so with highly supercharged aero engines using hydrocarbon fuels?

(c) What sort of maximum power would they expect from such a supercharged engine and would they recommend it with its extra complication for competition with with a 3 litre unsupercharged unit which is also permitted and from which we know that it is possible to obtain approximately 430 b.h.p. given suitable cylinder proportions?

Mr P. Parker, B.Sc. (*Graduate*)—There are three points on which I would like to comment. The first is in regard to engine breathing. A piston engine with high pressure supercharging is similar to a gas turbine in that, once air has been compressed by the expenditure of a large quantity of valuable work, quite small pressure losses cause a severe reduction in output.

The authors conclude that the reason the engine did not give the expected power with the original boost pressure

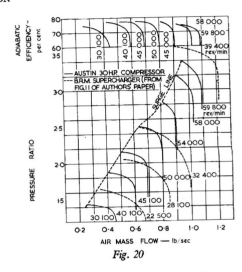

Fig. 20

was a deficiency in breathing capacity, which, after all, must have been caused by pressure loss somewhere in the engine cylinder head.

Since, as the paper clearly shows, the original boost pressure had been very carefully selected to give the required power, coupled with an engine power curve suitable for road racing, an improvement in the engine air flow would have given better results than raising the boost pressure.

The second point is on single stage compressors. The final performance of the two stage compressor, shown in Fig. 14, is excellent by any standards but, for the pressure ratio values actually required by the engine, the single stage compressor is dismissed too lightly.

As described by Dr Weaving (**3**) the single stage compressor of the 30-hp gas turbine developed by the Austin Motor Company produces a peak pressure ratio of 3·4:1 coupled with a mass flow of 0·95 lb/sec and an adiabatic efficiency of 75 per cent.

Fig. 20 shows the BRM supercharger characteristics from the authors' Fig. 11 plotted on the same graph as those for the Austin compressor.

It is apparent that the mass flow of the two compressors is very similar and that up to its maximum pressure ratio the cheaper and lighter single stage compressor would have been as good.

The third point is on vortex throttling or, as it is often called, variable prewhirl. An approximate formula for the effect of intake prewhirl on the temperature rise of a centrifugal compressor stage is

$$\Delta T = \Delta T_{\beta=0} \left[1 - \left(\frac{d_2}{d_{0D}} \right)^2 \frac{\tan \beta}{\tan \beta + \tan \alpha} \right]$$

ΔT Stage temperature rise with prewhirl.
$\Delta T_{\beta=0}$ Stage temperature rise with no prewhirl.
α Inducer tip blade angle.
β Prewhirl angle.

Vol 179 Pt 2A No 1

d_2 Inducer tip diameter.

d_{0D} Impellor tip diameter.

Applying this formula to an impellor with similar proportions to those in the BRM shows that, for 50 deg of prewhirl, a reduction in stage temperature rise of 15 per cent occurs. This figure is supported by the experimental results given by Anderson and Shouman (4).

For the BRM supercharger, with prewhirl on the first stage only, this result indicates that a 9 per cent reduction in compressor temperature rise should be obtained with 50 deg of prewhirl. Fig. 12 shows only 5½ per cent, which is disappointing.

In their conclusions the authors recommend an extension of the vortex throttle principle by using a three stage supercharger, with impellors having a higher ratio of intake to tip diameter.

The above formula supports the latter part of this statement, but it also shows that for geometrically similar impellors the percentage reduction in temperature rise from vortex throttling is the same whether it is applied to a single stage compressor or each stage of a multi-stage compressor.

REFERENCES

(3) WEAVING J. H. 'Small gas turbines', *Proc. Instn mech. Engrs* 1961–62 **175**, 6.

(4) ANDERSON, J. R. and SHOUMAN, A. R. 'The use of compressor inlet prewhirl for the control of small gas turbines', *Trans. A.S.M.E., J. Engineering for Power* 1964 (April).

Mr F. H. Stark (*Associate Member*)—In submitting one or two remarks I feel rather the odd man out in this exercise because I had nothing to do with the BRM project, and only watched from the side-lines, so I hope you will treat my remarks with some indulgence.

I was surprised to learn from the paper that the BRM engine was deficient in breathing capacity, as suggested by the measured charge flow being 12 per cent less than expected. If one assumes that a high supercharge pressure swamped the port flow shortcomings the lesson to be learned is that highly supercharged engines need high-flow inlet and exhaust ports no less than do naturally aspirated engines.

I want to try here to draw the authors on one aspect of their preliminary Merlin work.

Independently of the work carried out at Rolls-Royce in connection with Merlin performance, Professor Taylor at Massachusetts Institute of Technology, as a step in a more general investigation into four-stroke engine performance, estimated that the Inlet Mach Index of the Merlin engine was 0·30 at 3000 rev/min. Since it has been established that engine performance does not deteriorate appreciably until the Inlet Mach Index exceeds 0·50, this suggests that at 3000 rev/min the Merlin engine was breathing with low losses and would not be in trouble in this respect until the speed was increased by something like 50 per cent. If the inlet ports were as good as Professor

Taylor suggests, and the engine performance above 3000 rev/min was no better than the paper reports, the exhaust provisions must have been very inadequate under those conditions. From memory, the Merlin exhaust ports could not be claimed to possess any considerable aerodynamic refinement. Could the authors remember if the exhaust was responsible for any large proportion of the performance deterioration at high revolutions? Was any regard paid to the possibility of exhaust tuning on the car engines?

A significant point mentioned in the paper is that the engine maximum speed had to be reduced from the intended 14 000 rev/min to a practicable 12 000 rev/min, at which speed the cams and followers had an acceptable life. Is it not unreasonable in any engine of the highest possible duty, when opening a valve, to require the cam and follower in combination, at the same time also to supply the additional force to compress the valve springs in order that subsequently a force may be available for the negative acceleration of the valve? The replacement of the valve springs by the second cam of a desmodromic valve operation is a reasonable way of circumventing this and other problems of valve operation and port effectiveness. If a satisfactory design for such a mechanism has not yet been achieved, I feel that here is a worthwhile target that, with care, cannot be unattainable for future engines of high output, supercharged or not.

Mr M. Ransome, B.Sc. (*Graduate*)—I have some comments and questions to put to the authors. Did they ever consider the possibility of using the vortex throttle in the opposite sense as a variable inlet guide vane device, to extend the useful operating torque range of the engine?

I have heard that one of the more unpleasant characteristics of the BRM was for it to spin its wheels on occasions, very suddenly, at over 100 mile/h. This presumably would not have happened had vortex throttling been fitted.

If one refers to Fig. 7 in the paper it can be seen that a side effect of limiting the boost pressure by vortex throttling is to give the engine a characteristic similar to that of a positive displacement blown unit.

Presumably at the time of the V.16 BRM a centrifugal supercharger was an obvious choice, with the knowledge that had been accumulated at Rolls-Royce on the Merlin engine during the war, and anyway, the degree of boost required could not have been obtained on a positive displacement machine, without resorting to a considerable amount of heavy multi-staging.

Today, however, things are different. For anybody considering supercharging for the 1966 Formula, a positive displacement supercharger capable of high boost pressures in a single stage is a reality. Whether a high boost can be usefully employed with a 100 R.M. petrol–air mixture remains to be seen.

For an 8-cylinder 1½ litre engine I would expect such a supercharger to occupy less space than the BRM unit

DISCUSSION

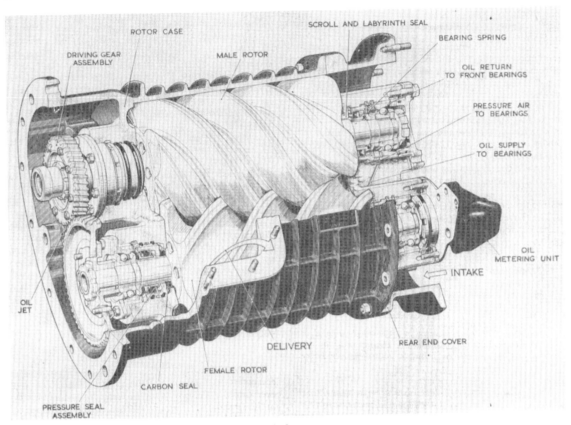

Fig. 21. Typical screw compressor

and to weigh about the same. Adiabatic efficiency at a boost pressure of 45 lb/in² would be slightly better than 70 per cent and a flat torque curve would be available without having to resort to any complicated control mechanisms.

Mr D. Bastow, B.Sc. (Eng.) (Bolton)—I would like to ask a question from ignorance. Was the fuel specified to the authors when they were asked to design their supercharger, or could they have considered the possibility of using a fuel which had a very much higher energy release per unit volume of mixture? Did they consider this as an alternative?

If you are using a normal petroleum-base fuel the amount of energy you can get from a given volume of air-fuel mixture is perhaps one and a half times as much as if you are using an alcohol fuel; even though in the case considered it was not all alcohol, something between these two ratios, probably nearer to the alcohol figure, was applicable. Intercooling in place of that otherwise provided by the fuel would have been implied, but the overall weight might have been reduced because of the reduced

fuel consumption, and the required indicated horsepower would have been much less because of the reduced air consumption and hence reduced supercharger power.

In a naturally aspirated engine the amount of air flow, and hence the amount of power, can be very much increased by exhaust tuning and, to a lesser extent, by inlet tuning in conjunction with the appropriate valve timing. I think the total effect of this may be equivalent to somewhere between ½ and 1 atmosphere of supercharge in terms of the amount of air going through. It would seem to me that this, as a means of assisting a supercharger, would be a worthwhile method of again reducing the effort which is required from the supercharger itself, and, therefore, the power it consumes. Was this considered at all in the engine development?

Mr R. W. Corbett, M.Sc., Wh.Sch. (*Associate Member*)—The authors found the volumetric efficiency of the BRM engine to be 12 per cent less than the Merlin, although the inlet valve area was double. I think that the induction manifold shown in Fig. 21 would account for a 30 per cent loss of power.

Proc Instn Mech Engrs 1964–65

Vol 179 Pt 2A No 1

The Schneider Trophy R engines had, in effect, a flat box connecting the supercharger and all the cylinders with four hand-holes to get at some of the inside sparking plugs. In fact, the V-engine was 80 per cent induction. It will be seen that in the V-engine only 30–40 per cent of the area available was occupied by the induction system.

We tried a variety of systems on the Merlin and there was only one that was better and that one was just a bit too big; in fact, there was not room to change the sparking plugs while the engine was running, so that was ruled out.

I think that the lack of induction volume is responsible for the lack of volumetric efficiency.

Communication

Mr E. H. Warne (*Associate Member*)—In reference to the authors' comments on the surface area to volume ratio associated with the small cylinders, I am interested in the change this might have on the detonation properties of the engine due to the relatively large cooling effect attributable to the large area. I am also interested to know if there were any noticeable effects due to the proximity of relatively cold walls in the combustion zone. I realize the extraction of these factors from general performance results would have its difficulties in view of the large number of independent variables which must have contributory effects on the properties in question.

In reference to surging conditions I am surprised at the proximity of the inlet valve to the compressor and wonder whether in fact this led to any serious maldistribution at the inlet and if so what effects this had on the performance characteristics of the compressor with particular regard to the surge characteristic which was known to be susceptible to inlet conditions. Also on the subject of surge, I wonder whether sharp closure of the throttle resulted in any surging or whether in fact the delivery volume of the compressor was sufficiently small to be able to accommodate the rapidly changing pressure conditions in a sufficiently short time, such that the compressor did not have to work even transiently at high pressure ratios. I am very interested in the authors' reference to the ability to transgress over the surge line when inlet and outlet volumes were small in comparison to the supercharger throughput. It is interesting to note the magnitude of the shift in the design air mass flow for a given $\mu_e/\sqrt{T_1}$ occasioned by the increase in gear ratio of the supercharger drive gear. The attainment of a pressure ratio greater than 9 from such a supercharger must also, I feel, be regarded as a very creditable achievement.

Finally I would make reference to the problems of turbo supercharging where there would obviously be a response problem and possibly an associated requirement for some form of speed control on the high power installation which would be necessary for this kind of engine. I would be interested in the authors' comments on any factors which they considered when the original decision was taken to adopt an engine-driven compressor. Compared to an exhaust-driven turbo supercharger it would seem that, on the face of it, higher powers can be achieved from the exhaust-driven unit, whilst interference with the exhaust air flow might be less important on a highly supercharged engine than on a normal aspirated engine where it is obviously most undesirable to interfere detrimentally with the exhaust flow pattern.

70

Authors' Replies

Mr F. J. Allen—I have had a brief look at some of the points raised by Mr Mundy and generally I am inclined to say that you can achieve the same power with the same boost at the same charge temperature. The fuel for the proposed new Formula 1 is going to have a higher calorific value and lower latent heat of evaporation, and so water injection or after-cooling will have to be used if the same high boost pressures are to be successfully used in the engine. I do not think it would be necessary to cool at different stages in the course of compression, whether by water injection or by heat exchangers, unless such high boosts are required that interstage cooling is necessary to protect the later stages of the supercharger from over-heating.

If you want to cool by water injection, I made a rough estimate that you might have to carry, in terms of volume, something like half as much water as you do fuel. I dare say that might be a serious handicap.

Would we recommend a similar system of super-charging? I think that is the gist of the question. As far as I can see it would be difficult to use any other. The Rootes by itself, as we know, has a very low efficiency for high pressure ratios. If you split it down into multi-stages the thing might become very bulky and prohibitive on that score. The centrifugal compressor can be made to compress reasonably well over the speed range. If you have these multi-gear transmission gear-boxes (the BRM had five speeds), so that the engine speed can be kept within a reasonably narrow range and the variation in boost controlled as explained in the paper, you can mitigate it to a reasonable extent by the variable swirl applied to both or all stages. The multi-stage blower has the energy equivalent of a single impellor whose diameter is the square root of the sum of the squares of the constituent impellors. This means that if you only pre-swirl at the first intake that is a relatively small diameter and, of course, it won't count so much as a proportion of the total change of angular momentum, which is what the impellor does to the fluid going through it. You must therefore apply the variable swirl to all stages and thus get quite an appreciable control over the boost without too drastic a reduction in efficiency. When you remember the lightness, compactness and mechanical reliability of the centrifugal compressor, and also the fact that it is less subject to wear than the displacement machines, it seems to have the balance of advantages.

May I just add that the prime object of using methanol fuel was to get the charge cooling without the bulk and

complication of the heat exchanger type of radiator. The heat exchanger was used on the Merlin engine but then it had a very much lower relative duty. The air–fuel ratio on a mass basis is about 6 to 1. We ran our supercharger rig tests with fuel using a weaker mixture purely because it saved fuel, having found that with the richer mixtures you did not get very much more temperature drop. I might remark that we did some preliminary tests with a sample of this fuel on a Merlin supercharger to get an idea as to what temperature drop we might expect. It did roughly confirm the very large values for which we had hoped.

Mr G. L. Wilde—I agree with Mr Allen's remarks and would like to add a few myself. Firstly, I was very interested to hear Mr Mundy's comments because some new figures were produced which I had not had before. It is very encouraging to know the power that was, in fact, achieved.

With regard to the breathing which Mr Mundy mentioned, this is also an encouragement because you must understand that we were not cloistered like monks in a nice research laboratory doing this work. The car was put on the track and brought back, and engines were exchanged. We were not able to do the step-by-step methodical investigation kind of work we were accustomed to on the aero engines. Therefore, our conclusions about the breathing were given with a little diffidence and to hear Mr Mundy say that the breathing was, in fact, deficient substantiated our conclusion.

Mr Mundy asked what was the maximum boost that we could have on 100 octane fuel for the future. We have given a little thought to this and our considered opinion (although, as I say, it is an opinion and not a calculation) is something of the order of 45 to 50 lb/in² absolute if the charge is not after-cooled.

Mr Allen has answered the question of water injection. I do not think that intercooling is necessary. I think if you had to cool it would be after-cooling, and then the boost pressure limit could be raised.

With regard to whether we would recommend a centrifugal supercharger again for such a project, this depends upon a number of factors, which are touched upon in our paper. I think the answer is that we would recommend a centrifugal supercharger redesigned to make more effective use of the variable swirl features and so give a less steep rising boost-with-speed characteristic. If the boost pressure for which the engine is designed is reduced, this problem becomes relatively easier. If boost pressures as high as those used in the BRM are to be used, then I think that a 3-stage supercharger designed in a special way to make the maximum use of variable swirl will be a practical solution. The additional supercharger stage will not increase the bulk significantly in the overall installation of the power plant in the car.

With a 3-stage centrifugal supercharger the pressure rise per stage can be limited to quite a moderate value, and it would be possible to employ the vaneless type diffusers in the high pressure stages in order to maintain a sufficiently large mass flow range to achieve good flow matching with the engine.

We accept the point that the volumetric efficiency must be good for supercharged engines, and certainly as good as it ought to be for naturally aspirated engines. The valve timing requirements for supercharging are different from normally aspirated engines, but the breathing capabilities should be as good. It is not good policy to supercharge an engine which has a basically poor volumetric efficiency.

I am not well acquainted with Professor Taylor's work, but I was one of the people involved in the performance analysis of the Merlin. My recollection is that at 3000 rev/min, which is 3000 ft/min mean piston speed, the breathing of the Merlin was good; in that respect we would agree with Professor Taylor. The highest speed reached on the Merlin engine was approximately 4200 rev/min; the normal speed, I think, was 3600 rev/min. My recollection is that the breathing was starting to degenerate at this speed. This was what worried us when we did the estimate for the BRM. That had, in fact, a designed piston speed of 4432 ft/min but in fact it never ran much above 3600 ft/min. So I would say that if the Merlin had had to run at such high speeds I would question whether the breathing capacity would have been acceptable.

I cannot answer the question as to whether the limitation was in the inlet or exhaust valves nor can I answer the question regarding mechanically operated valves for the BRM.

We agree that it would have been better to raise the air flow through the engine than to put up the boost pressure. This, however, could not be done in the time scale and, indeed, the problem was not thoroughly understood. We had to do what we could to get more power, and we did the obvious thing. I do not think we can defend it as a principle.

An important point, and I do not know whether or not it was taken into account in this comparison, is that if you are matching a centrifugal supercharger to a piston engine the locus of the pressure and flow operating points as you go up in speed is such that the flow relative to the surge gradually moves to the right or to a higher proportion of maximum flow. The working lines move over to the right-hand side of the characteristics. You therefore fall down the pressure characteristic. For comparison, in the case of a turbine engine you feed the gas into a turbine which behaves like a choked nozzle. In this case the working line is more or

less parallel to the surge line; in fact, it can move into surge at high engine speed—the converse of the situation in the piston engine. This is a very important factor in matching the supercharger to any device, either a piston engine or a turbine engine, and I suggest that if you put the matching lines of a piston engine on the characteristics you might have an unpleasant shock, and that to avoid surge at the low speeds you would be right down the pressure characteristics at high speeds.

We were well aware of this problem because of the work we had done on the supercharging of the Merlin engine. At high altitude where the inlet temperature falls very considerably, the corrected speed of the supercharger is extremely high and the flow matching with the engine is such that the operating point falls a long way down the pressure curve and therefore operates at a very inefficient condition. At such high corrected speeds the mass flow range of the supercharger is very small because the impellor intake is probably choked, or very near to it.

A two stage supercharger designed for the same pressure ratio as a single stage machine exhibits a much wider mass flow range at the high speeds, and this enables the boost pressures to be maintained. This is a direct result of improved flow-matching between piston engine and supercharger.

With regard to the comparison of temperature drop due to swirl, I would draw attention to the fact that the 5 per cent reduction we quote is on the total temperature rise.

A comment was made about geometrically similar impellors, with which I agree, although in fact the second stage should not be a scale of the first. They are running at different thermodynamic conditions, and the area ratio across the impellor passage should not be the same in each case because the pressure ratios of the two stages are not the same.

At the beginning of this project we were assuming we would have to operate on normal fuel, and we had worked out that we needed an after-cooler. It so happened that as the project went along the use of alcohol fuel was in fact proposed. I cannot quite remember the origin of how it came about, but it certainly came about, and in the process of working out the power and our knowledge of the effect of this on the performance of the supercharger, we discarded the after-cooler, but we were in doubt as to where this evaporation took place. Even now I think it was more by luck than good judgement that the evaporation effect came out so close to prediction.

With regard to normally aspirated engines and tuning exhaust and inlet systems, I am afraid that this was not considered at all. At one point it was suggested that the exhaust system might be treated like the Kadenacy system in some way, but this was never actually done, as far as I know.

If the BRM engine had been properly calibrated as a normally aspirated engine we feel that it would have shown up poorly on power produced. We had, in fact, a programme which included tests as a normally aspirated engine in order to find out the basic breathing characteristics. There just was not time, and A.D. Limited were in a very difficult position indeed. They had the problem of co-ordinating all this work in the face of much ill-informed publicity and the press, the supporting enthusiasts and the contributing firms all pressing for the car to race. This was not conducive to methodical work and I think that it may be a very good object lesson for any other group tackling a project with such difficult technical problems.

With regard to the question about counter-swirl, this was not really of use on the BRM because we were already geared to a speed which would not have benefited by counter-swirl. Another point is that we have always found, on practical tests, that counter-swirl decreases efficiency. Therefore I do not think it is a thing which would be of use in this case. I think these devices are perhaps of more use in special applications where low speeds and low pressure ratios are being used and, indeed, if you go to the water turbine field of work you can see their use in the Francis turbines. They have a large exhaust-to-intake diameter ratio, and the effect of pre-swirl is correspondingly greater.

Car wheel spinning at 100 mile/h at full throttle would certainly be eased by the development of the automatic vortex throttling system. I think there is no doubt about that since the excess torque available for acceleration could be limited.

Regarding the comment about Fig. 7 and the Lysholm blower, it sounds a good proposition, and I think it ought to be investigated, but that is all I can say about it. I am rather surprised to hear that the size of this type of compressor would be competitive with the small centrifugal.

However, I do not agree that a small single stage centrifugal would be as good an alternative as the two stage supercharger for the reasons I have already mentioned. It can give the pressure, but it cannot, in my opinion, give the range of mass flow required to match the engine properly over the whole speed range.

The large surface to volume ratio of the cylinder was considered by us to cause a basic loss of thermal efficiency, and in the calculation of power output we considered that the heat loss would be compensated for by the higher compression ratio of the BRM compared with that of the data at our disposal. The BRM exhibited unsteady running characteristics which were attributed mainly to poor fuel distribution in the induction system. Some of these effects may in fact have been due to processes in the combustion chamber itself.

I think the main butterfly throttle valve shown in Fig. 15 of the paper is rather close to the supercharger intake, and I would like to see it further upstream, space permitting. At full throttle the close proximity is of no consequence. At part throttle the maldistribution may have an adverse effect on the surge characteristics, although we have never found this to be critical. When throttled, of course, pressure losses are being intentionally introduced. With small intake volume between throttle and supercharger, surge frequency can be very high and surge may even be muffled.

The turbo blower was never seriously considered. Rapid speed changes and response rate are obvious obstacles in a racing car application. There is a more fundamental limit to their use in such an application, and that is in the limited expansion ratio that is available without raising exhaust back pressure on the cylinders.

Appendix 7

Bibliography

Birmingham, Dr. A. T., *The Riley Motor Car* (G.T. Foulis, 1965).

Borgeson, Griffiths (Griff), *The Twin Cam Engine* (Dalton Watson, 1981).

——, *The Alfa Romeo Tradition* (Haynes Publishing, 1990).

Buckley, J. R., *Cars of the Connoisseur* (B.T. Batsford, 1960).

Clarke, R. M., Editor, *ERA Gold Portfolio, 1934-1994* (Brooklands Books, undated).

Earl, Cameron C., *Investigation into the Development of German Grand Prix Racing Cars Between 1934 and 1939* (HMSO, 1948).

Fangio, Juan, with Giambertone, Marcello, *My Twenty Years of Racing* (Temple Press, 1961).

Fusi, Luigi, *Alfa Romeo, Tutti le Vetture Dal 1910* (Emmetigrafica, Third Edition, 1978).

Hawthorn, Mike, *Challenge Me the Race* (William Kimber, 1958, reissued with corrections, Aston Publications, 1988).

Hodges, David and Mundy, Harry, *The V-16 BRM* (Profile Publications, 1967).

Jenkinson, Denis, *Motor Sport Racing Car Reviews, 1950-56.*

Lloyd, John, *The Story of ERA* (Motor Racing Publications, 1949).

Ludvigsen, Karl, *BRM V16* (Veloce, 2006, reprinted 2008).

Mays, Raymond, *Split Seconds* (G. T. Foulis, 1951).

——, and Roberts, Peter, *BRM* (Cassell, 1962, Second Edition 1963).

Moss, Stirling, with Nye, Doug, *My Cars, My Career* (Patrick Stephens, 1987).

Nye, Doug, with Rudd, Tony, *BRM, Volume 1, Front Engined Cars 1945-1960* (Motor Racing Publications, 1994, reprinted 2003).

Pomeroy, Laurence, *V16, The Story of the B.R.M. Engine* (Motor Racing Publications, 1954).

——, and Walkerley, Rodney (editors), *Motor Year Book* (Temple Press, 1950-56 editions).

Rudd, Tony, *It Was Fun! My Fifty Years of High Performance* (Patrick Stephens, 1993).

Salvadori, Roy and Pritchard, Anthony, *Roy Salvadori, Racing Driver* (Patrick Stephens, 1984).

Weguelin, David, *ERA* (White Mouse Publications).

Magazines: *Autocourse, Autosport, Motor Racing, Motor Sport, Road & Track, The Autocar, The Motor.*

Page numbers in **bold** include photographs. Entries for cars are listed under the manufacturer's name, followed by the model name eg 'Alfa Romeo *Tipo 158 Alfetta*'.

Abecassis, George 9
AIACR (Association Internationale de Automobile Clubs Reconnus) 33–4
Aintree inaugural race, 1954 242–6
Albi 1,500cc race 1936 27
Albi Grand Prix 146, 147–9, 197–201
Alfa Romeo
 Disco Volante 142
 Tipo 158 Alfetta 35, 79, 80, **84**, 86, 141
 Tipo 159 12, **134**, 141
 Tipo 162 **37**, 39, 79
 Tipo 512 79
 Tipo A 34
 Tipo B Monoposto **34**, 219
 withdrawal from Grand Prix racing 142
Allen, F.J. 303–31
Alta 9, 151, 291
Alvis **248–9**
Ambrose, Arthur **105**
AMOC Trophy, Formule Libre 206, 240–1
Amon, Chris 289
An Engineering Exercise (Pomeroy) 298–302
Argentine Automobile Club 285
Argentinian Grand Prix, 1953 150
Armstrong Siddeley 25
Ascari, Alberto 104, **130**, 150
Aston Martin
 DB2 86
 DB3S **201**
Austin Lodestar 86, **87**, 103, 270
Austin Motor Company 126
Austro-Daimler 23
Auto Union
 C-Type 34
 D-Type **37**

Autocar, The 15, 43, 67
Automobile Developments Ltd 39
Automovil Club, Argentina 146
Autosport 170, 176, 187, 240, 266, 277

B. Bira
 BRDC *Daily Express* Trophy 1952 155, **156**
 BRM testing session 1950 114, 115
 Coupe de Prince Rainier Voiturette race 23
 Daily Express International Trophy 1955 269
 Daily Graphic Goodwood Trophy 1950 97
 ERA R2B 27
 Ulster Trophy 1952 152
 White Mouse Racing Team 44
 Woodcote Cup 1950 95
Banks, F.R., Air Commodore 43
BARC *Daily Telegraph* 200 242–6, **243**
BARC International Meeting
 1950 95–103
 1952 177–86
 1953 192–5, 211–15
 1954 227–39, 259–62, 266–8
BARC Trophy 262–3, 276–7
Barratt, Aubrey 22
Beart, Francis 262
Behra, Jean 243, 244, 283
Berthon, Peter
 British Grand Prix 1951 **112**, **119**, **129**
 BRM project **9**, 11, 39, **58**, 103, **146**
 career 17, 20
 Chichester Cup 1954 **230–1**
 criticisms of 15, 18
 death of 22
 ERA 22, 23, 26, 27, 30
 Monza 1952 **143**
 Penya Rhin Grand Prix 1950 **109**
 private life **22**
 Whitsun Trophy 1954 **247**
Bhanubandh, Prince Birabongse *see* B. Bira
bibliography 332
Bira, Prince of Siam *see* B. Bira
Bolster, John 176

Bonnier, Joakim 283
Borgonovo, 'Pancho' 146
Bourne works 20, 21, 23, 95, 177
Bowmaker Racing Team 289
Brabham, Jack **221**, 275
BRDC
 British Empire Trophy 1953 201
 Daily Express Trophy 1952 155–61
 International Trophy 1950 86, **87–9**, **91**
Bristol, 450 30
British Grand Prix *see also* European Grand Prix
 1951 **31**, **112–13**, 115–35, 291
 1952 155, 284
 1954 253
 1955 271, 285
 1956 283
British Grand Prix support race, 1953 202–5
British Motor Racing Fund 26
British Motor Racing Research Trust 39, 64, 177
British Racing Drivers' Club (BRDC) 86, 176
British Racing Motors Ltd *see* BRM (British Racing Motors Ltd)
British Trial Drivers' Championship 292
BRM
 P25 15, 225, **282–3**
 P48 283
 Type 15 41
 V16 *see* BRM V16
 V16 Mk I *see* BRM V16, Mk I
 V16 Mk II *see* BRM V16, Mk II
BRM (British Racing Motors Ltd)
 Board of Trustees 80, 83, 86, 104, 114, 116, 151, 291
 ceased racing 283
 drivers' confidence in 15
 financing of project 11, 39, 139, 142
 public confidence in 87, 163
 sale of 12, 176–7
 sponsorship 86, 87
 suppliers 297
 supporters 11, 18 *see also* Owen Racing Motors Association (ORMA)
 team drivers 146, 283

BRM (Mays/Roberts, 1962) 182
BRM: The Saga of British Racing Motors, Volume 1, Front-Engined Cars 1945-60 (Nye) 15
BRM V16
 chassis 45, **46–7**, **55**
 cockpit **54**
 crankcase **51**
 crankshaft **50**
 disc brakes **56**
 driveshaft failure 87–94
 engine **38**, 41–2, **48–9**, **63**
 exhaust system insulation failure 116, 131, 132–3
 first public appearance **10**, **11**
 first win 97
 gearbox **51**
 handling issues 25, 97, 104, 247, 288
 Mk I **218–19**, 225, 227, **239**, 253
 Mk II **218–19**, 225–6, 227, **228–9**, **230–1**, **232–3**, **239**, 240, **241**, **242**, **243**, **244–5**, **248–9**, 253, **264–5**, **272–3**, **274**
 press launch **60–1**, **64–5**, **66–7**, **74–5**
 race results 294–6
 reputation 176
 specification 293
 testing sessions 114, 138–9, 142, **143**, **144–5**
 transmission 42
 transportation of 86, **87**, 103, **220**
Brooks, Tony 14, 277, 282, 283
Brown, Alan **178**, **180–1**, **184–5**
Brown, David 14, 104
Buckley, J.R. 21
Bugatti
 Brescia 20
 Type 54 34
Bugatti Owners' Club Prescott Hill Climb **28**
Bushell, Fred 44

Campbell, Mrs Patrick 18
Caracciola, Rudolf 33, 35
Castle Combe International Meeting, 1955 278–9